CORPORATE VIEWS OF THE PUBLIC INTEREST

Perceptions of the
Forest Products Industry

JEFFREY A. SONNENFELD
Harvard University

 *Auburn House Publishing Company*
Boston, Massachusetts

Library of Congress Cataloging in Publication Data

Sonnenfeld, Jeffrey A., 1954–

   Corporate views of the public interest.

   Includes index.
   1.   Wood-using industries—United States. 2.   Lumber
trade—United States. 3.   Public interest—United States.
4.   Industry—Social aspects—United States. I. Title.
HD9756.S7   674'.0068   81-10863
ISBN 0-86569-060-X   AACR2

Printed in the United States of America

*This book is dedicated to my parents
as a modest tribute to the inspiration
and confidence which they have
always offered.*

PREFACE

This book suggests a map to guide the corporate executive through the increasingly important but largely uncharted terrain of public affairs. This territory is defined in a broad sense to include such non-market constituencies as state and federal regulators, legislators, the press, trade unions, public interest groups, trade associations, and community civic associations. The recent experiences of the oil and the transportation industries provide convincing evidence that increased appreciation of the limited supply of productive resources and zealous sentiment to relax and revise business regulation in no fashion indicate that firms should abandon efforts at upgrading their public affairs performance. On the contrary, it can be argued that the present state of the business environment calls for heightened awareness of a firm's public image and constituent relations and for the development of political skills.

We can, for example, presently observe leading U. S. financial institutions developing a much broader appreciation of competitive threats and advantages inherent in various regulatory moves. The introduction of electronic equipment, NOW accounts, money market funds, and regulatory reforms, as well as large mergers, has led to new inter-institutional alliances and rivalries. The long-standing differences between thrift institutions and commercial banks, and between large and small banks, have intensified. At the same time, strategic splits have divided the largest U.S. banks as interstate interests, emphasis on retail business, international commitments, and executive ideology lead these firms in different public affairs directions. Furthermore, while federal deregulation may have exacerbated such inter-firm rivalries, it has also not dampened the demands of the many local and national stakeholders.

These sorts of concerns are no longer fully remedied by trade association activities alone. The role of the modern corporation in its external social milieu is a much-discussed topic. This discussion is evidenced by the proliferation of journalistic commentaries, scholarly articles, and prescriptive books which address topics such as "business and society" or "corporate social responsibility." These writings reflect the sentiments of concerned business managers, open up a forum for the exchange of ideas between practitioners, and expand a constructive dialogue between business and academic communities.

A good deal of this literature, however, merely recycles trendy, value-ridden proposals for action that consider only a fragmentary view of the range of corporate activities. This superficiality is partially due to over-reliance on single-issue or single-company anecdotal data; it is also partially due to an unbalanced fixation on external company actions to the neglect of internal company qualities. The literature in organization theory, a second tradition, is very abstract and has rarely considered public affairs. While this initial approach to business and society discussion has helped to highlight the salience of questions about institutional practices, the time has come to move the discussion toward more systematic levels of investigation.

Such a new research stage requires analysis of the total array of public issues faced by an industry. This book looks at some ways internal company chemistry can contribute to comprehension of company performance across various issues. Public affairs is a particularly complex and confusing area of managerial concern. In the past six or seven decades, we have come to understand the purpose of a company's marketing function and its sector of the environment. The public affairs sector, however, has a wider array of constituencies and a uniquely volatile quality. This new managerial frontier requires thoughtful delegation and coordination. Exploring internal company preparedness can help us to understand how companies organize their actions to gather, transmit inward, and share needed information throughout the firm before management acts. Ill-informed public affairs maneuvers tend to lead to corporate crises. Neither philanthropic donations nor regulatory stonewalling yield companies the needed understanding of their constituencies. Company learning can be enhanced only through its organizational structure.

For such internal exploration of external practices, this book considers six of the leading forest products firms. This industry has a history of addressing a challenging public affairs environment. Public stakeholders have long claimed interests that directly affect the supply, the processing, and the marketing functions of forest products companies. The firms studied, however, differ dramatically in their public affairs performance and internal structure. The studies were accomplished through (1) interviews with and surveys of 140 top executives, (2) surveys of 75 outside stakeholders, and (3) review of archival literature. The book begins with some discussion of the relevant shortcomings of organization-environment adaptations. A model is then offered to add consideration of company structure to business and society research.

Next, two chapters explore the importance of public affairs in this industry by summarizing the economic history and major current social issues facing the industry. Chapters 8 and 9 look at the internal structure of the firm. A new dimension is added in Chapter 10 by a lengthy discussion of company cultures. Chapter 11 presents the internal executive perception of external public affairs, while Chapter 12 presents external stakeholder ratings of company public affairs management. Finally, Chapter 13 ties the findings back to the original model. A revised model is then offered and generalized to other types of firms.

J.A.S.

ACKNOWLEDGMENTS

The necessary guarantee of anonymity for participants precludes a deserved tribute to the many individuals and organizations who so crucially assisted in this research. Seven companies, more than two hundred company executives and forest products industry association officials, and a host of outside industry experts generally greeted this study with honesty, enthusiasm, and good humor. Their gracious sharing of valuable time and insights are an uplifting testimony to the social commitment of the corporate executives, the public stakeholder group officials, and the civil servants involved in this industry.

Closer to home, I would like to express my gratitude to the Division of Research at the Harvard Graduate School of Business Administration for its generous financial support and to Professor E. Raymond Corey, Joanne F. Segal, and Kathryn N. May at the Division of Research. In addition, I acknowledge the generosity of the Western Electric Company, through its "Hawthorne Fellowship," and of Irwin Publications, through its "Richard D. Irwin Fellowship." These three major sources of support facilitated the gathering of the extensive data vital to the wide perspective of this investigation.

Another set of valuable contributors were my sources of inspiration and guidance—people who have the very deep sort of influence that is appreciated not only at the culmination of a project but throughout a career. Professor Paul R. Lawrence has been a major intellectual influence through his early invitation to join him in this style of organizational investigation, his creative enrichment of my conceptual models, and his continued encouragement of my research interests. Professor Thomas K. McCraw provided the important perspectives of external evaluation of corporate public affairs activities and concern for the practicality of social science theories. Professor Robert H. Miles contributed a constant detailed challenge to both my conceptual and methodological plans; through his complementary research in other industries and extraordinary personal dedication, Professor Miles maintained a daily awareness of the developments in this project which rivaled my own. Others who offered unselfishly of their time and ideas include Professor John P. Kotter, Professor Chris Argyris, Professor John Dunlop, Professor Leonard Schlesinger, Professor James Clawson, Arvind Bhambri, Wendy Mela, James Singer, Reid Drucker (all from Harvard); Professor James Post (from Boston University); and Professor Chris Lehman (from Brandeis). A last set of major intellectual influences are my parents, Burton and Rochelle Sonnenfeld and my brother, Marc Sonnenfeld, to whom I am indebted for my interest in the responsiveness of social institutions as well as for their constant encouragement.

Finally, I would like to thank those who facilitated the many mailings, callings, data storage, and manuscript preparation. These individuals include Carolee Weber, Victor Filippini, Robert Ware, John Lechner, Kate Fitzgerald, Gloria Buffonge, Rita Perloff, Kay Smith, Sally Westover, Olivia Fiske, and Valerie Kerr. This group served admirably as translators of my handwriting, as editors and mindreaders, and as librarians of my scattered files.

J.A.S.

CONTENTS

CHAPTER 1
Introduction   1

CHAPTER 2
Beyond the Market: Pressures from Public Affairs   9

Dimensions of the Organizational Environment   10
    Scarcity, or "Munificence" External Control   10
    Environmental Volatility   10
    Environmental Complexity   11
    Subjective Environmental Uncertainty   11
    Research Deficiencies   11
The Boundary to Public Affairs   13
Similarities Across Public Affairs Issues   14
    Government Relations   15
    Community Relations   16
    Labor Relations   17
    Investor Relations   18
Corporate Preparedness for Public Affairs Issues   19

CHAPTER 3
Models of Organizational Adaptation to Public Affairs   27

Adaptation and External Forces   28
    Evolutionary Approaches   28
    Strategic Choice Approaches   30
Adaptation and Internal Preparedness   34
    Business Policy Approaches   35
    Contingency-Theory Approaches   39
Evaluation   43

CHAPTER 4
Model for Perceiving Public Affairs   51

Environment of Public Affairs   53
The Sensory Mechanism   53
Influence (Transmission)   54
Integration (Assimilation)   55
Perceptions   57
Performance   57

CHAPTER 5
Methods   61

Multimethod-Multisource Design   61
Constituencies Beyond the Marketplace   61
The Company Interviews   64
The Company Survey   65
Survey Administration   66
Measurement of Company Structure   67
Measurement of Perceptions   69
Measurement of Responsiveness: Interviews and Survey   70

CHAPTER 6
Development of the Forest Products Industry   73

The Industry Setting   73
History of the Timber Industry   75
History of the Pulp and Paper Industry   76
An Economic Perspective   79
Effects of the Recession   82
Technological Advances in Forest Management   83
Summary   88

CHAPTER 7
Public Issues in the Forest Products Industry   91

Conservation versus Timber Supply   92
    The Politics of Protection   92
    Timber Harvesting and Public Affairs   97
    Forest Management Issues   99
The Industry's Response   99
Labor-Related Issues   103
Pollution Control   107
Energy and Transportation   114
Financial Considerations   115
The Marketing Perspective   117
Conclusions   119

CHAPTER 8
Departments as Receptors 127

Interaction with Stakeholders 127
   Interaction Time 128
   Breadth of Interaction 135
Appreciation 135
Attention 139
Listenership 139
Conclusions 141

CHAPTER 9
Structural Sensitivity of the Companies 143

Departmental Receptivity 143
   Interacting with Stakeholders 143
   Breadth of Contact 151
   Appreciating the Value of Source Information 152
   Attention and Listening 155
   Depth of Involvement 155
Public Affairs Influence 156
Internal Integration 156
Conclusions 159

CHAPTER 10
Cultural Sensitivity to Public Affairs 163

Pacific Timber 166
   Reputation 166
   Establishing Contact 170
   Executive Themes 171
New York Paper 173
   Reputation 173
   Establishing Contact 174
   Executive Themes 175
Central Paper 177
   Reputation 177
   Establishing Contact 178
   Executive Themes 179
Northwest Forests 182
   Reputation 182
   Establishing Contact 183
   Executive Themes 184

American Forests   187
   Reputation   187
   Establishing Contact   188
   Executive Themes   189
U.S. Paper   192
   Reputation   192
   Establishing Contact   196
   Executive Themes   196
Conclusions   199

CHAPTER 11
Executive Perceptions of Public Affairs   203

Receptor Bias   204
Differences in Company Perceptions: Priorities   211
Differences in Company Perceptions: Company Posture   213
Differences in Company Perceptions: Internal Consensus   221
Summary   221

CHAPTER 12
Company Social Responsiveness   225

Industry Responsiveness   226
Stakeholder Bias   228
Company Differences   231
Summary   237

CHAPTER 13
Conclusions   239

The Business Constituency beyond the Market   239
A Sensory System Model   241
Public Affairs and Corporate Structure   242
Responsiveness and Corporate Structure   244
Public Affairs and Corporate Culture   244
A Revised Model   246
Managerial Implications   248
Academic Implications   252

APPENDIXES
The Interview Instruments   257

Index   275

Chapter 1

INTRODUCTION

A growing number of corporate staff and management people are finding themselves responsible for keeping their companies responsive to public affairs challenges. Some of them are general managers, while others are experts on law, government, human resources, and communications. Although they sometimes react independently to outside pressures, these "corporate defenders" also interact among themselves and with other members of the organization. Accordingly, they are best viewed as parts of the corporation's total system for detecting and analyzing diverse societal developments.

Consideration of corporate social performance has usually focussed narrowly on the social responsibilities of management. In fact, however, the long-discussed ethical and legal aspects of "social responsibility"[1] are quite distinct from the corporation's need for "public affairs responsiveness."[2] Social *responsiveness* implies a continuing state of awareness of public affairs and a readiness to comprehend them. Social responsibility, on the other hand, generally refers to the ethics of the corporation in a particular situation. They differ in that social responsibility is assessed through external performance and its *consequences,* while social responsiveness is assessed in terms of the quality of the *response process.* The large corporation today needs a coordinated companywide facility for continuously scanning and monitoring public affairs and for planning policy. In this book we shall examine some important prerequisites for clear perception of public issues.

The unprecedented degree of change in the social environment over the past twenty years has left many business organizations disoriented. In addition to the uncertainty of the market environment, they must deal with a foundation that seemingly is giving way beneath them. Many social needs have become as important as the traditional primary objectives of business—profits, growth, prestige, and power. In the years between 1970 and 1975 there was a 25 percent increase in the number of federal "economic" regulatory agencies and a 42 percent

1

increase in the number of federal "social" regulatory agencies. It has been estimated that in 1965 "heavily regulated industries" represented 7 percent of the U.S. GNP; by 1978 this figure had grown to over 30 percent.[3] Now there are 116 agencies regulating such routine business activities as workforce recruitment, incentive schemes, securities transactions, competitive practices, workplace safety, product design, pollution by effluent and emission, plant location, advertising, and retirement plans. Local communities have also added restrictions reflecting their particular concerns.

Significant shifts in needs and public expectations have resulted as the children of the post–World War II baby boom have aged.[4] A highly educated, underemployed public that has witnessed a decade of violence and scandalous public leadership has become deeply disenchanted with and distrustful of big government and big business. Pollster Louis Harris reported recently in *Business Week* that the general population's confidence in business leadership has plummeted to 22 percent from 55 percent at the beginning of the decade.[5] Broad social issues tend to penetrate corporate strategy and policies so deeply that they transport the corporation beyond its market role to a role as a principal social institution. Hence, this external arena can be considered part of the organization's "institutional environment" as opposed to its market environment.[6] In this institutional environment, the organization must establish its social legitimacy. Dealing with public affairs is the predominant activity in this environment. The expectations of many diverse, external stakeholders of the corporation must be considered.[7]

Public affairs, then, are not merely peripheral concerns of management. Issues such as the controversy over the infant milk formula, redlining for urban banks and insurance companies, the fluorocarbon ban, price fixing, television violence, and the health risks of smoking all demonstrate the close interweaving of social concerns with the marketing and operations aspects of a business. Although an entire industry may face the same public issues, merely relying on industry associations for response is not enough. Rather, individual companies must prepare their own responses. Companies may, of course, share a common exposure to public claims within an industry as well as across industries. Corporate action through industry associations is practical in situations in which firms share highly similar fates. But when the differences among companies are fundamental, such as in terms of product lines, operations, geographic location, managerial ideology, and managerial style, awareness is needed at the level of the firm. Work by Post, Sonnenfeld, and Lawrence and by Miles has detailed how company responses to issues within the same industry show varied success.[8]

A *Wall Street Journal* article on the surprise legislation altering

NOW accounts for New York banks well dramatizes the spillover between sectors. This hybrid of checking and savings accounts had long been available in New England, but as the Wall Street Journal reported:[9]

> *Federal legislation extending the service to New York state was passed last weekend by Congress in a last-minute flurry of bill passing before recessing. Most bankers weren't even aware the bill would come to a vote. Those who were, moreover, believed passage was unlikely.*

Many bankers panicked when they realized that their institutions might need months to prepare for authorized services that were to begin at once. One bank executive complained, "This thing came out of left field!" Many banks had already begun to advertise elaborately prepared but now obsolete alternative services. Top executives, lobbyists, marketing managers, and operations people had all assumed that someone else was preparing the bank to meet this issue.

Who, indeed, should be responsible for handling public affairs? Many traditional writers on business policy have looked to the chief executive as the institutional leader to be the corporate ambassador to society.[10] During a conference at the Harvard Business School, Du Pont's chief executive officer (CEO), Irving Shapiro called on his peers to assume this responsibility:[11]

> *CEOs are now found tramping through the corridors of Washington and the state capitals, testifying, talking with elected representatives and administrative aides, pleading cases in the agency offices and occasionally in the White House. Reporters are learning our names, and finding that many more of us have our doors open.*

The chief executives of large American companies such as Pfizer, General Electric, Bendix, and Du Pont claimed, according to *Business Week*, that they spend more than 25 percent of their time monitoring and speaking on institutional matters. The effectiveness of such CEOs has been shown by the attention and force marshaled by the Business Round Table, a new dynamic group of 200 of the country's strongest CEOs.[12]

This CEO activism, however, is being challenged by many organization analysts. Peter Drucker has suggested that a long-term price is paid for the short-term effectiveness and commitment a chief executive might offer:[13]

> *The new demands thus argue for a fairly drastic change in top management structure and top management jobs. Traditionally, American top managers gave three-fourths of their time to managing day-to-day business. Most still try today, but they have only a fifth of their time available for the job. They thus tend to stretch themselves even more thinly—and in the end slight both the public activities and the strategic decisions.*

On top of this time limitations constrain the chief executive's skill and expertise.[14]

To compensate for the unavailability of the chief executive, there has been an increasing use of public affairs futurists, scanners, compliance officers, and planners. Recent reports, however, indicate a confused allotment of responsibilities among chief executives, lawyers, lobbyists, public relations people, compliance officers, public affairs scanners, and corporate planners. This confusion among practitioners has not been properly considered by the literature of theorists on organization. The literature generally considers responses destined for reaction to environmental events instead of dealing with advance preparation to meet new issues. Two leading scholars have stated that environmental scanning may be dangerous:[15]

> *One can imagine some advantages to ignoring environmental change. Knowing about the change puts the organization in the position of having to respond to it.*

The systematic bias introduced by one's particular window on the world from an organization is largely ignored in the literature.[16] Furthermore, organizational adaptation theory considers only market and technology issues, completely ignoring the important and pervasive environment of public affairs.

Our interest will be in trying to correct these two important oversights and to alleviate the practitioners' confusion. Perception of the public affairs environment is very much a function of the structure of an organization. Although many other variables such as executive attitudes, past corporate history, and basic strength in resources influence perception of the environment, the power of the dominant management coalition is largely the determining factor.[17] The professional breadth and internal influence of this group control how accurately and thoroughly the environment is comprehended. The task of understanding the environment has become so complex that differentiation of responsibility at top management levels is a necessity for scanning and feedback. At the same time, as environmental demands multiply and compete for limited resources, top-level coordination also becomes a necessity. As in the human sensory system, perception is clear only when the various sensory receptors carrying different messages about the environment are integrated.

Accordingly, any organization whose perception of the environment is primarily influenced by any single perspective such as that of the chief executive, of government lobbyists, of public relations experts, of lawyers, of engineers, or of operating officials would be likely to differ from organizations that have more balanced environmental scanning. For example, a company with a problem in disposing of toxic waste may not view its surrounding public terrain through merely one single window. Rather, many company officials may simultaneously have a different outlook on the same issue; the perceptions from the corporate windows vary by location and by who is looking out. Thus a company's environmental engineers may focus both on understanding the technical specifications needed to meet public demands and on internal technical capabilities. This may involve close interaction between state and federal regulators and company operating personnel. At the same time, public relations officers may be trying to shape public opinion, to persuade the media to be more empathic with the company, and to understand the different interests of various community segments (such as angry property owners, relatives of victims, town forums, civic groups, and the local press). Meanwhile various executives who handle government relations are likely the most interested in state and federal legislation. Thus they are most likely to lobby legislators and confront opposing lobbies and form alliances with sympathetic forces. Company lawyers may focus on judicial precedent and be cautiously exploring strategies needed to protect the company from present or potential courtroom events. Their position may involve an adversary stance and abstract principles. Operations executives may push for quick resolution of any public controversy that could mean costly production delays and process changes. Finally, the chief executive may make public pronouncements of corporate ideology and intentions when facing other institutional leaders.

While each of these officials is learning about conditions and acting on behalf of the corporation, it is easy to imagine scenarios in which they are working at cross purposes. Each department interacts with different external groups in forums that vary in formality, specificity, and emotional intensity. The professional languages, defensiveness, time pressures, and priorities are also likely to vary across departments. The mechanism of gathering data is akin to the physiological mechanism of sensory *reception*. For sensible interpretation, there must be forceful *transmission* of information to a central *integrative* body. Thus we shall examine transmission and integration as key internal ingredients of a company's design for responsiveness to public expectations.

The current relevant literature suffers from three severe methodological weaknesses in addition to the cited conceptual problems. First, much of the literature in business and public affairs traces single issues and single company responses. This approach fails to help the practicing manager who does not have the luxury of "one-issue thinking." As Irving Shapiro explained, "People in jobs like mine have similar sets of constituencies and overlapping concerns. We have to try to balance them all."[18] Second, the tendency to study single companies leads to a swapping of war stories and highly anecdotal learning.[19] Third, these anecdotal studies do not provide any systematic measurement of effectiveness. What is needed instead are studies that compare different companies facing similar issues.

This research effort is a study of the multiple public affairs pressures faced by several companies in a single industry, forest products. In the study, we have taken these methodological problems into account. The forest products industry is such that we can make a fairly smooth generalization relative to many other U.S. industries; from it, we can provide examples of the various types of exposure to public affairs that American industry is beginning to face. Forest products is a nationwide industry; it is fairly unconcentrated and not subject to any special revolutions in its technological or market environments. The industry is free of any special arrangements with an economic regulatory agency, although it has faced a growing array of community, labor, governmental, and legislative threats.

A company in the forest products industry frequently controls much of the lives and well-being of those who live in the small towns around its mills. Critical mill openings and closings have become troublesome events. The logging, sawing, and paper production processes are very hazardous. Labor relations are notoriously poor, as evidenced by a seven-month strike in West Coast paper mills in 1977. Serious environmental controversies surround the intense struggles over increased cutting on public forest lands, air pollution from pulp mills, water pollution from mills, aerial spray of dangerous herbicides and pesticides, and solid-waste issues (bottles, recycled paper). Many of these environmental concerns and also land taxation issues and labor issues have both local and national aspects. Antitrust prosecutions also have cost the industry several hundred millions of dollars in penalties, plus jail sentences for executives, morale loss, and recruitment problems in connection with fixing prices of folding cartons, fire papers, corrugated containers, and plywood.

Using data collected from seven of the top ten companies in the industry, this book examines "megacorporations," for which, owing to sheer size, exposure to public affairs is much like that in other industries. Each of the companies has a wide national base, even though three have headquarters in the West, two in the Midwest, and two in the East. Each of these companies employs more than 30,000 workers and has sales from multiple product lines exceeding $3 billion.

The first step in the study was to interview the chief executive and top vice presidents of line operations and public affairs units, along with their staffs—roughly 15–20 people per company. The interviews probed how responsibility for public affairs and for the perception of public issues was allocated. Secondly, a questionnaire was designed for uniform measurement across companies. Finally, interviews with roughly 100 outside industry experts led to creation of a panel comprising journalists, environmentalists, congressional staff members, regulators, investment community spokesmen, and trade association officials. The function of the panel was to evaluate the apparent responsiveness at participating companies. Our three objectives were as follows:

1. An improved understanding of how managers can design their organizations to be responsive to public issues and to remain responsive to them.
2. An expansion of theories of how an organization adapts to the environment of public affairs.
3. A demonstration of the bias that derives from the structure of an organization and how it affects the organization's perception of the environment.

Such mixtures of practical and academic knowledge are long overdue. The famous Kurt Lewin aphorism that "there is nothing so practical as good theory" is only half the story. Eminent social scientist Dorwin Cartwright has explained that the full context of that passage revealed the true meaning:[20]

Lewin's essential point was that the theorist and the practitioner share common interests, that they have interdependent tasks, and that it is the special obligation of the theorist to provide the kind of theory that can be used for the solution of social problems. It is therefore somewhat ironical that only his advice to the practitioner should have gained such widespread popularity.

To begin, we shall look closely at a definition of the competence required in an organization for managing the environment of public affairs. How adequate are the various theoretical perspectives on organizational adaptation to guide company behavior? The model we develop for analyzing the completeness of a firm's design for processing information on public affairs will be examined as it applies in the field. For the particular industrial environment studied (forest products), top executive views of public interest claims vis á vis their own corporations' interests, as well as their views of corporate behavior are enlightening. We expect our principal themes to have relevance to theory and practice. By the end of the book we hope to have demonstrated that public affairs occurances are in no way low management priorities, and that internal preparation for understanding these important events is certainly mandated.

Endnotes

1. M. Moskowitz, "Profiles in Corporate Responsibility," *Business and Society Review*, 17 (1975), pp. 28–42. Also H. G. Manne and H. G. Wallich, *The Modern Corporation and Social Responsibility* (Washington, D.C.: The American Enter-

prise Institute, 1972); D. J. Hargreaves and J. Dauman, *Business Survival and Social Change* (New York: John Wiley, 1975); C. C. Abt, *The Social Audit for Management* (New York: Amacom, 1977).

2. L. E. Preston and J. E. Post, *Private Management and Public Responsibility* (Englewood Cliffs, N.J.: Prentice-Hall, 1975). Also S. P. Sethi, *Up Against the Corporate Wall* (Englewood Cliffs, N.J.: Prentice-Hall, 1977).

3. D. M. Kasper, "Note on Managing in a Regulated Environment," Intercollegiate Case Clearinghouse, 1-379-032, (Cambridge, Mass.: Harvard University Press, 1978).

4. J. Sonnenfeld, "Dealing with an Aging Workforce," *Harvard Business Review*, 56 (November–December 1978), pp. 81–92.

5. "The Corporate Image, PR to the Rescue," *Business Week* (January 22, 1979), pp. 46–61.

6. P. Seleznik, *Leadership in Administration* (New York: Harper and Row, 1957). Also T. Parsons, *Structure and Process in Modern Societies* (New York: Free Press, 1960); R. H. Hall, *Organizations: Structure and Process* (Englewood Cliffs, N.J.: Prentice Hall, 1972).

7. F. D. Sturdivant, "Executives and Activists: Test of Stakeholder Management," *California Management Review* (1979). Also Sethi, *op. cit.*

8. J. E. Post, *Corporate Behavior and Social Change* (Reston, Va.: Reston Publishing, 1978). Also J. Sonnenfeld and P. R. Lawrence, "Why Do Companies Succumb to Price-Fixing?", *Harvard Business Review*, 56 (July–August 1978), pp. 145–157; R. H. Miles, *Macro Organizational Behavior* (Santa Monica, Ca: Goodyear, 1980).

9. E. P. Foldessey, "Passage of Bill Allowing NOW Accounts in New York Catches Banks Unprepared," *Wall Street Journal* (Oct. 17, 1978), p. 6.

10. Seleznik, *op. cit.* Also K. R. Andrews, *The Concept of Corporate Strategy* (Homewood, Ill.: Irwin, 1971). Also R. W. Ackerman, *The Social Challenge to Business* (Cambridge, Mass.: Harvard University Press, 1975).

11. I. S. Shapiro, with J. T. Dunlop, A. D. Chandler, and G. P. Schultz, "Business and Public Policy," *Harvard Business Review* (Nov.–Dec. 1979), pp. 85–102.

12. Kim McQuaid, "The Roundtable: Getting Results in Washington," *Harvard Business Review*, (May–June 1981), pp. 114–124.

13. P. F. Drucker, "Coping with those Extra Burdens," *Wall Street Journal*, (May 2, 1979), p. 22.

14. G. J. Aguilar, *Scanning the Business Environment* (New York: Macmillan, 1967).

15. J. Pfeffer and G. R. Salancik, *The External Control of Organizations* (New York: Harper & Row, 1977), p. 268.

16. W. H. Starbuck, "Organizations and Their Environments," in *The Handbook of Industrial and Organizational Psychology*, M. D. Dunnette, ed. (Chicago: Rand-McNally, 1976), pp. 1175–1199. Also J. Sonnenfeld, "Executive Apologies for Price Fixing: Role-Biased Perceptions of Causality," *Academy of Management Journal*, 24, 1 (1981), pp. 192–198.

17. J. D. Thompson, *Organizations in Action* (New York: McGraw-Hill, 1967).

18. Shapiro, *op. cit.*

19. Post, *op. cit.* Also J. K. Brown, *This Business of Issues: Coping with the Company's Environment* (New York: The Conference Board, 758, 1979).

20. D. Cartwright, "Theory and Practice," *Journal of Social Issues*, 34, 4 (1978), pp. 168–180.

Chapter 2

BEYOND THE MARKET: PRESSURES FROM PUBLIC AFFAIRS

Academicians, much like practicing managers, have long tended to view the business-society interface in a cursory and fragmentary manner. Over the past thirty years, however, theorists have increasingly come to appreciate the extent to which external environmental factors affect the behavior of organizations. Even though the trend has been toward analyzing the environment as it relates to a specific industry, public issues may place common demands on companies across industries. Theoretic development and increasingly turbulent business environments both have challenged the value of the rigid universalistic implications of "classical bureaucratic theory"[1] and of "scientific management."[2] This challenge also applies to the "human relations" movement in management theory, which considers the social context within organizations but not the external social context.[3]

The gauntlet has been picked up by theorists who favor more open systems and who have considered the effects of various dimensions of organizations' external environment.[4] A prominent group of these writers, the "contingency school" theorists have explained that different organizations are likely to face very different sets of external market and technological forces.[5] Therefore, they believe, a "one-best-way" concept of managing environments seems inadequate. The difficulty in accurately generalizing across the markets of various industries should not blind us to common patterns in the environment across industries that relate to public affairs.

9

Dimensions of the Organizational Environment

The "open systems" thesis seems to specify types of environments that fit into three objective categories—(1) scarcity, (2) volatility, and (3) complexity—and one subjective dimension, perceived uncertainty. (The following section will review these descriptions.) The fundamental scarcity of resources and subsequent difficulties in distribution is an axiomatic concern of political scientists and economists.[6] The distribution of resources is important for explaining competitor and customer-supplier relations. More generally, the importance of scarcity in resources to organizational analysis has been well portrayed in the "strategic choice" perspectives and "external control" perspective.[7]

Scarcity, or "Munificence" External Control

In handling scarcity, organizations try to change their patterns of dependence on resources (for example, by environmental domain, barriers to entry, cooperation, interlocking directorates, cartels, and mergers).[8] Support for such theory is found in works such as Chamberlain's on competitor behavior, Evan's on an "organization set," or interlocking networks of organization roles, Williamson's on "market failures," Stigler's on oligopoly pricing, and Staw and Swajakowski's and Sonnenfeld and Lawrence's on illegal corporate behavior.[9]

Environmental Volatility

Volatility is as important as scarcity in the firm's environment. Burns and Stalker have suggested that an investigation of the rate of change in scientific technology and markets can help explain different management practices in different industries.[10] Emery and Trist used the concepts of scarcity and volatility to derive a four-celled typology of environmental scenarios, labeled the causal texture.[11] These cells are:

1. Placid-randomized (calm, resources randomly distributed).
2. Placid-clustered (calm, predictable pattern of resources).
3. Disturbed-reactive (competitive interdependence).
4. Turbulent (the field itself rather than the components alone shifting, events outside immediate control of transacting organizations).

This typology attributes the frequency and magnitude of change toward the environment to the different availability of resources. This means that what the organization does, and the attendant consequences thereof, very much depends on the predictability it can expect from the environment and the depth of its relations to different factors.

Environmental Complexity

The four cells mentioned do not, however, indicate the nature of the actors or the events in the environment. This *complexity* can be interpreted as the number and variety of environmental components.

Along these lines, Thompson has created a four-celled typology of environmental uncertainty that uses the dimension of complexity (which he has termed *heterogeneity*) along with the dimension of volatility (which he has termed *stability*).[12] Both high volatility and great complexity are thought to contribute to the difficulty of getting certain information on the environment. A key management task then, it was suggested, is to lessen this environmental uncertainty that complex organizations face. Managing *environmental uncertainty*, it is held, is the fundamental challenge of complex organizations.

Subjective Environmental Uncertainty

Many researchers agree that the identifying of uncertainty is of critical importance to management, but they have relied on subjective measures for assessing environmental uncertainty. That individuals perceive things differently is the basis for a fourth approach.[13] Lawrence and Lorsch, for example, examined the perception of organization members with regard to clarity of information, time span, and predictability. The "external control" school has studied lack of information, knowledge of outcomes of events, and inability to assign probabilities to events. Duncan has postulated that the perceived routine of problems seems to closely relate to these other measures of perceived environmental uncertainty.[14] Such subjective measures have been dismissed as reflecting more the individual perceiver's attributes than objective attributes of the environment. Accordingly, Tosi, Aldag, and Storey, and Downey, Hellriegal, and Slocum reported difficulty establishing replicability and reliability with such measures.[15] For example, an individual's tolerance for ambiguity could be very much involved with such evaluations. However, it has also been frequently theorized that management's subjective perception of the environment, however biased, may be more important than objective realities in understanding an organization's behaviors.[16]

Research Deficiencies

An oversight shared by all the above research is the failure to consider the effect of organization members' roles and their environmental perspectives. The form of an organization frequently determines management windows to the outside world. Starbuck commented in his extensive review of the literature on the environments of an organization, "None seems to have analyzed how subjective perceptions systematically deviate from objective evidence, let alone how perceptual distortions vary from actual organizational characteristics; for sure this is research terrain awaiting cultivation."[17] Pfeffer and Salancik argue that how an organization sets up its information systems and related activities directs the firm's attention and can lead to "misreading of the environment."[18] Dearborn and Simon have shown how misunderstanding is possible in a classroom setting,[19] and Sonnenfeld has demonstrated systematic bias in explaining company criminal behavior.[20] Future research is needed to compare organizations that have tried to correct for bias with those that have not.

A second limitation in the literature is the failure to appropriately consider broader pictures of the environment than what market and technology present. Many years ago Parsons identified three levels of management issues: (1) technical, (2) managerial, and (3) institutional.[21] The institutional environment was identified as the arena in which an organization steps beyond its market purpose and assumes a social role equal to other foremost forces in the community, such as governmental bodies, other business organizations, the church, and public interest concerns. The environmental typologies that have helped in studying how an organization adapts to the environment are much more related to what Hall called the "specific" environment, or what others have called the "task environment."[22] The actors in such an environment include only those forces with direct product-exchange relations. The initial literature on adaptation has focused on the market-technology issues, which were perhaps more pressing in past decades.

Despite the growing importance of other outside influences on businesses besides the market and technology, recent research on organizational adaptation still fails to consider the full complex nature of the environment. Miles and Snow, for example, impressively integrated structural, strategic, and environmental analyses in a study of almost 100 firms, yet never looked at the social involvement of these firms in any context broader than the "entrepreneurial" level—that is, the environment as it related to marketing the product.[23] The recent broadened perspective of the "external control of organizations" accordingly considers relations with regulatory agencies and methods of enhancing interorganizational arrangements (cartels, price fixing, protective agencies, and the like).[24] Yet while the government has been recognized as an important environmental factor of organizations there has been little cognizance of other social factors such as interest groups, journalists, and civic associations. Even the governmental influence has been largely regarded as centered around the older economic regulation of the market mechanisms, while the effect of newer, more

pervasive "social regulation" on businesses has essentially been neglected.[25] Pfeffer and Salancik state that "organizations act to achieve
social legitimacy," but they acknowledge that their methods of reducing dependence on resources have not been tested in an environmental
context wider than the marketplace.[26] The great advances in adaptation
theory must be broadened to consider the increasingly prominent
forces beyond the marketplace.

The Boundary to Public Affairs

While those who write about organization adaptation have often neglected the institutional environment, writers on social performance
have directly discussed this business-society relation. An expanded
concept of the environment, however, can lead to confusion over who
is on the outside and who is on the inside of an organization. Almost
thirty years ago, Lem Boulware, a prominent executive of General
Electric, declared that the primary work of managers was to consider
the interests of five separate publics: (1) customers, (2) employees, (3)
shareowners, (4) community neighbors, and (5) governments.

It has been noted that the boundaries as sketched by the theorists on
social performance are "even more ambiguous than those of clouds and
magnetic fields. A boundary between the outside and the organization
can be seen as largely a construction of the perceiver."[27] Downs
suggested that since all organizations are really part of large social
systems, drawing boundaries is really for analytic convenience.[28] Several other theorists have consciously adapted that perspective.[29]

The multitude of overlapping roles and organizational identities for
individuals has caused systems theorists to think of organizations as
limited to the "partial inclusion" of organization members.[30] The notion here is that individuals are defined by their overlapping roles or
memberships rather than by membership in any particular organization. This concept of partial inclusion interprets the organization as a
structure designed to control *behavior* instead of *individuals*. Reason-
ing from this, Pfeffer and Salancik have appropriately used *"activities"*
as their boundary criterion.[31]

> *The boundary should be drawn where the discretion of the organiza-
> tion to control an activity is less than the discretion of another organiza-
> tion or individual to control that activity.*

The environment that provides public affairs can be more usefully
defined for our purposes by applying this "activity" criterion.

Every business leader must respond to "stakeholder" groups, whose
collective activity may affect the company's figure.[32] Business and soci-

ety researchers customarily look at interactions between corporations and stockholders, employees, consumers, the news media, public interest groups, special interest groups, public values, community programs, and various governments.[33] These outside interest groups, the stakeholders, evaluate the *process* and the side-effects, as opposed to evaluating the intended products of the operations.[34] It is the outside forces that primarily grant social legitimacy to the operations.[35] Parsons spoke of three organizational subsystems having relations with the outside: (1) The *technical* interface, which defines the distinctive productive competence of the enterprise; (2) the *administrative* subsystem, which provides managerial support and coordination; and (3) the *institutional* interface, which negotiates and maintains the license from society to operate.[36] Preston and Post condensed both the technical and the administrative subsystems into one concept, "primary involvements," which is characterized by exchange activities.[37] The remaining, institutional subsystem, however, is characterized by secondary involvement that is generally "not intrinsic to the character of the organization but generated by its primary involvement activities."[38] The outside stakeholder groups naturally have varying interests. Researchers on social performance therefore run the risk of overemphasizing specific issues, failing to generalize appropriately about public affairs.

Similarities Across Public Affairs Issues

The earlier discussion about the causal texture of the environment may be a helpful basis for considering the great turbulence and complexity of the current public expectations from big U.S. corporations. Simple notions about the environment may have been justified in earlier times, but they are inappropriately narrow now as sectors of the environment have become intertwined and volatile. Institutional activities or secondary involvement have become increasingly important with the growing connection between organizations and expanding public expectations.[39] An interesting example is found in Post.[40] He charted the insurance industry's evolution from the "placid-randomized" environment of the colonial waterfront to a more competitive, and eventually a complex, "turbulent" environment composed of state and federal regulations along with a multitude of pressures from regional and national interest groups. Several other researchers have found that organizational environments are becoming increasingly turbulent through the proliferation of interorganizational pathways and obligations.[41] Coalitions, trade associations, and new channels of interorganizational communication proliferate to help manage environmental constraints.[42]

This increase in the interconnection of our big organizations is correlated with shifting public expectations. It has been suggested that we have moved from the eighteenth- and nineteenth-century value system of profit maximization, idealized by Calvinism and Adam Smith's invisible hand on the market, and the early-twentieth-century notion of trustee management, or the visible hand of detached management, as first noticed in American railroads to a more pluralistic, "quality-of-life" management, representing collectivist, or "communitarian," values.[43] Andrew Hacker, a political scientist, commented about the past two decades:[44]

> *Executives found it increasingly difficult to claim they were merely running a business. Accepting a military contract meant abetting an Asian war. Investing in overseas subsidaries could strengthen repressive regimes. Ordinary industrial processes might adversely affect the environment. Traditional hiring practices denied careers to millions of Americans. Besieged with reasoning of this sort, corporations could no longer insist on the rights of private enterprise.*

Recent surveys suggest a continuation of this philosophical trend. A Harris (1977) poll of *Harvard Business Review* readers over the past decade found that managers paradoxically reported both increases in political activity by businesses and little effectiveness in this activity.[45] A survey of opinion leaders, industry figures, scholars, journalists, congressional staffers, and agency chiefs concluded that egalitarian and humanistic-environmental values are slowly becoming public policy.[46]

Government Relations

This ideological shift has been manifested by complex and unstable public events. Between 1970 and 1975 there was a 25 percent increase in the number of big federal "social" regulatory agencies.[47] It has been estimated that in 1978, "heavily regulated industries" represented over 30 percent of the GNP.[48] Hansen explained that this new legislation is much harder for management to respond to than the older, commission-based regulation of the marketplace:[49]

> *The greatest difference is the existence of multiple governmental actors who can influence corporate operation. Most commission-based firms have had to deal with only a single actor. Secondly the rapidity of social and public policy changes in recent years has necessitated quick and continuing shifts in corporate policy and action.*

In addition to this federal regulation there has been even greater regulatory growth during the last two decades at the state and local levels.

Leone has pointed out that the diversity of ways in which such government regulation affects companies differentially within an industry indicates that policy formulation must develop beyond delegation to industrywide consideration.[50] He illustrated how this newer regulation fundamentally affects the competitive structure of industries through differential cost burdens and changes in relations with other institutions. Leone and Jackson have added that the dynamic quality of this interaction suggests that the political and technical phases of the regulatory process are intertwined.[51] Technical assessments of how various regulatory standards affect cost and efficiency ultimately affect policy. Self-interest dictates that firms think with both technical and political sophistication about regulation. Public policy initiations have been essential through the development of many industries (for example, railroads, aerospace, oil, utilities, and health). Now many more must consider the strategies and implications of public policy.

A new piece of legislation that highlights the need for careful thinking is the "bubble concept" of allowable offsetting air pollution emissions.[52] This sort of regulation involves continual interchange among several businesses and government agencies. This requires shrewder political skills and communication skills than mere lobbying. The many parties must negotiate in large groups and in informal arenas. The capacity to understand each other's needs becomes critical, since there is small chance of being able to rely on bureaucracy for objective resolution. Such an interactive approach to public policy is difficult however, since business has tended to internally centralize its contact with government, while government has tended to become more diffuse in dealing with business.[53]

Community Relations

In addition, the response of an organization to public issues is made difficult by the number of issues that are on the edge of formal governmental involvement. These have to do with community pressure groups, local economic and demographic changes, and public interest forces. A good example of such an issue is the mandating of the social behavior of large corporations. This was actively supported by a broad alliance of consumer, labor, religious, and environmental groups as they lobbied for legislation on standards in a demonstration on "Big Business Day 1980."[54] Schmenner has illustrated why actors on multiple public affairs must be used in assessing the prevailing business climate when an operating site is being sought.[55] The lack of well-staffed regional and local departments of public affairs in large corporations does not allow a firm to draw a cogent and sensitive picture of local public affairs. Many law firms and consulting firms have eagerly responded to this need, filling a rapidly growing ambassadorial function in representing a company's interests in distant locations.

Labor Relations

Conflicting hierarchical styles of management and trade unions have made it hard to monitor sensitivity to external labor voices. Walton and McKersie outlined a continuum of collective bargaining postures, from very antagonistic, distributive battling to more integrative, cooperative approaches that appreciate mutually beneficial negotiations.[56] An effective negotiator must understand and accommodate the needs of his opponent to strip away irrelevant conflict and give proper attention to actual disagreement. In particular, the negotiator should not behave in a way that undermines the long-run interest of the relation.[57] Researchers have found that one of the reasons workers join trade unions is for better communication with management.[58] Such communication is inhibited in an atmosphere of hostility and distrust. The last decade has witnessed increased joint labor-management approaches to issues about the quality of work life, and to tax cuts, trade policies, and energy planning. Ill-informed business hostility to the legitimacy of labor's role, however, has partly led to a dangerous cooling off between labor and management. Labor expert D. Quinn Mills explained:[59]

> By and large, U.S. unions have not challenged the moral and political legitimacy of private business, but the contest over labor law reform has suggested to them that private business does not accept them as partners. Would it be surprising if they ceased to recognize the legitimacy of private enterprise in turn? What would the political landscape be with a leftist trade union movement? Or what would be the consequence of vigorous union support of proposals to reform corporate governance or to limit mergers and acquisitions, which the unions have not yet chosen strongly to support?

Much of this new animosity has stemmed from miscommunication at the structurally uneven business-labor boundary. The battle over the Labor Reform Act of 1978 was seen by labor as providing minor fine-tuning of existing guidelines. It dealt with representation, election proceedings, and extension of various powers of the National Labor Relations Board. The thunderous crushing business response was seen by labor as a rejection of their right to represent the labor force.

Such miscommunication and conflict can be related to the organizational structure of the bargaining bodies. The opposite hierarchical forms of unions and corporations can show up in negotiations—not only in the promotion of harmful stereotypes but also in the impairment of information transfer and in delegation of authority. Executives not designated as negotiators may receive filtered information or may disruptively intervene in the bargaining. Glueck has commented that[60]

> ... important as the socioeconomic and educational background of these two groups are, the differences in the nature of their organizations can

strongly affect the perceptions, motivation, and behavior of these two groups in collective bargaining.

Union officials are far more laterally oriented than democratic personnel experts in corporations, who tend to be oriented in a vertical relation with superiors.[61]

In addition, the negotiator, as a staff specialist, tends to be remote from central activities of the organization and to have low status in principal decisions. Perry and Angle thus warn that:[62]

> . . . as the psychological distance of labor and management negotiators from their respective constituencies increases, the quality of joint decisions will decrease, . . . and the labor-management relationship pattern will be increasingly marked by conflict.

More specifically, poor rapport may result from ambiguity about goals, shown in conflicting messages from organization subunits. Negotiators may respond by assuming an overly tough stance against opponents to impress their constituencies with their strength. Further, such negative actions may be intentional efforts to create conflict and crisis, with the idea of increasing the importance of the negotiator's role in the organization. Crisis-free approaches that try to allow for future situations are possible but rare in managing such human resource issues as changing workforce expectations and demographics and manpower planning.[63] Progress in agreement on these issues and on issues such as privacy, flexitime, and worker dislocation has demonstrated the great value of union-management cooperation.[64] Lost momentum on these efforts leads to crisis and formal government intervention.

Investor Relations

Even relations with the investment community have become more difficult. The sharp decline in the number of brokerage houses has made it more difficult for specialized analysts to follow businesses closely.[65] As outside observers, analysts can easily misclassify or misinterpret company efforts. Analysts feel most confident when they have the chance to meet with company executives in small groups at regular intervals.[66]

The shareholder is no longer passive, silent, or indifferent. This is well demonstrated by the many proxy battles today over corporate social responsibility and merger activity. In addition, lobbying for fuller disclosure on overseas government activities, currency exchanges, and illegal activities has influenced standards established by the Securities and Exchange Commission, the Financial Accounting Standards Board, and the big stock exchanges. Chatlus has commented that despite such new shareholder activism:[67]

> *. . . few companies really know their stockholders. This in itself is a paradox of good public relations techniques. A public relations department properly devotes much of its energy to studying and researching its "publics" prior to planning its activities. Yet many companies expect to have good stockholder relations programs without researching or knowing their shareholders at all.*

Credibility and awareness here, as with the other groups discussed, is achieved, in part, through a closer interactive involvement.

Corporate Preparedness for Public Affairs Issues

Post has argued that a sophisticated public affairs perception, besides depending on merely looking at the forces of public affairs, is possible only after the history of the various issues has been acknowledged. He charted civil rights, environmental, and consumer protection issues through a four-stage "public issues life cycle," composed of (1) changing public expectations, followed by (2) political controversy, which is followed in turn by (3) development of legislation, and (4) litigation.[68] Identifying the relevant actors in a conflict and developing appropriate company positions require consistent corporate attention along with a knowledge of where to intervene. A centralized approach involves setting company priorities and the appropriate allocation of internal resources. Since issues have various phases, the primary responsibility for managing issues may be passed from operations along to public relations, and to government relations and the legal department within a company.

Therefore a company management should have at least as good an understanding of its public affairs environment as of its market environment. The academic community must help by filling the gap in the theoretical and empirical knowledge about this environment. Unlike affairs in the market environment, public affairs are not industry-specific. Although the precise issues vary by industry, *company size* is a better predictor of the type of stakeholder challenges company management must understand.

Despite vast differences in the primary, or market, environment of the very large corporations, or "megacorporations," they face a similar type of exposure to public affairs.[69] These megacorporations all face a complex and volatile public affairs environment. Public interest groups, state and federal agencies, changing legislative bodies, uneasy labor leaders, remote voices in community affairs, and a changing community of investors all represent a highly diverse variety of actors with extremely volatile positions. To be aware of events requires continuous close monitoring and daily involvement by a skilled specialist, as well as maintenance of a centralized company posture and a strategic appreciation of public events. Grunig's penetrating study of the various publics represented in a community indicates that effective communication requires "dialogue sessions with the active public" as opposed to low-key advertising of the corporate image.[70]

Preston and Post mentioned three stages of corporate response: (1) awareness, (2) commitment, and (3) selection and implementation.[71] Chase and Jones have outlined a more detailed process of managing public issues, which roughly falls into the categories (1) issue identification (2) issue analysis and priority setting, (3) issue strategies, (4) issue action programs, and (5) evaluation.[72]

Such procedures reflect a need for realistic corporate *responsiveness* to public affairs in place of dated responses. Such responsiveness should not be confused with "social responsibility."[73] The term *social responsibility* means many things to many people—from legal, exchange, and charitable obligations to fundamental ethical positions.[74] The concept of responsibility is a dimension of the corporate *purpose*. Social responsibility, then, should be measured by examining company outcomes. The present consideration of *responsiveness* to public affairs describes a corporate *process*. Performance in this sense cannot be evaluated by examining specific outcomes to issues but rather by taking a wider view.

Carroll has suggested, in fact, that *social responsibility* (economic, legal, and ethical), *social issues* (consumerism, environmentalism, discrimination), and *social responsiveness* (attentiveness) represent three independent contenders for social attention.[75] The company's social behavior can be plotted for each issue, for the ethical commitment of the company, and finally for the type of corporate attentiveness. What remains to be considered is how each company must be organized to achieve the required responsiveness. It is possible that certain structural modifications will yield richer perceptions toward public affairs. Somehow companies must foresee how their structure will distort their views of the environment, and they must correct for this distortion.

In essence this chapter has suggested that literature on organization theory has increasingly begun to appreciate the external context of an organization's activity as well as its internal dynamics. This literature, however, has focused on market and technological sectors of the environment at the expense of purely institutional considerations. The business constituents of this institutional environment have become so vocal and influential that they can no longer be ignored. Analysts of corporate social performance have indeed focused on institutional considerations but have tended to be drawn toward issue-specific anecdotal views of a firm's exposure as an institution. The challenges to an organization can hit it on both strategic and tactical levels. Furthermore, their functionally specific nature threatens to fragment the public affairs posture of firms.

Although the literature on organization adaptation has focused on market and technological issues, this body of research may have some relevant contribution to the public pressure for both expertise and coordination within firms. Various models of processes and structures can be conceived to be applied to the institutional environment. The next chapter looks at such models of adaptation.

Endnotes

1. M. Weber, *The Theory of Social and Economic Organization* (New York: Oxford, 1907, transl., 1947). Also H. Fayol, *General and Industrial Management* (London: Pitman, 1949, tr.).

2. F. W. Taylor, *The Principles of Scientific Management* (New York: Harper, 1911). Also L. F. Urwick, *The Elements of Administration* (New York: Harper, 1943).

3. F. J. Roethlisberger and W. J. Dickson, *Management and the Worker* (Cambridge, Mass.: Harvard University Press, 1939). Also D. McGregor, *The Human Side of Enterprise* (New York: McGraw-Hill, 1960); R. Likert, *New Patterns of Management* (New York: McGraw-Hill, 1961).

4. W. R. Dill, "Environment as an Influence on Managerial Autonomy," *Administrative Science Quarterly*, 2 (1958), pp. 409–443. Also A. N. Turner and P. R. Lawrence, *Industrial Jobs and the Worker* (Boston: Harvard Graduate School of Business Administration, 1965); F. E. Emery and E. L. Trist, "The Causal Texture of Organizational Environments," *Human Relations*, 18 (1965), pp. 21–32; W. M. Evan, "The Organization Set: Toward a Theory of Interorganizational Relations," in *Approaches to Organizational Design*, J. D. Thompson (ed.) (Pittsburgh: University of Pittsburgh Press, 1966), pp. 173–191; D. Katz and R. L. Kahn, *The Social Psychology of Organizations* (New York: Wiley, 1966); W. Buckley, *Sociology and Modern Systems Theory* (Englewood Cliffs, N.J.: Prentice-Hall, 1967); P. R. Lawrence and J. W. Lorsch, *Organization and Environment* (Boston: Harvard Graduate School of Business Administration, 1967).

5. J. D. Thompson, *Organizations in Action* (New York: McGraw-Hill, 1967). Also T. Burns and G. M. Stalker, *The Management of Innovation* (London: Tavistock, 1961); Lawrence and Lorsch, *ibid.*; R. B. Duncan, "Multiple Decision-Making Structures on Adapting to Environmental Uncertainty," *Human Relations*, 26 (1973), pp. 273–291; J. Galbraith, *Designing Complex Organizations* (Reading, Mass.: Addison-Wesley, 1973).

6. R. Hobbes, *Leviathan* (Oxford: Blackwellis Political Texts, 1946, orig. 1651). Also K. Marx, *Das Kapital* (1867), as excerpted in *Marx and Engels: Basic Writings on Politics and Philosophy*; L. S. Fever, ed. (Garden City, Ca.: Anchor, 1959); R. Dahl, *Who Governs?* (New Haven, Conn.: Yale University Press, 1962); R. E. Caves, "Uncertainty, Market Structure and Performance: Galbraith as Conventional Wisdom," *Industrial Organization and Economic Development* (Boston: Houghton-Mifflin, 1970).

7. J. Child, "Organizational Structures, Environment and Performance: The Role of Strategic Choice," *Sociology*, 6 (1972), pp. 1–22.

8. J. Pfeffer and G. R. Salancik, *The External Control of Organizations* (New York: Harper & Row, 1977).

9. N. W. Chamberlain, *Enterprise and Environment* (New York: McGraw-Hill, 1968). Also W. M. Evan, "Due Process of Law in Military and Industrial Organizations," *Administrative Science Quarterly*, 7 (1962), pp. 187–207; O. E. Williamson, *Markets and Hierarchies* (New York: Free Press, 1975); G. Stigler, "A Theory of Oligopoly," *Journal of Political Economy*, 72 (1964), pp. 44–61; B. M. Staw and E. Swajakowski, "The Scarcity-Munificence Component of Organizational Environments and the Commission of Illegal Acts," *Administrative Science Quarterly*, 20 (1975), pp. 340–354; J. Sonnenfeld and P. R. Lawrence, "Why do Companies Succumb to Price Fixing?" *Harvard Business Review*, 56, No. 4 (1978), pp. 145–157.

10. Burns and Stalker, *op. cit.*

11. Emery and Trist, *op. cit.*

12. Thompson, *op. cit.*

13. Burns and Stalker, *op. cit.* Also Duncan, *op. cit.*; Lawrence and Lorsch, *op. cit.*; Galbraith, *op. cit.*; V. Hage and M. Aiken, "Relationship of Centralization to Other Structural Properties," *Administrative Science Quarterly*, 22 (1967), pp. 72–92.

14. R. L. Tung, "Dimensions of Organizational Environments: An Exploratory Study of Their Impact on Organization Structure," *Academy of Management Journal*, 22 (1979), pp. 672–693. Also R. Jurkovich, "A Core Typology of Organizational Environments," *Administrative Science Quarterly*, 19 (1974), pp. 380–394.

15. H. Rosi, R. Aldag, and R. Storey, "On the Measurement of the Environment: An Assessment of the Lawrence and Lorsch Environmental Uncertainty Subscale," *Administrative Science Quarterly*, 18 (1973), pp. 27–36. Also H. Downey, D. Hellriegal, and Y. Slocum, "Environmental Uncertainty: The Construct and its Application," *Administrative Science Quarterly*, 20 (1975), pp. 613–639.

16. K. E. Weick, *The Psychology of Organizing* (Reading, Mass.: Addison-Wesley, 1969). Also W. H. Starbuck, "Organizations and Their Environments," in *Handbook of Industrial and Organizational Psychology*, M. Dunnette, ed. (Chicago: Rand-McNally, 1976); S. Allen, "Understanding Reorganization of Divisionalized Companies," *Academy of Management Journal*, 22, (1979), pp. 641–671; Tung, *op. cit.*; R. M. Miles, *Macro Organizational Behavior* (Santa Monica, Ca.: Goodyear, 1980).

17. Starbuck, *op. cit.*

18. Pfeffer and Salancik, *op. cit.*

19. D. C. Dearborn and H. A. Simon, "Selective Perception: A Note on the Identification of Executives," *Sociometry*, 21 (1958), pp. 140–144.

20. J. Sonnenfeld, "Executive Apologies for Price Fixing: Role Biased Perceptions of Causality," *Academy of Management Journal*, 24 (1981), pp. 192–198.

21. T. Parsons, *Structure and Process in Modern Societies* (New York: Free Press, 1960).

22. Dill, *op. cit.* Also Thompson, *op. cit.*

23. R. E. Miles and C. C. Snow, *Organizational Strategy, Structure and Process* (New York: McGraw-Hill, 1978).

24. Pfeffer and Salancik, *op. cit.*

25. D. Vogel, *Lobbying the Corporation: Citizen Challenge to Business Authority* (New York: Basic Books, 1978).
26. Pfeffer and Salancik, *op. cit.*
27. Starbuck, *op. cit.*, p. 1071.
28. A. Downs, *Inside Bureaucracy* (Boston: Little, Brown, 1967).
29. Weick, *op. cit.* Also Child, *op. cit.;* and Duncan, *op. cit.*
30. F. H. Allport, "A Structuronomic Conception of Behavior: Individual and Collective," *Journal of Abnormal and Social Psychology*, 64 (1962), pp. 3–30. Also Katz and Kahn, *op. cit.;* Weick, *op. cit.*
31. Pfeffer and Salancik, *op. cit.*, p. 32.
32. J. R. Emshoff and R. E. Freeman, "Stakeholder Management," Working Paper (Wharton Applied Research Center, July 1978).
33. G. A. Steiner, *Business and Society* (New York: Random Books, 1974). Also L. E. Preston and J. E. Post, *Private Management and Public Responsibility* (Englewood Cliffs, N.J.: Prentice-Hall, 1975); R. Ackerman and R. Bauer, *Corporate Social Responsiveness: The Modern Dilemma* (Reston, Va.: Reston Publishing, 1976); S. P. Sethi, *Up Against the Corporate Wall* (Englewood Cliffs, N.J.: Prentice-Hall, 1977); J. E. Post, *Corporate Social Performance* (Reston, Va.: Reston Publishing, 1978).
34. Preston and Post, *ibid.*
35. Parsons, *op. cit.*
36. *Ibid.*
37. Preston and Post, *op. cit.*
38. *Ibid.*, p. 11.
39. D. Votaw and S. P. Sethi, "Do We Need a New Corporate Response," *California Management Review* (Fall 1969), reprinted in D. Votaw and S. P. Sethi, *The Corporate Dilemma* (Englewood Cliffs, N.J.: Prentice-Hall, 1973), pp. 170–190. Also Pfeffer and Salancik, *op. cit.*
40. Post, *op. cit.*
41. S. Terreberry, "The Evolution of Organization Environments," *Administrative Science Quarterly*, 12 (1968), pp. 590–613. Also H. Turk, "Interorganizational Networks in Urban Society," *American Sociological Review*, 34 (1976), pp. 1–19.
42. Pfeffer and Salancik, *op. cit.*
43. A. D. Chandler, *The Visible Hand* (Boston: Belknap, 1977). Also H. Hay and E. Gray, "Social Responsibility of Business Managers," *Academy of Management Journal* (March 1974), as it appeared in A. Carroll, *Managing Corporate Social Responsibility* (Boston: Little, Brown, 1977); G. C. Lodge, "The Uses of Ideology for Environmental Analysis," Intercollegiate Case Clearing House, 9-377-147 (Boston: Harvard Graduate School of Business Administration, 1976).
44. A. Hacker, "The Press vs. the Corporation," *New York Times Book Review* (Feb. 25, 1979), p. 9.
45. S. N. Brenner, "Business and Politics—An Update," *Harvard Business Review*, 57 (Nov.-Dec. 1979), pp. 149–163.
46. J. O'Toole, "What's Ahead for the Business Government Relationship," *Harvard Business Review*, 57 (March-April 1979), pp. 94–105.
47. W. Lilley and J. C. Miller, "The New 'Social' Regulation," *The Public Interest*, 47 (1977), pp. 49–61.
48. D. M. Kasper, "Note on Managing in a Regulated Environment," Intercollegiate

Case Clearinghouse, 1-379-032, (Cambridge, Mass.: Harvard University Press, 1978).

49. K. Hansen, *The Social and Political Dimensions of Corporate Strategy: The Auto Industry and Fuel Economy*, unpublished doctoral dissertation (Cambridge, Mass.: Harvard Graduate School of Business Administration, 1981), p. 3.

50. R. A. Leone, "The Real Costs of Regulation," *Harvard Business Review*, 55 (Nov.-Dec. 1977), pp. 57–66.

51. R. A. Leone and J. E. Jackson, "Toward a More Effective Organization for Public Regulation," unpublished working paper (Boston: Harvard Graduate School of Business Administration, 1980).

52. A. O. Sulzberger, Jr., "New Air Pollution Policy to Give Industry Flexibility on U.S. Rules," *New York Times* (Dec. 4, 1979), p. A1.

53. Chandler, *op. cit.* Also D. H. Fenn, Jr., "Finding Where the Power Lies in Government," *Harvard Business Review*, 57 (Sept.-Oct. 1979), pp. 144–153.

54. P. Shabecoff, "Law Against Business Abuse Urged," *New York Times* (Dec. 13, 1979), p. D4.

55. R. W. Schmenner, "Look Beyond the Obvious in Plant Location," *Harvard Business Review*, 57 (Jan.-Feb. 1979), pp. 126–132.

56. R. E. Walton and R. McKersie, *A Behavioral Theory of Labor Negotiations* (New York: McGraw-Hill, 1967).

57. *Ibid.*, p. 284.

58. D. Bok and J. Dunlop, *Labor and the American Community* (New York: Simon and Schuster, 1970). Also V. C. Sherman, "Unionism and the Non-Union Company," *Personnel Journal* (June 1969), pp. 413–422.

59. D. Q. Mills, "Human Resources in the 1980's," *Harvard Business Review* (July-August 1979), pp. 153.

60. W. F. Glueck, *Personnel: A Diagnostic Approach* (Dallas: Business Publications, 1974), p. 572.

61. R. Stagner, *Psychology of Industrial Conflict* (New York: Wiley, 1956). Also R. Stagner and N. Rosen, *Psychology of Union Management Relations* (Belmont, Ca.: Wadsworth, 1965).

62. J. L. Perry and H. L. Angle, "The Politics of Organization Boundary Roles in Collective Bargaining," *The Academy of Management Review*, 4 (1979), p. 493.

63. E. M. Burack and T. G. Gutteridge, "Institutional Manpower Planning: Rhetoric versus Reality," *California Management Review*, 20 (Spring 1978), pp. 13–22.

64. J. Casner-Lotto, "Plant Closings: Relocations Increase, Federal Legislation Proposed to Reduce Disruption to Communities and Employees," *World of Work Report*, 4 (December 1979), p. 64.

65. S. L. Hayes, "The Transformation of Investment Banking," *Harvard Business Review*, 57 (Jan.-Feb. 1979), pp. 143–171. Also W. Chatlos, "What Is Investor Relations?" *Investor Relations*, A. R. Roahman, ed. (New York: Amacom, 1974), pp. 3–19.

66. Chatlos, *ibid.*

67. *Ibid.*, p. 119.

68. Post, *op. cit.*

69. P. Blumberg, *The Mega Corporation in American Society* (Englewood Cliffs, N.J.: Prentice-Hall, 1976). Also Post, *op. cit.*

70. J. E. Grunig, "A New Measure of Public Opinions on Corporate Social Responsibility," *Academy of Management Journal*, 22 (1979), pp. 738–764.

71. Preston and Post, *op. cit.*

72. Witt, Chase, "The Issue Management Gauntlet," *Journal of the International Public Relations Association*, 2 (April 1978), pp. 24–27.

73. K. Davis, "Can Business Afford to Ignore Social Responsibility?" *California Management Review*, 2 (1960), pp. 70–76. Also H. G. Manne and H. G. Wallich, *The Modern Corporation and Social Responsibility* (Washington, D.C.: The American Enterprise Institute, 1972); C. C. Abt, *The Social Audit for Management* (New York: Amacom, 1977); A. B. Carroll, ed., *Managing Corporate Social Responsibility* (Boston: Little, Brown, 1977).

74. Votaw and Sethi, *op. cit.* Also Preston and Post, *op. cit.;* Ackerman and Bauer, *op. cit.*

75. Carroll, *op. cit.*

Chapter 3

MODELS OF ORGANIZATIONAL ADAPTATION TO PUBLIC AFFAIRS

We have argued that megacorporations need an internal capacity to meet the highly uncertain public environment they face. To be responsive to public affairs, corporations must be prepared before a crisis. They need to appreciate the complexity and overlapping of public concerns, and they must establish, a reputation for reliability through adherence to commitments across company departments and over a period of time. Responsiveness to public affairs requires that a company develop expertise in discerning issues and also in coordinating a response. Theoretical models can be established for such adaptive capacities.

We suggest that initially, a company structure affects how it perceives its environment of public affairs. Post has explained that managing public affairs is really a task of closing the gap between public expectations and corporate behavior, regardless of whether the company chooses to close the gap by changing public expectations or by changing its own behavior.[1] Each of these avenues is externally oriented, in that either the external actions themselves or external consequences of these actions are considered. Since many internal company actors are involved in institutional affairs also, internal dynamics can fundamentally affect external awareness.

We can broaden the range of corporate actions under consideration if we include the internal consequences of corporate action. In a broad review of the literature on strategic choices, Miles has pointed out that organizations may choose the internal or the external environment as a target for change. They may also choose between reactive (crisis-driven) or proactive (crisis-avoiding) motives in change.[2] We hold that organizations should consider the internal (structural) and proactive (anticipatory) avenues first.

27

Adaptation and External Forces

An internal focus is quite distinct from the external focus of many current theoretical approaches. Externally oriented approaches can be grouped into those that rely on evolutionary forces and those that rely on strategic choices by the firm. Let us discuss each of these categories, in turn.

Evolutionary Approaches

Some of the theory and research on how an organization learns has embraced the evolutionary perspective of change and response.[3] The sum of this literature is that organizations existing today are those that have best adapted to given environmental conditions. The most extreme "ecology" theorists suggest that organizations that have survived environmental threats to their industry were environmentally favored at their birth and have therefore survived more through their good beginnings than through favorable managerial action.[4] Such a premise depends on a large, diverse "gene pool." These theorists refer to large populations of small organizations, but their findings do not explain the environmental interactions of small populations of large organizations, such as Chrysler, Lockheed, IBM, Exxon, and ITT, whose effect on the environment is considerable.

Furthermore these theorists do not distinguish phylogenetic change (evolution) from ontogenetic change (maturation), an error that biologist Stephen Gould has highlighted as common among the true ecologists concerned with populations.[5] Such an error translates to a confusion in any study concerned with development over time, because differences attributed to genetic transformation over many life spans may actually represent changes due to age within a normal life span. The present design of mass retail operations may reflect normal maturation (proliferation or streamlining, and the like) rather than the survival of superior forms.

Evolutionary theory has also been taken less literally and more as a standard from which to propose how a single organization learns.[6] The three essential processes that operate are (1) random environmental variation, (2) rational selection, and (3) routine retention. Irrational learning (the superstitious linking of actions to outcomes contrary to available evidence) is possible but pathological, given the need to adapt to unyielding external conditions, the company theoretically cannot survive over time by this method. This belief in ultimate rationality presumes that an organization can perceive the environment objectively. The organization, however, does not respond objectively to the environment. Distorted perspectives within the organization and a loose correspondence between organizational actions and environmental events can create subjective internal perceptions which tend toward inaccuracy. Consequently, nonadaptive, inconsistent learning may prevail.

The traditional model of evolutionary adaptation has been modified by proposing a perceived environment rather than the actual one. Weick has suggested that random environmental variation be replaced by environmental "enactment," in which the relevant environment is created instead being perceived as it actually is. Weick states:[7]

> *The human creates the environment, to which the system then adapts.*
> *The human does not react to an environment, he enacts it. It is this*
> *enacted environment, and nothing else, that is worked upon by the pro-*
> *cess of organizing.*

Weick does not explain who exactly the "human actor" is who brings about this "enactment" to which the system then adapts. The enacted environment might be either the product of a single individual's perceptions, the product of a small dominant coalition, or the pooling of a larger array of environmental perspectives. A failure to define the individuals who are directing the organization's attention and the knowledge it retains can lead, in a sense, to crediting the organization with abilities it cannot have in itself.

Thus Weick joined traditional-evolutionary theorists when he suggested that organizational structure should be viewed primarily as a response to the environment. There is a strong basis to indicate that the reverse relation—that organizational structure can influence the environment as it is perceived—might be equally plausible.[8] Understanding organizational structure can reveal just how the environment comes to be perceived. Starbuck argued that this failure to appreciate "how perceptual distortions vary with organizational characteristics" represents research terrain awaiting cultivation.[9] Accordingly, Miles has theorized that organizational factors influence adaptation.[10] Sensitivity to structural factors has a basis in earlier works. Cyert and March have theorized that environmental perception and learning is really biased by the perspective of each subunit in the parent organization.[11] Dearborn and Simon found in a study that the functional role of executives tended to bias their perception of a problematic setting in a hypothetical business case. They concluded that "each executive will perceive those aspects of a solution that relate specifically to the activities and goals of his department."[12] More recently, the research of Lawrence and Lorsch has demonstrated how structurally determined interactions with the environment contribute to specific expectations of a subunit.[13] Sonnenfeld found vertical organizational bias, in that top executives tended to blame difficulties in corporate-environment relations on the incompetence of lower-level personnel, and that divisional general managers blamed such problems on unfair environmental pressures.[14]

Thus, in summary, evolutionary theories of an organization's response to the environment tend to be unfoundedly deterministic. Different-sized populations, systemic slack as a direct result of the environment, and the contribution of management strategy and organizational structure on the perceptual process have been consciously but incorrectly neglected. Finally, the greatest limitation to the evolutionary models of organizational adaption is that they are strictly models of organizational response. These models may describe the ways in which organizations have reacted to an environment, but *reaction* neglects "proactiveness." That is, these models offer no explanation about how organizations detect change in their environments. This detection is what Vickers called the "appreciative system."[15] Evolutionary models do not explain the acquisition of new information. Often the organizations may retain responses based on historical rather than current perception of the environment.[16] In slower-moving times, it was enough to see the past as the key to the present, but such a reactive stance is no longer adequate for effective adaptation. Megacorporations today do not operate in a tranquil environment with isolated temporary disturbances. The turbulent institutional environment is actually characterized more by constant change rather than change followed by long periods of stability. Foresight has become vital as organizations no longer can afford simply to respond to isolated events in the environment; they now must expect to respond to a steady flow of events.

Strategic-Choice Approaches

Like the evolutionary perspective, theories about strategic choice in responding to the environment begin with a review of how existing organizations have responded to survive over time. The theorists who uphold strategic choice, however, believe that the organization can form its own environment and hence avoid dependence on random environmental variation.[17] Strategic-choice theorists document the ways by which organizations can reshape their environments rather than passively accept the given objective environment, or even the enacted environment. These theorists have attempted to merge literature on environmentally determined structure with literature on strategy-determined structures in an effort to allow for environmental influences without permitting them to become overly deterministic.

An important first step in such a manipulation of the "corners" of the environment is the act of "domain choice"—that is, the selection of technology, target population, and intended output.[18] Miles and Snow used a four-cell typology of strategies (prospector, analyzer, defender, and reactor) to show that normative statements about structure and process must consider the strategic decisions top managers make in selecting the market environment.[19] For example, a book publishing company determined to defend its domain may adopt a strategy and a structure that are different from those of a publishing house that decides it would rather be in mass communications, in general, with sales in various media. Similarly a tobacco producer might defend its old domain or could prospect a future as a consumer-products company.

Further environmental manipulation is suggested by perceiving "external control" as a method of organization-environment relations. This perspective offers a framework in which one can understand how organizations can make strategic choices and thereby reduce dependence on outside forces for critical resources.[20] Theorists argue that the struggle to control resource dependencies are the most revealing way of describing the behavior of organizations. Pfeffer and Salancik essentially have applied Cyert and March's "organizations as coalitions" perspective to relations within organizations.[21] Cyert and March believe that many organizational decisions result from the exercise of power by various coalitions and subcoalitions within the overall organizations.[22] The power of these coalitions is a function of the degree of control that they can exert over critical resources.

Pfeffer and Salancik, placing this coalition perspective in an interorganizational context, argue that it becomes clear that the organization is far from an autonomous actor pursuing its independent goals or strategy.[23] Examples of the types of relations in these coalitions are found in Selznick's study of the TVA's survival through co-optation of threatening outside interests; Litwak and Hyton's research on cooperative groups such as trade associations; Aiken and Hage's research on joint ventures; Pfeffer's study of co-optation of external threats; and studies of collusion, and collaboration by Hirsch and Staw and Swajakowski.[24] Kotter has summarized these mechanisms of reducing external dependence to:

1. Choice of domain (market shift, diversification).
2. Establishment of favorable relations with external elements (advertising, personal contact, co-optation coalitions).
3. Control of who operates in the domain (barriers to entry).
4. Decoupling or decentralizing the organization to be more responsive to external pressures.[25]

The "strategic choice" theory postulates more than mere environmental reaction; it includes the attempt to act on and alter the perceived environment. A new environment so created, however, is merely a response to a perception of the original environment. Thus while the organization may be considered proactive in that it is acting strategically before any crisis or any special event arises, it may also be considered structurally reactive in that there is no demonstrable effort to see that it has foreseen and corrected for a structurally induced bias. Perhaps a given strategic proactive behavior was really unnecessary but seemed essential only from a distorted corporate vantage. A psychologist would diagnosis such unrealistic external fear as neurotic instead of proactive.

Argyris and Schon have argued that managerial attitudes determine responses to the environment.[26] Thus along with the given objective environment, the theories that an organization is using about the environment must be challenged. The likely perceptual bias associated with organizational configuration certainly has relevance but is inadequately considered in the adaptation literature.[27] A truly forehanded, proactive organization needs more than crisis-avoiding strategies. It also requires the accurate foresight that comes from a prescient *structure*. Organizations so built do not merely respond to given environmental factors; they act on information netted from an environmental scanning mechanism that corrects for perceptual distortion and allows receptivity to environmental change.

This is not to suggest that all "strategic choice" researchers have ignored organizational structure. Pfeffer and Salancik state that the structure of the organization, its information systems, and the activities of the organization all shape the attention of organization members.[28] Internal power structures, it is acknowledged, cause misreadings of the environment through varied internal definitions and priorities.

However, Pfeffer and Salancik did not suggest any means for avoiding this perceptual distortion. In fact, their structural proposals would only exacerbate such subunit bias.[29] They suggested that organizations can best respond to external demands by loosening resource dependencies through greater decentralization of the organization. They claim that specialized subunits can be designed to deal with subsegments of the environment. These subunits serve two purposes for the organization: (1) They can act as buffers against the heterogeneous environment; and (2) they can lessen the effect of external influences through the co-optation of outside challenges. The authors state:[30]

> *Each subunit must be in a position to take actions unconstrained by the actions taken by other subunits. Loose-coupling assists organizations in coping with their environments by permitting new subunits to absorb protest without a requirement to rationalize the relationship among all the various subunits.*

Further they suggest that general management can handle external affairs on their own:[31]

The expertise required to manage the organization's interdependence is often present in the organization. It is already possessed by the various operating managers themselves. Constantly confronted with problems from their own interactions with the environment, it is unlikely they are aware of the environment.

This is a naive blind trust in the abilities of specialized "buffering" subunits or busy general managers to solve external issues independent of other corporate actions. In particular, it certainly reflects a sharp departure from the sensitivity to organizational politics and structural bias referred to earlier in their work. In addition, Pfeffer and Salancik seem to be unaware that because public issues cut across organizations, companies cannot reduce external dependence by such decentralized responses as these authors suggest.[32] Environmental pollution, legal compliance, antitrust violation, labor difficulties, taxation, and administrative interactions all are issues that call for an organization-wide sensitivity and an organization-wide reaction. The company's many boundary spanners on these issues need to see core company goals to be effective. Secondly, and more important, an intelligent understanding of public issues requires the input of many varied technical, professional, and managerial perspectives. As we suggested in the previous chapter, the technical and policy levels of these issues are inseparable.[33] At the same time, issues still pass through discernible stages— from changing public expectations, through political negotiation and legislative action, to litigative enforcement.[34] Therefore organizations need a corporatewide perspective so they can marshal appropriate company resources. Finally, a company needs to speak with a single voice to the outside; otherwise belief in it will be destroyed and it can easily wind up fighting itself.

Thus the strategic-choice explanation, like the evolutionary explanation, is reactionary as it pertains to the environment and is naive about the role or organization structure. An organization's effort to respond actively to a perceived environment demonstrates that the strategic-choice explanation is not passive to a given environment. There is nothing, however, to indicate that the strategic-choice explanation is in any way concerned with how to guarantee foresight on a company's part rather than perception based on history. No statement could better represent the core of this reactive stance than the following passage:[35]

It may also be that scanning the environment is, in fact, not that necessary. One can imagine some advantages to ignoring environmental change. Knowing about the change puts the organization in the position of having to respond to it.

This myopic approach does not make the issues disappear. Ostriches with their heads in the sand certainly do not respond to environmental threats. An awareness of issues is not necessarily followed by an immediate compulsion to act. Rather, awareness permits analysis, priority setting, and preparedness. Hasty compulsion to act occurs when management responds to a crisis instead of anticipating it. The fact that organizations have historically done little environmental scanning, as Pfeffer and Salancik suggest, does not indicate that it is unimportant.[36] Such efforts are well under way in improving market research and technological research. More important, the environment is changing in such a way as to make awareness more important—in particular, the public environment is becoming more complex and volatile.

We thus have highlighted a third weakness of both evolutionary and strategic-choice theorists: They seem to be wearing blinders when they regard the external environment from the narrow perspective of how the market defines the business environment. Public issues, which make up the institutional subsystems of Parsons, have been routinely ignored—as the determining environmental pressures (of the evolutionary school) and the strategic responses (strategic choice) reflect.[37] As we saw in our review of concepts of the external environment, this is a failing organizational theorists share widely.

Adaptation and Internal Preparedness

The evolutionary and strategic-choice literatures are grouped as external adaptation targets because they focus on specific reactions to the external environment. "Business policy" and "contingency" schools of thought, however, understand better how the internal structure of an organization influences actions and how environmental forces influence actions. Proponents share a belief in certain structural prerequisites for adaptation; these were first identified in the organic-systems theory[38] and the process-systems theory.[39] Summarizing such systems theory, Buckley outlined some of the conditions necessary for the kind of structure an organization should have if it would adapt to new environmental conditions:[40]

1. Sensitivity to a continual flow of information from the environment.
2. Flexibility in structure, to allow differentiation in the face of diverse environmental stimuli, including:

- Sensitivity to continuous flow of information from the outside.
- A differentiated structure, which allows for selective sensitivity.
- A method of evaluating external conditions and how these would imply deviation from organizational goals.
- A system for retaining and propagating successful adaptation.

Thus, for perceptions of the environment—and hence strategies—to change, the organization must have a responsive basic form.

Business Policy Approaches

Business policy theory on organizational adaptation has focused more on internal responsiveness than on structural variables. Contingency organizational theorists have focused more on the structural variations than on internal processes. Both groups demonstrate a long-standing interest in structural preparedness. Barnard wrote:[41]

> *The direct environment of executive decisions is primarily the internal environment of the organization itself. The strategic factors of executive decisions are chiefly and primarily strategic factors of organization opera-tion. It is the organization, not the executive which does the work on the external environment.*

Thus the executive should design a structure that allows for efficient and effective operation, but the executive should not be the primary external contact. Simon (1946) similarly saw that the chief problem of managing external affairs is in placing an investigatory unit so "that the information received will be promptly transmitted in a usable form to the appropriate points in the organization."[42]

A much more active role for the chief executive was envisioned by business policy writers. Selznik argued that the chief executive, rather than specialized analysts, is the institutional leader of the organization and should therefore have the primary relation with the outside. He explained:[43]

> *The leader, sensitive to internal pressures and to the heavy price that must be paid for co-optation, is impatient with the analyst whose narrow logic of efficiency leads to proposals for change that are irresponsible from the standpoint of the institution.*

Similarly, Andrews suggested that the executive alone must gain "an awareness of society's expectations and determine the corporate re-sponse." He further stated:[44]

> *In short, in his role as an architect of strategy, the general manager examines and becomes informed about the environmental external to his company; he examines his own organization, he examines himself, and he determines his own responsiveness to the multiple demands being made upon his company by elements of the community at large. In his role as strategist, he must often think and decide for himself.*

Thus prominent writers on policy agree about the need for internal preparedness but differ over whether this preparedness should focus on the organization or the executive.[45]

This focus on executive initiative has been supported by Ackerman and by Murray.[46] Ackerman and Bauer presented the following three-stage model of corporate response to public issues: (1) The chief executive recognizes the importance of an issue to the company and perceives the need to develop a company position; (2) the chief executive appoints staff specialists to research the issues and coordinate information on them; and (3) through formal policies, potential procedures, and subsequent structures such as task forces and a permanent department, the company develops its response.[47]

This focus on executive initiative does demonstrate an appreciation of the need for organizational skills before responding to environmental perceptions.[48] However, it overlooks some important problems. First, it assumes that the organization has the time to wait for external change and then time for mangerial deliberation before carefully selecting the proper response. Second, it ignores an organization's vulnerability to highly biased perception—a likely consequence of dependence on the skills, background, time, and perception of a single executive.

On the first point, the issues often move too fast for a company that is not already prepared. Votaw and Sethi have illustrated how this "top-down" model usually produces very reactive fire-fighting techniques.[49] Votaw and Sethi argue that on its own, general management tends to wait for the "pickets at the plant gate" rather than anticipating issues. They term this reaction a *pressure-response* style of behavior and call for a more proactive style.[50] By the time management has identified a problem, it has often grown to a crisis. Sethi has demonstrated the great costs in money, morale, public image, employee relations, litigation, and unfavorable legislation that companies have suffered by reactive response to environmental change.[51]

Post examined the evidence of proactive corporate behavior found by Ackerman and Bauer and reactive corporate behavior cited by Sethi.[52] He concluded that each approach was possible but that neither was an accurate portrait of what always happens. Post looked especially at issues such as changing demographics and the response of the baby-food industry, the bauxite cartel and the aluminum companies, the fluorocarbon ban and the chemical and toiletry industry, television violence and the advertising industry, red-lining and the banking industry, political payoffs and big multinationals, and the infant-formula controversy and makers of the product. Through these investigations he showed that at least three types of responses exist: (1) a reactive (or "adaptive") mode, (2) a proactive mode, and (3) an interactive mode.

This three-way classification is different from previously described reactive-vs-proactive modes, because he defined these two responses as single-issue responses only and not an enduring response style. The third mode, the interactive mode, moved beyond one-shot responses to issues and involved a wider preparedness for the continuing nature of public issues. This three-way classification may be unnecessary, however, as both reactive and proactive modes may have both issue-specific and enduring, response-style components. Thus, for example, a firm may be reactive on all issues or on just a few. More intensive study of the behaviors of Aetna Life and Casualty and Polaroid over several issues, and of the infant-formula industry, indicated that more systematic work is needed to identify under what conditions a company is likely to undertake one of these responses. One clear message from this consideration was that when "matters are not well understood by top management, a structure must be created from within from which a strategy can emerge."[53]

The second weakness of the *executive-initiative* approach is that likely distorted perceptions and biased strategies are not anticipated. Substantial evidence suggests the reality of such bias. Cyert and March and Lawrence and Lorsch have studied subunit biases on readings of events and of priorities in the external environment.[54] Dearborn and Simon have found a systematic bias by functional role in classroom case analysis.[55] Sonnenfeld has identified a hierarchical role bias between senior and divisional executives in how they perceived their company's involvement in illegal activity.[56]

Other researchers have noted how structure affects strategy, although according to Aguilar, limitations plague the general manager in scanning the environment.[57] Aguilar observed that managers tend to overlook evidence and protect themselves from challenges to their notions of reality. Argyris has termed this *single-loop learning*.[58]

This single-loop learning is a way of avoiding the frightening complexity of reality. Cyert and March elaborated on this point, stating that "the organization seeks to avoid uncertainty by following regular procedures and a policy of reacting to feedback rather than forecasting the environment."[59] Aguilar, in his research, found that managers tended to overemphasize the importance of market conditions to avoid dealing with important broad issues. Thus he inferred from his findings that:[60]

> *the heavy emphasis on market activities by managers of specialties and all levels would seem to lend support to the sometime stated view that companies tend rather to react to current conditions than to innovate. Certainly the data suggest that much more attention is focused on trying to ascertain the existing pattern of events in the industry than on trying to anticipate such pattern.*

Aguilar noted that general managers lack, besides such perceptual distortion, (1) an awareness of all the issues on the outside that are important to the organization, (2) the time to track all these issues, and (3) the ability to understand the information. Developing the various aspects of the external environment requires the organization to have access to many information sources, both professional and informal.

General managers, because of their general training, do not have the necessary background for understanding the relevance of particular developments. They lack the technical knowledge of the appropriate specialists, the relevant jargon, the access to information, the interest in the specialty, and demonstrated expertise in the field.

It seems that the business policy approach to adaptation to the public environment has always appreciated the importance of internal preparedness before external response. Further it seems that the focus of attention for this preparedness has shifted from the organization[61] to the executives[62] and then back to the organization.[63]

Recent surveys of large U.S. companies suggest that this return to focusing on the organization has left the theory stage and engaged managerial practice.[64] Several years ago, Mazis and Green noted the beginning of a trend toward structural preparation for social issues as opposed to structural reaction.[65] Mazis and Green noted three predominant structural mechanisms for understanding public affairs: (1) ad hoc, temporary task forces, (2) a permanent top-echelon committee, and (3) a department of social affairs. Mazis and Green strongly favored a permanent department. In citing various drawbacks to the first two approaches, they mentioned crisis appeasement, the limited time and expertise of executives for dealing with current problems, and the lack of established channels of communication to effectuate plans. They suggested a social affairs department as the best way of monitoring, verifying, and transmitting information about the environment. Holmes found further evidence, in her survey of 192 "*Fortune 500*" firms, of a likely trend from temporary task forces toward more permanent departments of social affairs.[66] Large companies (those with more than 10,000 employees or over $1 million in sales), more than smaller companies, seem to rely on permanent structures. Holmes also found that industries such as oil, gas, financial services, and utilities tend to prefer permanent departments, whereas manufacturing firms tend to prefer relying on an individual executive to manage public issues. Such an industrial pattern is demonstrated in Newgren.[67] A Conference Board study found that size (over $1 million in sales) and industry patterns indicated the likelihood that a government relations unit existed in a firm.[68]

This structural formalization was found to be related to more sophisticated environmental forecasting, as Mazis and Green would expect.[69] With great fanfare, many business publications have heralded the appearance of new boxes on organization charts with such titles as *vice president of external affairs, environmental scanners, futurists,*[70] and *compliance officers.*[71] The Conference Board has presented thorough and wide-ranging case studies of successful corporate programs for identifying and analyzing issues and has elaborated on scanning topics, such as environmental taxonomies, priority setting, outside sources, and internal reports.[72] In another important Conference Board study, McGrath illustrated new procedures for acting on the issues once they have been identified and analyzed.[73]

What is lacking in all the exploratory literature is a comprehensive view of an organization. Brown, for example, noted the lack of coordination between the departments of public affairs and of corporate planning in identifying public issues. "The current state of planning public affairs liaison among companies represented in this study is something of a potpourri."[74] Similarly, McGrath found a lack of a clear delineation between the responsibilities of the staff and of the chief executive in managing external affairs.[75] Whereas the literature suggests that the chief executive can best contribute to plans for action by formulating a company commitment, chief executives seem to be more interested in identifying issues.[76] Fleming further found that the corporate counsel has a similar outlook:[77]

> There is a need for managerial coordination and designation of areas of responsibility in the public activity to avoid duplication of effort and gaps in coverage. Clear interface definitions need to be established between the public affairs and the legal departments, between public affairs and corporate planning, and between the corporate and divisional levels within public affairs.

Supporting this concern, McGrath's survey of 256 large corporations found that committees on public affairs who coordinated legal operations, public relations, technical planning, and government relations represented less than 15 percent of the sample.[78]

Thus, we can see that theoretical research and field investigations are beginning to recognize that the proper structure is an important prerequisite for an awareness of public affairs. The business policy approach has identified the importance of the chief executive officer in committing the company to managing public affairs. It simultaneously recognizes that the chief executive has limitations as a primary scanner or analyst. Specialized corporate departments are assuming this role, yet the literature on policy and practice does not provide an organizationwide picture that shows appropriate delegation of responsibilities and necessary coordination. Finally, the structural changes are rarely linked with any consideration of how effective such arrangements are. Where effectiveness is demonstrated, it has been supported with strictly unsystematic, anecdotal data.

Contingency-Theory Approaches

Writers on contingency theory can contribute to this investigation in that they have long recognized the importance of the internal structure (such as reporting relationship, job design, appraisal, selection, and reward.[79]) Dill found a relation between managerial decisions and the external environment—the more heterogeneous the environment, the more autonomous the decisions.[80] Burns and Stalker found that "mechanistic," rigid managerial systems were most appropriate for stable environmental conditions, and that looser, "organic" systems were most appropriate for rapidly changing market and technological environments.[81] Lawrence and Lorsch applied the first systematic measurement to this emerging concept and found that varied degrees of "differentiation" and "integration" were appropriate, depending on the degree of uncertainty management perceived in the task environment.[82] Duncan has extended such notions to intra-departmental analysis.[83] Lorsch and Morse have found that the personal predispositions of organization members must also be considered in designing the organization for adaptiveness.[84] Negandhi and Reimann, Kandwalla, and others continued to demonstrate the applicability of this perspective which highlights the "fit" between organizations and their environments and subsequent organizational effectiveness.[85]

These researchers on contingency theory, however, have relied on narrow definitions of the external environment, definitions based on market and technology. This reliance has often led to their reluctance to generalize too broadly across industrial categories. Yet, if their criteria of environmental analysis were applied to the environment of public affairs, company size rather than kind of industry would be a more important delimiting factor than industry. Regardless of the marketplace or the production technology, large corporations as important social institutions face highly complex and unstable conditions. As Thompson briefly mentioned:[86]

> *Uncertainty would appear to be greatest, at least potentially, in the institutional level. Here, the organization deals largely with elements of the environment over which it has no authority . . . it is subjected to generalized norms ranging from formally codified law to informal standards of good practice, to public authority, or to elements expressing the public interest.*

Whereas this discussion was parenthetical to Thompson's theories, it has been largely ignored by other writers of the contingency school.

Specifically, Thompson foresaw the need for specialized anticipatory scanning, which has only very recently been appreciated as a vital managerial concern. He stated that concerns at the institutional level require active monitoring of the environment, or "opportunistic search."[82] Thus he realized that environmental perceptions, particularly of public affairs, can be affected by organizational structures. He suggested that environments requiring serious judgment should have broad dominant coalitions too. He suggested that the dominant coalition's understanding of a complex environment depends on the sophistication of its boundary-spanning units. Various typologies of boundary spanning can be found in the works of many authors.[88] Miles offered the most complete range of activities. He has identified six "institutional-adaptive" functions of boundary spanners:[89]

1. *Representing* the organization to external constituencies.
2. *Scanning* and *monitoring* environmental events.
3. *Protecting* the organization from environmental threats.
4. *Processing information* to inform other internal or communication units.
5. *Transacting* with other organizations for procurement and disposal of outputs.
6. *Coordinating* activities with other organizations.

Miles cautioned that boundary spanners, while conceptually distinct, are likely to perform more than one function.[90] It has been suggested that the degree of differentiation or specialization in the boundary-spanning roles a firm develops depends on the size and technology of an organization and the environmental complexity and volatility.[91]

Differentiated boundary-spanning units often experience difficulty in influencing public policy. Often they are created in the wake of some serious event and viewed as narrow flack-catchers, interested in appeasement rather than solution and understanding.[92] In some firms, important information from environmental scanners is ignored because they are viewed with skepticism and considered abstract futurists.[93] In addition, Perry and Angle have noted that such boundary spanners may encourage external crisis to increase their internal strategic importance.[94]

This difficulty is to be expected, since the structural configuration that allows the spanners of public affairs the needed flexibility and proximity to outside information also inhibits their influence in the parent organization. Boundary spanners are, by the nature of their function, removed from the core of the organization.[95] And thus their power follows what has often been demonstrated—that power and influence of departments are related to the degree of centrality and control of critical resources.[96]

Many traditional bases of organizational power, such as coercion, rewards, and formal authority, tend not be used by boundary spanners. Accordingly, it has been found, boundary spanners tend to rely on their personal "expertise" as the source of their influence.[97] If this base of influence is to be effective, the particular expertise not only must be achieved but must be valued by the organization. Jemison has found that the degree of influence a boundary-spanning unit has is related to the boundary-spanning function it assumes.[98] More specifically, Jemison has noted that boundary-spanning units that are involved in "domain determination" tended to have the greatest influence in an organization. Next in order of influence are those involved in "physical input control," and lastly those involved in "information acquisition and control."[99] This relation proved true across the three technology types studies (long-linked, mediating, and intensive) but was particularly strong in long-linked industry, such as food processing.

This finding is consistent in that information acquisition and control is the primary type of activity of units on public affairs in their role as scanners and monitors. Therefore, these units primarily aim toward expertise in an area less valued or central to the organization than the other two types.[100] Domain determination and control of physical input are readily seen as immediate "strategic contingencies," but the longer-range anticipatory concerns of a proactive public affairs system is not likely to be recognized as important unless a crisis needs resolution.

Therefore the chief executive, as the architect of the corporate strategy has the duty to give more stature to these activities by regarding them as essential elements of corporate strategy.[101] Brown (1979) has indicated that the corporate culture very much affects the receptivity of public affairs executives.[102] The prestige of the sponsor and leaders of new departments is an important component of their initial political clout.[103] For enduring strength, their importance to the organization must be demonstrated. If public affairs are shown to be an important part of planning appraisals and training managers, and to have the attention of senior management, then the professionals who deal with public affairs will have formal authority and appreciation of their expertise.

A second problem with boundary spanners is that they develop a certain shortsightedness because of the nature of their work. Organizational roles can lead to functionally biased[104] or hierarchically biased perceptions.[105] As differentiated public affairs sub-units gain expertise and professionalism, they are likely to become identified with their work in itself to the detriment of how they look at things from the organization's point of view. Their developing professional standards, the times in which they are functioning, the type of external sources, and their stage of involvement may lead them towards a technocrat's lack of appreciation for what they contribute to the organization.[106] Pfeffer and Salancik argued, for example, that:[107]

> *Scanning highlights and narrows the organization's attention to the assignment of specialized individuals to scan specific environmental segments . . . may leave the organizations more isolated and less informed than before. The scanners focus on routinized quantitative data collection, prepare reports filled with jargon and complexity, and then struggle with operating personnel to have their efforts considered.*

Thus boundary spanners may pursue dysfunctional activities having lost touch with organizational objectives.

Such insights are certainly not novel to public affairs, nor to scanning in general. Nor is such behavior unavoidable. Contingency theorists have identified other structural concepts besides mere differentiation. Lawrence and Lorsch defined differentiation as the "difference in cognitive and emotional orientation among managers in different functional departments."[108] This was a useful concept in understanding sub-unit behavior in areas completely unrelated to scanning public affairs. Secondly, they found that the environment poses varying demands on the "integrating" efforts an organization should undertake. This integration was defined as the "quality of the state of collaboration . . . among departments." Varied degrees of integration can be employed depending on the degree of interdependence across departments. They discussed planning, the manager's role, special cross-cutting individuals to act as integrators, and coordination committees.

Similarly, Thompson has suggested that environments requiring substantial judgment should have a broad dominant coalition; this would limit the distortion that might characterize the perception of just a few top managers if they are the only ones doing the judging. In actual practice, recent literature on issue managers[109] highlighting internal bulletins and multilevel public affairs steering committees[110] indicate that integrating mechanisms are beginning to be used in managing public affairs.

Thus we see that while contingency theorists have not directly considered the specific demands of the public environment, their concepts can provide a helpful framework for designing structures to manage public issues better. Because the public environment is complex and volatile, differentiated boundary-spanning units have to keep the organization adaptive to avoid a crisis. The difficulties of establishing organizational influence for the differentiated boundary-spanning units present an important responsibility for top managers. The latter must confer and maintain the perceived significance of these units that are oriented to the long run. Finally, integrating mechanisms are needed to combat the tendency for isolated specialists to transmit conflicting, confusing, and irrelevant information.

Evaluation

There is a value, then, in those adaptation theories that focus primarily on internal preparedness, contrasted with external responses, as a way for organizations to be proactive in managing public issues. Theorists who are externally oriented believe in "evolutionary" approaches and "strategic choice." Each of these externally oriented groups has specific theoretical weaknesses, but jointly fail to appreciate how organizations gain a perception of the external environment. They tend to focus more on behavior toward a single issue in the outside world. There is little consideration of how responses to one issue can be related to responses to another and how organizations can seek accurate views of the outside.

Internally oriented adaptation theories such as the business policy approach and the contingency approach focus on the need for developing structural prerequisites for effective external responses. Business policy approaches have recently moved away from relying on the agency of the chief executive and have acknowledged that managing public affairs has to be delegated and coordinated as other environmental sectors have been handled. Contingency theorists, while silent on how to apply their findings to the public environment, have provided evidence that differentiation, integration, and influence are important design variables in managing such environments effectively. Units that span the boundary between the firm and the constituents in the external environment seem to keep firms responsive to the public environment, even though it is complex and volatile. The effectiveness of these units, however, is threatened by their lack of influence and involvement in company decisions as well as by their tendency to be short-sighted. Missing from all these theories is any systematic research on the effectiveness of this form of managing the public environment.

Endnotes

1. J. E. Post, *Corporate Social Behavior* (Reston, Va.: Reston Publishing, 1978).
2. R. H. Miles, *Macro Organizational Behavior* (Santa Monica, Ca.: Goodyear, 1980).
3. A. L. Stinchcombe, "Social Structure and Organizations" in *Handbook of Organizations*, J. G. March, ed. (Chicago: Rand-McNally, 1965), pp. 142–193. Also H. Aldrich and A. Reiss, "Continuities in the Study of Ecological Succession: Changes in the Rare Composition of Neighborhoods and their Businesses," *American Journal of Sociology* (January 1976), pp. 846–866; D. T. Campbell, "Variation and Selective Retention in Socio-cultural Evolution," *Social Change in Developing Areas* (Cambridge, Mass.: Schenkman, 1965), pp. 19–49; M. Hannan and J. Freeman, "The Population Ecology of Organizations," *American Journal of Sociology*, 82 (March 1977), pp. 929–964; H. W. Aldrich, *Organizations and Environments* (Englewood Cliffs, N.J.: Prentice-Hall, 1979); Spencer, 1897.
4. Stinchcombe, *ibid.* Also Hannah and Freeman, *ibid.*; Aldrich, *ibid.*
5. S. Gould, *Ontology and Evolution* (Cambridge, Mass.: Harvard University Press, 1977).
6. Campbell, *op. cit.*

7. K. E. Weick, *The Social Psychology of Organizing* (Reading, Mass.: Addison-Wesley, 1969), p. 64.

8. *Ibid.*

9. W. H. Starbuck, "Organizations and Their Environments," in *Handbook of Industrial and Organizational Psychology*, M. Dunnette, ed. (Chicago: Rand-McNally, 1976), pp. 1979.

10. Miles, *op. cit.*

11. R. M. Cyert and S. G. March, *A Behavioral Theory of the Firm* (Englewood Cliffs, N.J.: Prentice Hall, 1963).

12. D. C. Dearborn and H. A. Simon, "Selective Perception: A Note on the Identification of Executives," *Sociometry*, 21 (1958), pp. 142.

13. P. R. Lawrence and J. W. Lorsch, *Organization and Environment* (Boston: Harvard Graduate School of Business Administration, 1967).

14. J. Sonnenfeld, "Executive Apologies for Price Fixing: Role Biased Perception of Causality," *Academy of Management*, 24 (1981), pp. 192–198.

15. G. Vickers, *The Art of Judgement: A Study of Policy Making* (New York: Basic Books, 1965).

16. J. Pfeffer and G. R. Salancik, *The External Control of Organizations* (New York: Harper & Row, 1978).

17. J. Child, "Organizational Structures, Environment and Performance: The Role of Strategic Choice," *Sociology*, 6 (1972), pp. 1–22.

18. S. Levine and P. E. White, "Exchange as a Conceptual Framework for the Study of Interorganizational Relationships," *Administrative Science Quarterly*, 5 (1961), pp. 583–601. Also J. D. Thompson, *Organizations in Action* (New York: McGraw-Hill, 1967); Child, *ibid.*; Miles, *op. cit.*

19. R. E. Miles and C. C. Snow, *Organizational Strategy, Structure and Process* (New York: McGraw-Hill, 1978).

20. Pfeffer and Salancik, *op. cit.*

21. Pfeffer and Salancik, *op. cit.* Also Cyert and March, *op. cit.*

22. Cyert and March, *op. cit.*

23. Pfeffer and Salancik, *op. cit.*

24. M. Aiken and J. Hage, "The Organic Organization and Innovation," *Sociology*, 5 (1971), pp. 63–82. Also J. Pfeffer, "Merger as a Response to Organizational Interdependence," *Administrative Science Quarterly*, 17 (1972), pp. 382–394; P. M. Hirsch, "Organizational Effectiveness and the Institutional Environment," *Administrative Science Quarterly*, 20 (1975), pp. 327–344; B. M. Staw and E. Swajakowski, "The Scarcity-Munificence Component of Organizational Environments and the Commission of Illegal Acts," *Administrative Science Quarterly*, 20 (1975), pp. 345–354.

25. J. P. Kotter, "Managing External Dependence," *Academy of Management Review*, 4 (1979), pp. 87–92.

26. C. Argyris and D. Schon, *Organizational Learning: A Theory of Action Perspective* (Reading, Mass.: Addison Wesley, 1978).

27. Starbuck, *op. cit.* Also Dearborn and Simon, *op. cit.*; Sonnenfeld, *op. cit.*

28. Pfeffer and Salancik, *op. cit.*

29. *Ibid.*

30. *Ibid.*, p. 274.

31. *Ibid.*, p. 271.

32. *Ibid.*
33. R. A. Leone, "The Real Costs of Regulation," *Harvard Business Review*, 55 (Nov.-Dec. 1977), pp. 57–66.
34. Post, *op. cit.*
35. Pfeffer and Salancik, *op. cit.*, p. 268.
36. *Ibid.*
37. T. Parsons, *Structure and Process in Modern Societies* (New York: Free Press, 1960).
38. L. J. Henderson, *Pareto's General Sociology* (Cambridge, Mass.: Harvard University Press, 1935). Also W. B. Cannon, *The Wisdom of Body* (New York: W. W. Norton, 1939); G. C. Homans, *The Human Group* (New York: Harcourt Brace Janovich, 1950); Parsons, *ibid.*
39. R. M. Ashby, *An Introduction to Cybernetics* (London: Chapmann Hall, 1956). Also L. Von Bertalanffy, "The Theory of Open Systems in Physics and Biology," *Science*, 3 (1950), pp. 23–29; W. Buckley, *Sociology and Modern Systems Theory* (Englewood Cliffs, N.J.: Prentice-Hall, 1967).
40. Buckley, *ibid.*
41. C. I. Barnard, *The Functions of the Executive* (Cambridge, Mass.: Harvard University Press, 1938), p. 211.
42. H. A. Simon, *Administrative Behavior* (New York: Free Press, 1946), p. 167.
43. P. Selznick, *Leadership in Administration* (New York: Harper & Row, 1957), p. 75.
44. K. R. Andrews, *The Concept of Corporate Strategy* (Homewood, Ill.: Irwin, 1971).
45. Selznik, *op. cit.* Also Andrews, *ibid.*
46. R. W. Ackerman, *The Social Challenge to Business* (Cambridge, Mass.: Harvard University Press, 1975). Also E. A. Murray, "The Social Responses in Process in Commercial Books," *Academy of Management Review* (July 1976), pp. 5–15.
47. R. Ackerman and R. Bauer, *Corporate Social Responsiveness: The Modern Dilemma* (Reston, Va.: Reston Publishing, 1976).
48. Selznik, *op. cit.* Also Andrews, *op. cit.*; Ackerman, *op. cit.*; Ackerman and Bauer, *ibid.*; Murray, *op. cit.*
49. Votaw and Sethi, "Do We Need a New Corporate Response" *California Management Review* (Fall 1969), reprinted in D. Votaw and S. P. Sethi, *The Corporate Dilemma* (Englewood Cliffs, N.J.: Prentice-Hall, 1973), pp. 170–190.
50. *Ibid.*
51. S. P. Sethi, *Up Against the Corporate Wall* (Englewood Cliffs, N.J.: Prentice-Hall, 1977).
52. Post, *op. cit.* Also Ackerman and Bauer, *op. cit.*; Sethi, *ibid.*
53. Post, *op. cit.*, p. 248.
54. Cyert and March, *op. cit.* Also Lawrence and Lorsch, *op. cit.*
55. Dearborn and Simon, *op. cit.*
56. Sonnenfeld, *op. cit.*
57. L. E. Fouraker and J. M. Stopford, "Organization Structure and the Multinational Strategy," *Administrative Science Quarterly*, 13 (1968), pp. 47–64. Also F. J. Aguilar, *Scanning the Business Environment* (New York: Macmillan, 1967).
58. Argyris, *op. cit.*
59. Cyert and March, *op. cit.*, p. 113.
60. Aguilar, *op. cit.*, p. 54.

61. Barnard, *op. cit.* Also Simon, *op. cit.*
62. Selznik, *op. cit.* Also Andrews, *op. cit.*; Ackerman and Bauer, *op. cit.*
63. Aguilar, *op. cit.* Also Votaw and Sethi, *op. cit.*; Sethi, *op. cit.*
64. M. Mazis, and R. Green, "Implementing Social Responsibility," *MSU Business Topics* (Winter 1971), as it appeared in *Managing Corporate Social Responsibility*, D. B. Carroll, ed. (Boston: Little, Brown, 1977), pp. 216–225. Also P. S. McGrath, *Managing Corporate External Relations* (New York: The Conference Board, No. 679, 1976) and *Action Plans for Public Affairs* (New York: The Conference Board, No. 733, 1977); S. L. Holmes, "Corporate Social Performance: Past and Present Areas of Commitment," *The Academy of Management Journal*, 20 (1977), pp. 433–438 and "Adapting Corporate Structure for Social Responsibility," *California Management Review*, 21 (1978), pp. 47–54.
65. Mazis and Green, *ibid.* Also Ackerman, *op. cit.*
66. Holmes, *op. cit.*
67. K. Newgren, "Social Forecasting: An Overview of Current Business Practices," in *Managing Corporate Social Responsibility*, A. B. Carroll, ed. (Boston: Little, Brown, 1977).
68. P. S. McGrath, *Redefining Corporate-Federal Relations* (New York: The Conference Board, No. 757, 1979).
69. Mazis and Green, *op. cit.*
70. *Business Week*, "Capitalizing on Social Change" (Oct. 29, 1979), pp. 105–106.
71. T. J. Murray, "A New High-Level Executive," *Dun's Review* (November, 1979), pp. 63–64.
72. J. K. Brown, *This Business of Issues: Coping with the Company's Environment* (New York: The Conference Board, 758, 1979).
73. McGrath, *op. cit.*
74. Brown, *op. cit.*, p. 64.
75. McGrath, *op. cit.*
76. Newgren, *op. cit.* Also McGrath, 1977, *op. cit.*; J. E. Fleming, "Public Issues Scanning," presented at the *39th Annual Meeting of the Academy of Management* (Atlanta, August 1979).
77. Fleming, *ibid.*, p. 17.
78. McGrath, *op. cit.*
79. W. R. Dell, "Environment as an Influence on Managerial Autonomy," *Administrative Science Quarterly*, 2 (1958), pp. 409–443. Also T. Burns and G. M. Stalker, *The Management of Innovation* (London: Tavistock, 1961); Lawrence and Lorsch, *op. cit.*; Thompson, *op. cit.*; R. B. Duncan, "Multiple Decision-Making Structures in Adapting to Environmental Uncertainty: The Impact on Organization Effectiveness," *Human Relations*, 26 (1973), pp. 273–291; J. W. Lorsch and J. J. Morse, *Organizations and Their Members* (New York: Harper & Row, 1974).
80. Dell, *ibid.*
81. Burns and Stalker, *op. cit.*
82. Lawrence and Lorsch, *op. cit.*
83. Duncan, *op. cit.*
84. Lorsch and Morse, *op. cit.*
85. A. R. Negandhi and B. C. Reiman, "A Contingency Theory of Organization Re-examined in the Context of a Developing Country," *Academy of Management Journal*, 2 (1972), pp. 77–101.
86. Thompson, *op. cit.*, p. 12.

87. *Ibid.*, p. 151.

88. J. S. Adams, "The Structure and Dynamics of Behavior in Organization Boundary Roles," in *The Handbook of Industrial and Organizational Psychology*, M. D. Dunnette, ed. (Chicago: Rand-McNally, 1976). Also E. J. Miller and A. K. Rice, *Systems of Organization: The Control of Task and Sentinent Boundaries* (London: Tavistock, 1967); Aiken and Hage, *op. cit.*; J. A. Wall, Jr., "Managing Negotiators," *Business Horizons* (February 1975), pp. 41–44; E. Goffman, "The Nature of Deference and Demeanor," *American Anthropologist*, 58 (1956), pp. 473–502; D. Katz and R. Kahn, *The Social Psychology of Organizations*, (New York: Wiley, 1966); H. Aldrich and D. Herker, "Boundary Spanning Roles and Organization Structure," in *Academy of Management Review*, 2 (1967), pp. 217–230; A. G. Kefalas, "Environmental Management Information Systems," *Journal of Business Research*, 3 (1975), pp. 253–263; Lawrence and Lorsch, *op. cit.*; R. P. Leifer and A. Delbecq, "Organizational/Environmental Interchange: A Model of Boundary Spanning Activity," *Academy of Management Review*, Vol. 3 (1978), pp. 40–50.

89. Miles, *op. cit.*

90. *Ibid.*, p. 38.

91. Miles, *Ibid.*, Thompson, *op. cit.*

92. Mazis and Green, *op. cit.*, and W. H. Chase, "The Issues Management Gauntlet," *International Public Relations Association Review*, 2 (1978), pp. 24–27.

93. Brown, *op. cit.*

94. J. L. Perry and H. L. Angle, "The Politics of Organization Boundary Roles in Collective Bargaining," *The Academy of Management Review*, 4 (1979), pp. 487–496.

95. Thompson, *op. cit.* Also Perry and Angle, *ibid.*; Miles, *op. cit.*

96. P. M. Blau, *Exchange and Power in Social Life* (New York: Wiley, 1964). Also M. Crozier, *The Bureaucratic Phenomena* (Chicago: University of Chicago, 1963); Katz and Kahn, *op. cit.*; Cyert and March, *op. cit.*; D. J. Hickson, C. R. Hinnings, C. A. Lee, R. E. Schneck, and J. M. Pennings, "A Strategic Contingencies Theory of Interorganizational Power," *Administrative Science Quarterly*, 16 (1971), pp. 378–397.

97. R. Speckman, "Influence and Information: An Exploratory Investigation of the Boundary Role Person's Basis of Power," *Academy of Management Journal*, 22 (1979), pp. 105–117. Also M. Patchen, "The Locus and Basis of Influence on Organizational Decisions," *Organizational Behavior and Human Performance*, 11 (1974), pp. 195–211.

98. Jemison, "Strategic Decision Making Influence in Boundary Spanning Roles," presented at the *39th Annual Meeting of the Academy of Management* (Atlanta, Georgia, 1979).

99. Jemison, *ibid.*

100. Fleming, *op. cit.* Also Brown, *op. cit.*; McGrath, *op. cit.*; Homes, *op. cit.*

101. Andrews, *op. cit.* Also Ackerman, *op. cit.*

102. Brown, *op. cit.*

103. A. M. Pettigrew, *The Politics of Organizational Decision Making* (London: Tavistock, 1973). Also "Towards a Political Theory of Organizational Intervention," *Human Relations*, 28 (1975), pp. 191–208.

104. Dearborn and Simon, *op. cit.*
105. Sonnenfeld, *op. cit.* Also S. Lieberman, "The Effects of Changes in Role on the Attitudes of Role Occupants," *Human Relations*, 9 (1956), pp. 385–402.
106. Selznik, *op. cit.*
107. Pfeffer and Salancik, *op. cit.*, p. 270.
108. Lawrence and Lorsch, *op. cit.*
109. Brown, *op. cit.*
110. Holmes, *op. cit.* Also Fleming, *op. cit.*; Mazis and Green, *op. cit.*; McGrath, *op. cit.*

Chapter 4

MODEL FOR PERCEIVING PUBLIC AFFAIRS

The highly turbulent and complex set of demands by corporate stakeholders has made it essential for American business managers to become responsible to interests beyond merely those of the marketplace. Current theory about organizations is more strongly concerned with reactive behavior than with an organization's foresight and receptiveness. Since investigating existing organizational structure could yield valuable insight, we present a basic model of corporate interaction with public affairs. This model applies across industries, up to the megacorporations. It parallels the biological stages observed in the perceptual process of human beings. Accordingly, we must portray the perceptual process of the corporation, noting analogous stages.

The essential components of the perceptual process for a corporation are (1) events in the environment, (2) structural sensitivity of the internal system, (3) perceptions about the outside, (4) actions, or company performance, and (5) results of the actions. The feedback loops in Figure 4-1 indicate that this process is not unidirectional. Changes in any one of these components can alter the circumstances of any of the other four components. A review of existing literature on the subject has clearly revealed that only three of these factors have been recognized as relevant—environmental events, performance, and effectiveness. Wide-ranging debate has centered around the wisdom of actions by companies in response to particular issues. Vigorous discussion has evolved and highlighted strategies that enable companies to exert greater control on the environment; these strategies emphasize that a company be exposed early to the environment to prepare for critical environmental encounters. An inward, diagnostic focus by the company on its sensory mechanism, and a thorough appraisal of the company's processes in formulating a perception of the outside world, are conspicuously less often found in the body of theoretical and practical literature. Let us now examine each of these five components that comprise the perception.

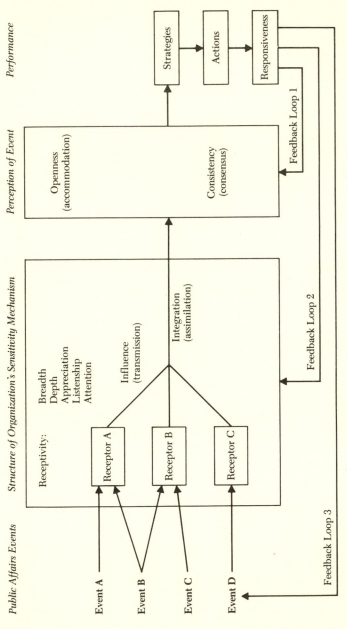

Figure 4-1   Perceptual Model of an Organization's Responsiveness to Public Affairs.

Environment of Public Affairs

The first of these components, the public affairs environment, is in many ways as dramatic a sector as the marketplace and the technological milieu—the two primary considerations in theories about organizations and their environment. The megacorporations have become a prominent, if not dominant force in American life. These companies, through their actions as producers, purchasers, employers, marketers, landowners, investors, competitors, taxpayers, and resource consumers, fundamentally affect the lives of very diverse segments of the population. Changing public expectations and the evolving roles of our social institutions have empowered special-interest groups to successfully challenge managerial discretion over traditionally private corporation activities, for example employment practices, equipment purchases, plant location, product design, marketing practices, shareowner communication, the aggregate effect of economic actions, and the rise of externalities and social costs due to technological change.

The Sensory Mechanism

The existing and potential outside influences on corporate behavior are detected and interpreted by the specific mechanism the firm has established for acquiring such information. Large companies rely on many diverse boundary-spanning units, resembling the differentiated receptors of the human nervous system, to detect important signals and forward this information inward to a central authority.* These units are receptive to new information in their fields, and are primarily responsible for keeping the firm up to date, enabling it to respond appropriately to the environment. Their general diversity is coordinated with a number of functional departments; however, independent units for gathering specialized information may be established in some companies where there is special need. Generally, departments oriented to public affairs, such as the legal department, the public relations department, and the government relations department, are the primary sources of information about public issues. They are not, however, the exclusive source of public information in large firms. Since such issues are complex and volatile, many other executives from technical areas, line operations, finance, human resources, and general management must be involved in public affairs.

Large volumes of information generated by courts, the mass media,

---

* The human nervous system is composed of sensory receptors, which with sensory nerve axons are distributed throughout the body and are especially sensitive to particular types of stimuli.

and the legislature regarding a firm's involvement in public issues may be controversial and incomplete. Insight into both the historical background of these issues and their implications to the firm is often more fully available in offices of the firm not primarily concerned with public affairs. These offices can probably provide a more compact and internally directed analysis that can be prepared more quickly. However, the importance of a department for public affairs is well recognized; there must be a primary unit to keep track of issues and to know the appropriate language and relevant skills for communication. Largely because of the nature and persistence of public issues that U.S. corporations must face, it would be unrealistic to burden chief executive officers with primary responsibility for scanning and interpreting an institution's environment. Besides time constraints, other constraints such as one's professional training, unconscious bias, and the limitations of personal and professional contacts are good reasons chief executives must delegate more broadly their traditional ambassadorial responsibilities.

There are specific activities and attitudes that can indicate the *receptor* quality of the boundary-spanning units in a firm. For example, experts who are receptive will be expected to initiate greater contact with outside stakeholders than will less receptive units. This greater outside contact would be shown by the breadth and variety of outside sources as well as by the total time spent in such interaction. These important factors affect the depth and quality of the information gathered.

It is equally important that once the information is acquired, these units are able to appreciate clearly the potentiality for information that outside sources represent. Thus, outside stakeholders should not be viewed merely as passive, target audiences. Ability to listen is therefore an important but often undervalued quality in units concerned with information. Firms frequently emphasize espousal at the expense of listening. Information-gathering tasks such as scanning for new issues or monitoring existing issues should not be overshadowed by information-disseminating tasks like representing the firm to outsiders and protecting the firm from outside threat.

Influence (Transmission)

Two components of structural sensitivity besides the receptivity of company units are the *influences* of public concerns on the firm and the *integration* of the information from the units within the firm. We recall the comparison with the human sensory system; once the information is received, there must be a strong transmission signal (influence) from the receptor to indicate that the information gained is being passed along the proper channel. In this process, diverse fragments of information must be assimilated so that the firm can interpret them (integration).

Examining first the contribution of influence, we can refer to the earlier discussion (end of Chapter 2) that showed how boundary-spanning units are often on the periphery of company decisions. If boundary spanners are seen strictly as reactive agents of the chief executive, they will be unable to alert the organization to issues the chief executive does not first identify. Units concerned with public affairs are especially seen as of dubious critical importance since they lack control over vital physical inputs and involvement with market activities. There is danger that the long time frame of public issues can cause their strategic significance to be undervalued. Information about public issues must be made relevant to organizational needs to be accepted throughout the firm. Any messages from receptors that are too abstract or that are politically threatening to more powerful internal units will be ignored.

Chief executives and corporate boards of directors can remedy the inadequate influence of public affairs units by ceding to them a greater amount of formal authority. Another way would be to promote a less formal culture, which presumably would appreciate the significance and legitimacy of these units within the firm. The executives can approve and endorse public affairs units by giving them attention, involving them in performance appraisals and in planning by other units, in the status of public affairs executives, and in career paths of public affairs personnel.

Integration (Assimilation)

Finally, all the information that is compiled, processed, and disseminated to appropriate departments must also be assimilated to be understood. While general managers suffer from a lack of expertise, public affairs executives, when blinded by excessive expertise, may tend towards shortsightedness. It is possible to encourage expertise while correcting for the possible side effects from the technocrat. The tasks of the specialized public affairs scanner do not automatically provide corporatewide perspective. These specialists can coordinate their actions on issues and thereby limit the drift toward unproductive routines and jargon. Contradictory company impressions of the outside world can be revealed and resolved. Limited resources (such as the time and attention of political figures, regulators, and activists, advertising dollars, and lobbyist efforts) can be properly allocated. The relative compartmentalization that exists in companies means that different departments hold the separate pieces of information needed for a comprehensive view of the social environment. Once these different pieces of the informational puzzle are combined, a realistic picture of the environment is created. Primary responsibility for steering the firm through each stage in the public interaction on an issue can be determined as needed. Furthermore, corporate subunits will be in the position to initiate action as well as to react more consistently to the initiative of constituents. Some methods for achieving this integration are through a coordinating top manager (vice president of external affairs), company planning processes, project managers, temporary task forces, and top-level steering committees.

The quality of structural sensitivity to public issues consists of three components: (1) receptivity, (2) influence, and (3) integration; that, in turn, should directly contribute to how responsive a firm is. Human perceptions are directly proportional to the quality of the sensory system, which internalizes the information about the environment. Similarly, an organization's concepts are limited by the sensitivity of the structure that acquires, transmits, and organizes information. Inaccurate perceptions may result from departmental or other bias. Certain departments may consistently foster an adversarial view towards all public affairs issues, while other departments may regularly be conciliatory. Some receptor units may overplay the threat from particular outside groups, and others overemphasize the concerns of a narrow interest in the firm. Despite such bias, a firm with a structure that is sensitive to its environment may be successful in detecting important new information and in relaying it to challenge any prevailing misconceptions within the firm.

It is, of course, counterproductive to elevate and place total trust in an organizational process while endowing it with virtues it does not have. The sensory process comparison we have been using helps us to remember that all organizational processes are merely the coordinated concepts and actions of organization members. The number of windows on the world, giving exposure to the outside environment, determines the degree of perceptual distortion an organization will be subject to; in any case, it increases the complexity of distortion beyond what is likely on an individual level. A chief executive, a labor relations officer, a line general manager, a public relations officer, compliance officers, lobbyists, public affairs scanners, and the like, all may view the same issues differently, and either selectively ignore issues or act on them differently. William James noted a century ago that "genius means little more than the faculty of perceiving in an unhabitual way."[1] Mechanisms must be designed that will free organizations from the distortions induced by the perceptual habits of their individual members.

Perceptions

The character of an organization's perceptions can be reached through examining the openness, the receptivity to outside critics, the understanding of diverse positions, and the consensus, or internal consistency of the organization, in formulating these perceptions. The term *accommodation* is appropriate here as it is used in cognitive psychology—to refer to the openness to new and different concepts. This is in contrast to the meaning of *accommodation* that suggests capitulation to outside demands. Accommodation as a perceptual quality in an organization can be identified by examining what attitudes a company has towards the public affairs. How does the company perceive outside stakeholders? How important does it consider an interchange of ideas with outside stakeholders? How does it rate emerging issues? Consensus is evinced most distinctly when there is a high degree of accommodation.

Performance

These perceptions are important in that they affect the actions of the firm. As the organization responds to its dynamic environment, an accommodating perspective may allow enlightened actions whereby firms can both shape their environment and anticipate the consequences of their actions. Thus, the firm will be less likely to react blindly to crises and more likely to display actions (strategies and behavior) that reflect foresight and analysis. Furthermore, companies with a high degree of internal consensus are likely to present a consistent and reliable image to the outside. Companies with internal dissension lack coherent policies and disregard commitments, while those with differing, more balanced and constructive perceptions come to power.

These strategies can lead to company actions best seen as changes in internal process.[2] In such a setting, we should expect changes in forest practices, mill operations, marketing practices, and the like. The system does not end with internal actions. The feedback loops in Figure 4-1 indicate three possible targets of company actions and strategies beyond internal processes. Company efforts may be directed toward external events (loop 1), as suggested by the "strategic-choice" perspective. Examples include attempts to help shape legislation, strengthen coalitions, and change public opinion. Companies can also direct their energies towards company structure (loop 2), as suggested by the "contingency" perspective.[3] This effort could be manifested through redesigning integrating structures, for instance, reporting relations, steering committees, and product teams; or it could mean altering differentiated units, for instance, changing the size and responsibility of public affairs departments. Finally, company efforts can have an internal influence, modifying company perceptions (loop 3) as suggested by organizational learning theorists.[4] An example is reassessing fundamental assumptions about outside stakeholder groups.

The success of a company's performance in the public affairs environment can best be appraised by those on the outside. Company officials, by nature, lack the objectivity for adequate self-analysis. Furthermore while adequate external data on market issues exist and are available for companies to use, this is not true for data on the public affairs environment. Even though the problems in both market and public affairs are not congruent, accurate information from both sources must be integrated by firms for formulating policy and for making effective decisions.

A combination of many subjective, geographic, and parochial factors also affect the quality of data available. For example, considerable quantitative data exist from legal compliance records and law suits, and time for construction permit clearance. Such figures may be distorted due to local political climate, pressures in the industry, limitations of the geographical environment, and other environmental variables. Consequently, "data" can be judged to be a product of a firm, reflecting the qualities of the particular firm. General evaluation methods may also prove deficient when it is found that firms with objectively bad records are actually performing well, given their setting. Although this disputes the usefulness of a particular set of data as a solid indicator, it is of paramount significance that there is no basis for adding or sealing such data. Serious problems might be associated with data that were oriented to administration and not to analysis, to inability to include certain values, to difficulty in measuring social and political trends, to skewing, to influence of company standards, or to limited techniques. Each variable does not merit equal weighting; many important dimensions of performance do not lend themselves to being measured at all. For example, elements of data may lack equivalent terms in some instances, or may run over longer periods; there may be essentially abstract qualities like influence, credibility, and reactiveness, that cannot be assessed or measured quantitatively.

If we turn to outside judges of the company performance, we overcome such obstacles. Large panels of diverse stakeholders can correct for the bias of any particular interest group. Such judges should represent interest groups that have a history of interaction with the industry in question. Thus they would have a knowledgeable basis for evaluating companies within an industry. The dimensions for evaluating the success of company performance should be drawn from the experience of these stakeholder groups. For example, these dimensions might include:

1. Degree of background preparedness on the issue.
2. Degree of credibility of company statements—for instance action will follow from the words of negotiators.
3. Degree of reliability of company behavior over time—it will maintain its commitments.
4. Whether the company can clearly distinguish its interest from the public interest.
5. Relative accessibility of corporate officials to outsiders.
6. Degree of perceived legitimacy of outside critics.

These dimensions of corporate performance in public affairs can be termed *responsiveness*. The term describes a state of behavior the organization achieves rather than an ethical evaluation of company actions.

In summary, the following four propositions relate to the proposed perceptual model for interaction between organizations and the public:

1. The public affairs environment of big corporations has become sufficiently complex and important that, in some industries, it rivals the marketplace as a critical environment sector.
2. It is therefore appropriate to analyze the sensitivity of the organizational structure that reads and interprets this environment. Departments are biased by their professional focus and personal distance from various issues. Companies are distinct in the components of this structural sensitivity (receptivity, influence, and integration).
3. Structural sensitivity contributes to aggregate company perceptions and a twofold consequence: openness to understanding information from outside stakeholders, and internally consistent notions of the company's reaction.
4. Perceptual qualities affect the company's responsiveness to public affairs as it is seen in outside appraisal of company performance.

Our proposed model recommends analyzing four phenomena: (1) the public affairs *environment*, (2) structural *sensitivity* to this environment, (3) the company's internal *perceptions* of this environment, and (4) the *responsiveness* of the company. Specific events and actions are given secondary emphasis; the model focuses primarily on the enduring qualities of the system.

Endnotes

1. William James, *The Principles of Psychology* (New York: Henry Holt, 1890), p. 19.
2. K. R. Andrews, *The Concept of Corporate Strategy* (Homewood, Ill.: Irwin, 1971).
3. J. P. Thompson, *Organizations in Action* (New York: McGraw-Hill, 1967). Also P.

R. Lawrence and J. W. Lorsch, *Organization and Environment* (Homewood, Ill.: Irwin, 1967).

4. K. E. Weick, *The Social Psychology of Organizing* (Reading, Mass.: Addison-Wesley, 1969). Also D. Argyris, "Double Loop Learning in Organizations," *Harvard Business Review*, 55 (Sept.-Oct., 1977), pp. 115–125; R. H. Miles, *Macro Organizational Behavior* (Santa Monica, Ca.: Goodyear, 1980).

Chapter 5

METHODS

The purpose of the research on which this book is based was to explore in detail the proposed theoretical model. The model has been applied to a particular industry—the forest products industry. The model suggests first that new, imposing forces are operating in the corporate public affairs environment that make it essential for a firm to make observations that go beyond the industry. The second proposition under this model holds that companies acquire and process information about public affairs differently, according to the environmental sensitivity of their structure. Third, the model proposes that this structural sensitivity contributes to the degree of openness and clarity with which companies perceive complex public issues. Finally, it is proposed that the quality and nature of perception influences the characteristics and responsiveness of company actions.

Multimethod-Multisource Design

Data were collected from five categories of source material: archives (for example, periodicals), interviews with company executives and outside stakeholders, and questionnaire surveys of company executives and outside stakeholders. The distinguishing aspects of this methodology are (1) its attempt to consider the richness and complexity of the total public environment instead of dwelling on a single issue, (2) its attempt to get many respondents from each firm, because single responses represent the individual more than the organization, and (3) its evaluation of individual company performance by relevant outside constituencies.

Constituencies Beyond the Marketplace

The first task, then, was to demonstrate that the public sector of the business environment has become as challenging and critical as other sectors, such as the marketplace. A comprehensive review of stakeholder sources, such as the general press, environmental publications, labor publications, and relevant books traced the infusion and exercise of "influence" into management decisions by forceful stakeholder interests. This survey of the industry's exposure to public affairs was not intended to criticize how particular issues are managed but to convey the variety and persistence of these issues.

Since it was presumed that company exposure to public issues is affected by size of companies, examination was limited to the ten largest companies in the industry. Each of these companies has reported an excess of $3 billion in sales, and each employs over 30,000 workers. Our first approach was to the chief executive in each firm. In our solicitation, we explained the premise that an undesirable gap exists between the needs of American managers and the current academic insights into the interactions between a company and surrounding public affairs. (See Appendix A.) We pointed out that the experience of the forest products industry can be useful in spurring American business to take the initiative in closing the gap. The advantages resulting from such efforts—considered a new venture by some firms—would consequently be highlighted. Companies were invited to participate in a study designed to overcome the deficiency; it was suggested that they permit interviews with a dozen top executives, and that they encourage responses to follow-up questionnaires by twice that many people. Finally, copies of relevant articles by the researcher, published in the *Harvard Business Review*, were enclosed to substantiate the integrity of the study and respect for the time and autonomy of the executives and for company confidentiality.

Seven of these ten companies responded favorably to this request; one declined, claiming to have been inundated with such requests; another declined, explaining that it was already involved in a similar internal study. The third company to decline stated it did not foresee enough gain to the company to warrant the necessary commitment of time. The nonparticipating companies showed no distinction from those that did participate in either size, location, or market performance.

Despite a general commitment to the research, the participating companies did vary in their enthusiasm throughout the study. Three companies, proud of their achievements, greeted the research project with eagerness, shown in their positive first responses and in their hospitality. Two chief executives, convinced that they had a lot to learn, embraced the study with equal zeal. Another company that declined initially cautiously reversed its position following telephone interchanges with the chief executive. This company, after careful deliberation, decided the study had some potential value to the company.

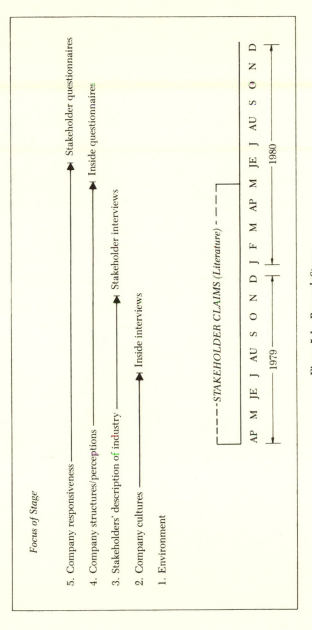

Figure 5-1 Research Stages.

In a sixth firm, which had been indifferent to the request, the executive who had first declined subsequently, after a personal meeting, agreed to cooperate. The other officers exhibited little general interest; although some were willing to help, they lacked the spontaneity of their counterparts in the three enthusiastic companies. Finally, a seventh company wavered from contact to contact. The company (through a particular executive) refused to cooperate in the study initially, but willingly agreed to do so after a second appeal. This particular company cooperated well with the first half of the field interviews but was more guarded on the second round; it broke contact entirely when the questionnaire survey commenced. After three months, contact was reestablished, yet the company formally withdrew from further participation.

Participating companies were widely diverse geographically: two had headquarters on the East Coast, three on the West Coast, one in the mountain states, and one in a Great Lakes state. Each of these companies has substantial land holdings and big facilities in the Pacific Northwest, the South, and the Northeast. According to interviews with outside stakeholders (union leaders, environmentalists, and regulators), the participating companies represented as wide a range of performance in public affairs (responsiveness) as any that could be found in the industry. Also, all these companies had fully integrated marketing and operating activities from forests through to finished wood and paper products.

The Company Interviews

The field interviews were conducted during three-day visits to each of the company headquarters, plus a week of interviews with company lobbyists in Washington, D.C. Included among the fifteen top executives interviewed in each firm were the chief executive, the vice president of finance, the vice president of the timber division, the vice president of the pulp and paper division, the corporate counsel, the vice president of human resources, the vice president of government relations, and the vice president of public relations. Listed below are the six chief purposes of these interviews:

1. To determine the effect of public issues on these firms.
2. To document the internal range of perceptions about such issues.
3. To get the view of the executive about the role of the companies—both at present and historically—in public affairs.
4. To identify the dominant coalition that defines organizational perceptions and strategies.

5. To learn about informal delegation for handling public affairs and coordination thereon.
6. To formulate questions for the follow-up questionnaire on company structure and perceptions.

Such extensive agenda required a minimum of one hour for an interview. The interviews were mostly congenial, and they generally followed the pattern of relaxed conversation in the privacy of the executive's office. The discussion began with a casual question, nonthreatening and generally reflecting on the fluctuations in public affairs. The participants progressed to a more sensitive consideration of the company, and then to a discussion of what part the executive has in managing relations with these outside forces.

Since public affairs are volatile, these interviews were carefully organized to be completed within six months. Fortunately, with the help of the companies, the interviews were successfully concluded between July and December of 1979. Coincidentally, during this period all the companies exhibited very strong market performance, even though recession threats had increased.

The Company Survey

The follow-up questionnaires were prepared and distributed by the end of the first quarter of 1980, which marked the onset of a recession. Each company received thirty questionnaires and an accompanying respondent list. The names on this list included all the top executives previously interviewed, along with representatives of the next level of management from the following fields: legal, finance, planning, general management, government, line operations, public relations, human resources, engineering, and environmental. This range was important, since the companies have broad exposure to wide-ranging public interests. The activities of each of these departments can be directly felt by outside constituencies. (See Chapters 2 and 6.)

The covering letter that accompanied each questionnaire (Appendix B) explained that this was a study of "how an industry confronts multiple pressures from the outside." The term *public affairs* was defined in a very broad sense, as "all those interactions with outside interest groups in non–product-market issues." Examples of issues were then given. It was explained that their company was participating along with six others in this undertaking, and that each executive selected to discuss internal responsibility for management of public affairs and the company's posture on several public issues was one of thirty executives selected from within his company. Furthermore, the questionnaire was presented as a product of interviews with many executives in this industry, including help from senior executives in their own firms. The instructions requested the executives to refrain from skipping questions and from delegating questionnaire completion and asked that approximately 30 minutes' consideration be given it. Finally, it was confirmed that both the executive and the firms would remain anonymous (through the assigning of fictitious names) although names of respondents were requested.

Survey Administration

The questionnaires were distributed through the office of the official assigned by the chief executive to coordinate the company's participation. This official was generally a vice president of public affairs. Responses were mailed back directly to the researcher, and 141 of the original 180 questionnaires (78 percent) were received by the end of the second quarter of 1980. Company affiliation was plainly marked on each questionnaire. All but three executives provided their names, and all provided departmental affiliation.

Each company returned from 15 to 28 of their 30 questionnaires, with all but one of the companies returning 75 percent of their questionnaires (see Table 5-1). The slight variation in response rate across the companies did not seem to be associated with any of the main study variables or with the executive status of the internal contact person. Overall, 89 percent of the respondents were based at the corporate headquarters. The range around this mean was fairly narrow (from 82 to 96 percent). Those departments with substantial representation outside the corporate headquarters tended to be Washington lobbyists (23 percent), engineers and scientists (7 percent), regional operations management (5 percent), and regional public affairs executives (43 percent). The field executives were quite similar to headquarters executives in most dimensions, including rank and experience.

Rank of executive officers did differ significantly across companies. In the simple categorization of officers (CEO, senior VP, VP) versus

Table 5.1 Percentage of Officers Among Company Responses

Company	Percentage
Pacific Timber	87%
American Forests	66
New York Paper	57
Central Paper	37
Northwest Forests	33
U.S. Paper	29

nonofficers (director/manager), there were very significant differences among the companies. The percentage of officers in each company sample were as shown in Table 5-1. In view of the high overall response rate and the rank lists balanced for questionnaire distribution, the explanation for company difference in rank participation is not evident. The pattern does not correspond with information on the meaning of the internal significance of public issues discussed later. Nor does the response pattern correspond with the access to top corporate officers. The first three companies were distinguishable from the second three companies in that the CEO and the other top officers of the first three companies tended to boast far less about the company's successes in public affairs. It is possible, however, that different response patterns by rank across the companies might indicate the importance to the companies of this particular study as a possible instrument of change.

Fortunately, executive rank did not significantly relate to any of the important variables of the study. Half of the sample were officers (chief executives, 3 percent; senior vice presidents, 11 percent; vice presidents, 34 percent). The other half were nonofficers (director/manager). Officers did tend to have greater company tenure (17.97 years) than nonofficers (12.54 years). In group-by-group comparisons, nonofficers had significantly less tenure than every other group (CEO, $p < .001$); senior VPs, $p < .01$; divisional VPs, $p < .001$).

Measurement of Company Structure

The ten-page questionnaire tried to measure *structural sensitivity* through the three dimensions (defined in Chapter 4) unit departmental *receptivity*, internal public affairs *influence*, and companywide *integration*. An early question (question 2) on receptivity asked for an estimate of time spent per week (1–10 hours) with each of seventy outside interest groups. This list of groups was compiled from cross-industry studies in public affairs management as well as from interviews in the current study with 200 industry executives, trade association officials, nine environmentalists, two union leaders, eight regulators, and six journalists.[1] The list included national and regional industry associations, professional associations, federal and state regulators, federal and state legislatures, the investment community, environmental groups, civic associations, unions, and the press. In addition to this activity measure, several cognitive measures were used. Building on the pioneering work of Aguilar, question 3 inquired about the extent to which executives relied on various sources of information on public affairs issues (using the scale 1 = not at all, 5 = a great deal).[2]

Another receptivity question, 8, sought to learn unit-level differences in time orientation by asking how much time the individual making the response generally spent working on public issues.[3] Five categories, ranging from one day or less to a year or more, were provided to allow uniform reporting of the information.

Finally, the measurement of *receptivity* was carried out by requesting information about the purpose, in the firm, of the respondent's function as a boundary spanner.[4] Self ratings in the measurement of "purpose" were defined through the assessment of six possible department roles with which the respondent might be associated; representing, scanning, monitoring, protecting, transmitting, and transacting. Each of the roles was placed on a five-point Likert-type scale, ranging from 1 = not at all, to 5 = a great deal. Thus, these questions allowed *structural receptivity* to be measured along several dimensions such as:

1. Breadth, the number of outsiders.
2. Appreciation, the information value of outside sources divided by time in contact with such sources.
3. Attention, total importance of all boundary-spanning roles.
4. Listenership, importance of scanning and monitoring function.
5. Depth, the average time on public issues.

In this procedure, executives were asked to indicate first how many influential executives have primary responsibility in managing public affairs (question 9). This approach, it was hoped, would supply a sample of public concerns among the members of the dominant coalition in a firm. Influence was also measured by how it operates within the company, particularly with reference to company characteristics that reflect an awareness of influence (question 11). These characteristics were measured by types of influence: the time and attention of the board of directors, the company's annual planning, the respondent's personal career progress, performance appraisals, career paths, and training programs. Each instance of how influence was used was rated

Table 5.2 Response Rate by Departments

Finance and planning	(14)	10%
General management*	(31)	22
Human resources	(21)	15
Engineering/environment	(14)	10
Public affairs	(61)	45
Legal	(10)	
Government relations	(20)	
Public relations	(18)	
Public affairs	(7)	

* Including line operations.

along a 5-point Likert scale, with categories ranging from "very unimportant" to "very important." These instances of influence were well correlated with each other (ranging from $r = .38$ to $r = .74$; the average was $r = .58$, $p < .001$, for each pair). Furthermore, there was a positive but somewhat weaker correlation between the overall score on these seven influence measures and question 7, the measure of how prominently public affairs rated among influential executives ($r = .24$, $p < .001$).

The last aspect of *structural sensitivity* was companywide integration. Several integrating mechanisms are possible, such as company planning, hierarchical coordination, and integrating managers and integrating teams. Data were collected on all such mechanisms wherever they existed and were used by firms. This was accomplished through the interviews. It was found from the emphasis given by each company and the extremely complex and dynamic nature of the environment (as analyzed in Chapter 6), the team mechanism was used the most. Other studies corroborate and support widespread use of this form in preference to the other mechanisms.[5]

The issues facing forest products companies in particular require a constant coordination of functional expertise such as law, technology, politics, communication, and costs and operating information. Thus the questionnaire was able to provide information about the quality of integration when the respondents were first asked to report how often temporary task forces were established to handle public affairs (question 12: a 5-point Likert scale, ranging from "never" to "quite often"), and next asked to report how well established top-level steering committees on public affairs were (question 13: a 5-point Likert scale, ranging from "not at all" to "well established"). There was a moderate positive correlation between these two dimensions of integration ($r = .37$, $p < .001$).

Measurement of Perceptions

The last set of questions had to do with executive perceptions of company performance in different dimensions of public affairs, and executive perceptions of the correct company position on public issues. Both perception questions had been formulated from the interviews with executives and from an analysis of the industry. The first question asked executives to rate their company's performance relative to (1) protecting the natural environment, (2) community relations, (3) federal affairs, (4) local affairs of government, (5) legal compliance, (6) labor relations, and (7) investor relations. In each of these areas, managers expressed the performance goals of their companies. And in each performance rating, a 5-point Likert scale, ranging from "very well" to "very badly," was used.

The second set of perception questions listed 46 specific public concerns voiced frequently (at least 10 times) in the interviews. These topics were presented in the form of one-sentence statements quoted directly from the interviews. This was intended to give more authenticity to extreme statements and to sample the strength of an opinion. The direction of negative to positive responses was frequently reversed across companies to correct for possible response-structured artifacts and to limit echo responses—those purporting to favor issues considered socially desirable yet with no real company support. All the categories of public affairs previously discussed were included, but the order of these issues was randomly sorted. Executives were asked to first respond to the *accuracy* of each statement (5-point Likert scale). They were next asked to evaluate the *priority* of the underlying issue which appeared in italics in the statement (high, medium, or low).

Measurement of Responsiveness: Interviews and Survey

The last important set of data came from outside stakeholders. First, 33 stakeholders were interviewed in the field and over the telephone to develop and guide ways for measuring company responsiveness. This group was compiled from the recurrence of names in the executive interviews (mentioned about 10 or more times in the study), and from an analysis of the industry. The soliciting letter was similar to the one sent to industry executives, except that respondents were apprised of (1) the difference between social responsibility and social responsiveness (as explained in Chapter 2), (2) the importance of answering, even if the information is incomplete, and (3) a shorter estimation of time required for completion (see Appendix C).

From the interviews with outside stakeholders and with industry executives, and from the environmental analysis of the industry (see Chapter 6), a group of 150 stakeholders was constructed. This list was composed of investment analysts, trade unions, environmentalist organizations, state regulators, federal regulators, congressional staffers, trade association officials, and academicians. It was presumed that each of these groups would perceive company performance differently. Questionnaires were mailed directly to respondents in June of 1980. By August of 1980, 50 percent (75) had been returned.

The questions on this four-page survey (see Appendix D) began by asking for an assessment of each of the 20 largest companies in the forest products industry (presented in order of size) in social responsibility and social responsiveness. The top 20 were selected so that it would be possible to compare how representative the seven closely studied companies were. Each assessment was on a 5-point Likert scale. Reliability among raters was .99 within each stakeholder group. Next, these judges were asked to rate the responsiveness of the forest products industry overall in relation to 11 other prominent industries. This allowed this set of judges to be compared with a national sample that responded to this same question in the same year. Furthermore, this procedure would permit a comparison of the responsiveness of the forest products industry with the responsiveness of other industries.

The next set of questions asked for ratings of seven particular companies by seven more precise measures of responsiveness (see Chapter 4 for definition). These answers were assessed on a 7-point Likert scale, ranging from "low" to "high." These seven more precise dimensions of responsiveness were all positively correlated with overall responsiveness ($r = .62$ on the average, ranging from $r = .45$ to $r = .81$). The overall average of these seven components was more highly correlated with the general measure of responsiveness ($r = .74$). Reliability was high ($r = .92$) within stakeholder groups. Finally, judges were asked in an open-ended question to predict the top three important public issues the industry was likely to confront in the next year.

In review, this methodology has drawn from six different sources: (1) published records, (2) industry executives, (3) interviews, (4) questionnaire survey of executives, (5) interviews with stakeholders, and (6) questionnaire survey of stakeholders. An underlying principle of this methodology was that a single, one-shot data reading on research variables is misleading and inappropriate. The common research approaches that study (1) isolated environmental issues, collecting (2) single executive responses, or (3) responses from single stakeholder groups, are by themselves insufficient indicators of the external or internal realities facing an industry. Perceptual bias exists in the observations of company executives and in the convictions of stakeholder groups and influences the identification of an issue. The differences in perception, and the associated opposing perspectives of each sector, should not be regarded as nonnegotiable impediments but should be acknowledged as an integral function of coexistence and the essence of informed corporate-public interaction.

Companies do not face a neat sequence of distinct public issues; rather they face a thrashing sea of complex, interrelated issues. Perceptual bias exists in the observations of company executives and in the positions of stakeholder groups. Rather than ignore such differences, research should embrace these conflicting perspectives as the essence of business-society interactions.

Endnotes

1. J. K. Brown, *This Business of Issues: Coping with the Company's Environment* (New York: The Conference Board, 758, 1979). Also P. S. McGrath, *Managing Corporate External Relations* (New York: The Conference Board, No. 679, 1976) and *Action Plans for Public Affairs* (New York: The Conference Board, No. 733, 1977).
2. F. J. Aquilar, *Scanning the Business Environment* (New York: Macmillan, 1967).
3. P. R. Lawrence and J. W. Lorsch, *Organization and Environment* (Boston: Harvard Graduate School of Business Administration, 1967).
4. R. H. Miles, *Macro Organizational Behavior* (Santa Monica, Ca.: Goodyear, 1980).
5. S. L. Holmes, "Adapting Corporate Structure for Social Responsibility," *California Management Review*, 21 (1978), pp. 47–54. Also M. Mazis and R. Green, "Implementing Social Responsibility," *MSU Business Topics* (Winter 1971), as it appeared in *Managing Corporate Social Responsibility*, A. C. Carroll, ed. (Boston: Little, Brown, 1977), pp. 216–225.

Chapter 6

DEVELOPMENT OF THE
FOREST PRODUCTS INDUSTRY

The institutional role of a business firm in society is a factor in that firm's success. Public affairs are neither peripheral to the corporation nor merely isolated questions of conscience. These issues fundamentally affect all the traditional business functions such as operations marketing, and finance. A thorough inspection of the range of external issues can reveal both the complexity and importance of the public issues facing managers.

To appreciate this pervasive influence we must understand some key developments both in the history of the traditional market/ technological environment and in the industry's public affairs environment. Accordingly this chapter outlines the economic development of the forest products industry. The following chapter, Chapter 7, then adds a public affairs overlay to this economic backdrop.

The Industry Setting

It is important to look at the range and depth of stakeholder claims on forest products companies, not to analyze the accuracy of the issues but to document the multitude of external criteria. Forest products are directly involved in the operations of virtually every U.S. industry, from construction and shipping to publishing and health care. This is evident when we consider the complex network of wood-based industries that produce such products as wood fuel, timber, lumber, flooring, furniture, tableware, plywood, chipboard, paper board, container board, folding cartons, corrugated containers, bags, packaging paper, printing paper, writing paper, newsprint, tissue paper, duplicating

73

paper, computer paper, bandages, and dinnerware (napkins, cups, and plates). During the 1970s, forest products industries accounted for 7.2 percent of all employment in manufacturing, 6.4 percent of manufacturing payrolls, and 6.5 percent of the value of all manufacturing.[1] Pulp and paper manufacturing alone is ranked as the seventh largest U.S. industry in sales, and it is also probably the largest private landowner in the country.[2] The size of companies forming this industry tends towards the median of U.S. manufacturing firms, although there are several very large companies and several hundred small paper-converting and timber-harvesting concerns.[3]

In many ways the forest products industry finds itself in the same economic situation as the average American manufacturing industry. As a large employer, a large landholder operating throughout the entire country, and an industry directly intertwined with many other industries involved with intermediate and consumer products, the forest products industry faces a market typical of American industry today. This market is dynamic for three reasons: (1) the close relation of lumber and paper demand to the business cycles; (2) the evolution of new technology in forest management; and (3) the discovery of new paper products and paper substitutes.

Its *nonmarket* environment, however, makes this industry unique. Producers of forest products face a particularly crowded and active collection of stakeholders in the industrial environment that lies beyond the marketplace. The growth of the industry not only has led to greater contributions to society but also has meant greater consumption of society's resources. Accordingly, each firm has had to respond not only to external market and technological events but also to external social objectives. These companies simultaneously face powerful pressures from the community, labor, legislators, litigants, and shareholders. A recent trade journal's survey of forest products executives showed that such non-market pressures produce much greater worry than do marketplace issues.[4] The types of non-market pressures in this industry, then, represent pressures that U.S. business is likely to experience. What are the technological, market, and institutional issues as seen in this environment?

To appreciate the present industry structure, it is helpful to consider briefly the history of the two main component sub-industries: timber, and paper and packaging. The large forest product companies have integrated pulp and paper sub-companies, lumber and plywood sub-companies, and timber-owning firms, while many independent landowners, loggers, sawmill operators, pulpmakers, and paper converters remain throughout the country. The timber industry is reportedly the oldest industry in North America.[5]

History of the Timber Industry

Eric the Red's saga of Leif Ericson describes the transportation of a cargo of wood from North America back to Greenland. European colonists quickly perceived the opportunity in sending wood products from timber-rich America to timber-starved Europe, and the first sawmill was erected in Jamestown in 1608. This industry developed raw materials for building ships and colonial frames and beams.

Transportation has always been a critical factor in that the products are very heavy and bulky in comparison with their value. Reliance on water transportation meant that the early water-powered and steam-powered sawmills in New England—particularly in Maine—were located along rivers. The good water transportation and new railroads were vital to the industry's expansion to the North Central lake states following the Civil War. Logging camps were established to process wood on large tracts of land, and they grew into company towns. Such destructive practices as overcutting of the tracts and reckless burning to clear stumps and slash left lasting scars. Large forest fires frequently spread through the countryside, resulting in further desecration of the land. When a firm had depleted the available timber supply, the owners closed the mill and either moved to another region or became involved in other businesses in the same locale. Some companies moved into pulp and paper production to take advantage of the pulp wood that remained after the logs were harvested for timber. The search for new timber led companies to the West Coast and to the Southeast.

The concept of a stable industry arose in the early 1900s, concomitant with the establishment of forestry schools and the U.S. Forestry Service. While early schools of forestry recognized the broad range of services and products relative to forests, they emphasized protection of the forests and harvesting for timber. Later, well in advance of popular environmental and aesthetic concern, professional forestry education programs integrated management of all forest resources on sound biologic and economic principles. The National Forest Products Association has long been an advocate of the Forestry Service, and has recognized its own obligation, as an industry, to maintain forest land in productive condition. They have relied heavily on intensive forest management and on research to safeguard the future supply of their basic raw material.

New Deal programs such as the Civilian Conservation Corps and the short-lived National Recovery Act helped spread consciousness of forest fires, conservation, disease and insect control, and replanting. Although the national forests were established at the turn of the century for purposes of timber and water supply, the "Multiple-Use Sustained Yield" Act of 1960 added that the national forests also had values as a means of preserving wilderness areas and their wildlife. Several eastern and Great Lake states acquired millions of acres for protection, and 17 states developed forest practice acts to limit abuse of private land.

The development of intensive forest management is comparatively recent. For many years the myths that the forests are inexhaustible and that most forest land is suitable for agriculture led to the practice of "cut and get out." Fear of an impending timber famine, however, was largely responsible for a movement to bring about regulation of forest cutting on lands under industrial ownership.[6] Although the Society of American Foresters, supported by the Forest Service, failed in their effort to secure federal legislation regulating cutting on privately owned forest lands, they did influence state regulation. The creation of Yellowstone National Park in 1872 brought about the first permanent restraints on forest land. Other extensive land withdrawals took place under forest reserve acts of 1890, 1901, and 1907.

In the late 1930s, the national industry associations such as the National Forest Products Association (then the National Lumber Manufacturers Association), the American Forest Institute (then the American Forest Products Industries), and the American Paper Institute (formerly the American Pulp and Paper Association) became active in promoting responsible forest management. The large landowning companies such as Weyerhaeuser and International Paper have joined the Forest Service as leaders in soil sciences, genetics, tree physiology, silvicultural systems of cutting, and control of fire, insects, and disease. Since the mid-1960s, the industry has been harvesting a "third forest" in the South—the result of the first serious reforestation. In the West, by contrast, the companies continue to liquidate timber from old growth. Orderly replacement with younger growth consumes more time because of the increased length of the growing cycle in the West. Further, as a result of the federal reserves created early in the century, which encompass more than half the timber land in the West, the industry is very dependent on public timber, which is not managed as intensively as the industrial timberlands today.

History of the Pulp and Paper Industry

Paper is thought to have been invented by the Chinese more than 2000 years ago.[7] Silk fiber was generally the raw material used at that time for paper production, but the Chinese also worked with vegetable fibers such as mulberry bark. The eighth-century Arab conquests of the

Orient led to the transfer of this technology. Since the original fibers were unavailable in their land, the Arabs substituted cotton and linen as the raw materials. The Moors brought papermaking to Spain in the twelfth century. During the Renaissance this technology spread to Europe. William Rittenhouse introduced papermaking to the United States at a mill outside Philadelphia in the 1600s.

Rags were the primary raw material for pulp at this time, but in the late 1800s wood became the chief source. Now over 98 percent of the fibrous raw material used in making paper is from trees, and the paper industry therefore depends heavily on the timber industry. It is significant that although lumber and paper companies actually own about 14 percent of the commercial forest land available, they do use 30 percent of the total forest land. Accordingly, the industry must buy approximately half its supply from non-industry landowners, who tend to be small private landowners in the South, and from the federal government lands, which contain more than half the nation's softwood timber volume.

The paper industry, originally based in New England and the Mid-Atlantic states, spread to the North Central states along with the timber industry as transportation improved.[8] The northern softwoods were particularly well suited to the early "groundwood" method of making pulp. Improved pulpmaking technology in the 1930s enabled the industry to move to the Southwest to begin pulping southern pine. More recent technology changes that permit the pulping of chips, slabs, and other residues of the timber industry drew the industry in the 1950s to the Douglas fir trees of the Pacific Northwest. Consequently the North's share of the total U.S. woodpulp production has dropped from 35 percent in 1947 to 17 percent in 1978. Mountainous terrain and distance from markets have limited the Western states' woodpulp production to 18 percent of the country's total. In the South meanwhile, further technological developments in the 1960s have helped this region become the predominant manufacturer of wood pulp; the South now produces 65 percent of all pulp in this country.

This generous supply of pulpwood has given the United States the lowest pulp costs in the world. The paper mills of the South and the West have pursued economies of scale with high-volume product lines. These regions produce much of the country's packaging products—for example, kraft linerboard, unbleached paper, and bag paper. The older paper mills in the northern states have become low-volume paper producers with a focus on customer service. They produce such items as folding cartons, coated and fine paper for printing and writing, and tissue paper. A 1972 survey by the American Paper Institute showed 200 paper and board mills and 281 pulp mills in operation. Up through the 1920s and the 1930s, these mills were owned by firms that specialized in single product lines such as newsprint, writing paper, paper bags, and folding cartons. Consequently, these mills rarely offered more than one big product line. When southern pine offered a new pulp supply in the 1930s, the industry began to integrate pulp production with papermaking. Now 90 percent of all pulp is internally consumed by producing firms. With further improvements in papermaking technology, these firms began to offer a wider range of product qualities.

Three additional types of vertical integration took place through the 1950s. First, containerboard companies integrated downstream in the converting process by acquiring manufacturers of folding cartons and corregated shipping containers. Similar integration from primary to secondary converters took place in other product lines. Thus many former containerboard companies became part of firms that were fully integrated, from tree to finished container. A second trend was a general movement towards the packaging industry, which attracted both forest products companies and can and glass manufacturers. Finally, the forest products companies of the Pacific Northwest began to build or purchase pulp and paper mills.

All told, this integration amounted to a substantial confluence of the timber-based and pulp-based forest products companies. The paper-based companies include International Paper, Crown Zellerbach, Mead, St. Regis, Westvaco, Scott, Kimberly-Clark, Great Northern Nekoosa, Hammermill, and Union Camp. The timber-based companies include Georgia-Pacific, Weyerhaeuser, Boise Cascade, Champion International, Diamond International, and Potlatch. The packaging-

Table 6-1   Forest Land Ownership by Company

	Est. 1979 Sales ($ Billions)	Est. 1979 Profit ($ Millions)	Acres Owned (Millions)	Percentage Self-Sufficiency
Boise Cascade	2.885	181	2.7	50
Champion International	3.760	252	3.4	50–55
Crown Zellerbach	2.750	125	2.1	57
Georgia-Pacific	5.100	340	4.8	50
Great Northern Nekoosa	1.140	90.5	2.7	30
International Paper	4.450	295	8.4⁻	40–45
Louisiana Pacific	1.325	107·	.84	39
Potlach	.825	79.5	1.3	55
St. Regis	2.500	155	3.1	39
Union Camp	1.380	152	1.7	34
Westvaco	1.240	76.9	1.3	35
Weyerhaeuser	4.450	545	5.9	90+

Source: Kathleen W. Weigner, "America's Green Gold," *Forbes* (December 24, 1979), p. 46.

Table 6-2   Balance of Timber versus Paper Products by Company

Company	Sales ($ Billions)	Pulp, Paper, Packaging		Lumber, Building Products	
		Percentage Sales	Percentage Operating Income	Percentage Sales	Percentage Operating Income
Georgia-Pacific	5.2	24	24	64	52
International Paper	4.5	76	71	16	27
Weyerhaeuser	4.4	33	22	57	76
Champion International	3.7	51	58	49	42
Boise Cascade	2.9	55	69	44	30
Crown Zellerbach	2.8	76	57	23	42
Mead	2.6	100	100	—	—
St. Regis Paper	2.5	75	59	14	19
Kimberly-Clark	2.2	99	100	—	—
Scott	1.9	92	88	—	—
Union Camp	1.4	83	91	—	—
Louisiana-Pacific	1.3	17	22	83	78
Westvaco	1.2	89	89	—	—
Great Northern Nekoosa	1.1	92	93	—	—
Hammermill Paper	1.1	100	100	—	—

Source: Standard and Poor's Compustat Services, Inc., adapted from "International Paper Tries Managing for the Long Run," *Business Week* (July 28, 1980), p.702.

based companies include American Can and Container Corporation of America.

Data from *Forbes* give the estimated 1979 sales and profit, the actual forest acreage owned, and the percentage of self-sufficiency of several of these large, integrated forest products companies. (See Table 6–1.)

Since these mergers fueled growth, some fully integrated companies have become quite large. Eighteen forest-products firms appear on *Fortune*'s 1979 list of the nation's 500 largest manufacturing firms. Despite the trend toward vertical integration, however, the industry remains competitive. It is noteworthy that this chart shows a dozen comparably sized competitors such as Mead, Scott, Hammermill, and Kimberly-Clark, which do not even appear on the above *Forbes* chart. Table 6-2 illustrates how differently these integrated companies balance the profits from their mixed operations.

An Economic Perspective

Concentration in the forest products industry has changed very little in the past twenty years. Census data indicate that the four largest firms represent 29 percent of industry sales and the eight largest firms represent 45 percent of sales.[9] The fifteen largest companies, however, account for only 58 percent of the industry's total. Several hundred converting companies are still active in the industry.[10] The timber side of the industry is also not highly concentrated, with the four leading companies representing only 17 percent of sawmill and planing-mill volume in 1972.[11] There are almost 3000 widely dispersed lumber companies and 200 plywood producers. These concentration rates are fairly low for an industry with such potential for economies of scale. The top twenty companies have been stable players for a long while, however, and small-scale oligopolistic behavior is possible. Individual firms can wield substantial power in various industry segments such as pulpmaking and sanitary paper products.

Despite a $2.9 billion trade deficit in forest products including paper and pulp, the United States is by far the largest and most efficient producer of these items.[12] A trade surplus in solid wood products, the first in ten years, was achieved in 1980. This country is by far the world's largest producer of pulp and paperboard, exceeding the total output of its three nearest competitors, Japan, Canada, and the USSR. Because of the tremendous U.S. domestic consumption, however, Canada, Finland, and Sweden export more pulp than the United States. Although the United States ranks behind the Soviet Union, Africa, Asia, Latin America, and Canada in total forest land, it is by far the world's largest timber producer, accounting for almost a third of the world's total harvest.

This high production is partly because the U.S. climate allows rapid tree growth and partly because the good transportation system in the United States allows timber to be brought to market fast and easily. In addition, this nation's technology has provided efficient use of forest land. In 1950, only 21 percent of a tree was used in the manufacturing process; now companies use 60 percent of a tree. Effective forest management and genetic research have also led to better and faster yields. Finally, the U.S. forest products industry has a relatively lighter debt burden and fewer labor costs; a recent industry study reported that the hourly cost of producing a metric ton of pulp is $51.35 in Sweden, $38.85 in Canada, and $30.43 in the United States.[13]

Labor costs represented roughly 25 percent of sales in 1979, an increase of only 8.9 percent over the past decade, in comparison with a 10.5 percent increase in revenues. Expenditures for plant and equipment, however, grew roughly 12 percent during the same period and now represent 7 percent of sales—almost $5 billion alone—with about 7 percent of this sum allocated to equipment for abating pollution.[14] Through the 1970s, the industry spent nearly half a billion dollars a year on such pollution-control equipment, and Environmental Protection Agency requirements for the best available technology are expected to keep such costs high.

Another important cost is the chemicals needed for pulping wood and making paper, although these have remained relatively stable in recent years. Higher energy costs, on the other hand, have placed a substantial additional burden on pulp and paper production. This industry is the largest user of residual oil in the country, and the fifth biggest consumer of all fuels.[15] With the price of energy jumping sixfold in the past few years, forest products companies are spending 10 percent of their capital striving for self-sufficiency. Most large integrated mills produce their own electricity today. Reserves of wood residues for burning, hydropower, and oil and gas on their forest land have become important sources of fuel. Burning of waste wood material to recover fuel represents only a secondary, residual opportunity for wood use and is not a primary focus of the industry. Expanding fuel reservoirs is not considered a reason for preempting other, more fundamental uses of forest resources. Wood is considered a relatively low-grade bulk fuel that demands considerable human effort in preparation for conversion to energy. Large-scale burning of wood requires installation of expensive smokestack "scrubbers" to cope with pollutants such as "fly ash."[16] Dr. Carl H. Reidel, the past president of the American Forestry Association and director of environmental programs at the University of Vermont, concedes that burning is the least efficient use of wood fiber.[17]

Despite both technological improvements in operations and new produce development, innovations have been gradual and the response to them foreseeable. Certain products such as newsprint, coated papers for writing and printing, and uncoated writing and duplicating paper have been in very strong demand, while tissues and linerboard have been in only fair demand. Finally, prices of industrial products such as corrugated containers, packaging and industrial papers, folding cartons, and construction papers have become competitive because of lower demand and substitute products.[18]

While the industry operated above 90 percent capacity through the 1970s (except during the 1975 recession), its history shows periodic bouts with overcapacity. Much of this problem is caused by the industry's extreme sensitivity to economic fluctuation. Forest products, as we have seen, are derived from a closely integrated manufacturing process and are high-volume items used in virtually every sector of the economy. Studies comparing the gross national product (GNP) to paper output show a remarkably consistent relation over the past century. From 1947 through the 1970s, roughly 79 thousand tons were produced per billion real (1958) dollars.[19] The consequent short-term industry swings have been severe. The construction, packaging, and planning applications of forest products mean that the products are used very early in the stages of distribution. At the end of the past decade, however, the gain in paper consumption outpaced the gain in real GNP (5.2 vs 4.0 percent).[20] While the large companies (top twenty) maintained a 5 percent sales margin and a 12 percent return on net worth, they engaged a 20 percent increase in earnings in 1978. This favorable situation persisted through 1979, with production up another 5 percent at yearend. Many forest products companies, both paper and timber-oriented, reported this as one of their best years ever. Substantial imports were required to meet the strong domestic demand.[21]

Effects of the Recession

Recent market surveys by the U.S. Department of Commerce, McGraw-Hill Econometrics, and Merrill Lynch Econometrics showed dramatic increases in the paper industry's spending of capital in 1979 (up 38 percent from the previous year).[22] Much of this expansion in capacity was targeted for the tight demand markets in linerboard, coated papers, and newsprint. This increased level of capital spending was more than twice the increase for all U.S. industry. Profits remained strong through 1979 despite threats of a recession, thereby inspiring the companies to maintain their high capital investment to take advantage of a presumed strong economic recovery in 1981.[23]

The long-awaited recession at last began to invade the industry in late 1979 and through the first quarter of 1980. Already by December 1979, hiring starts fell because scarce mortgage money reduced demand for western and southern lumber and plywood.[24] Profits in the whole industry dropped more than 4 percent in the first quarter of 1980, although a few of the paper-oriented companies reported record profits. Much of the decline was due to the continued softening of lumber and timber markets, which particularly hurt the timber-based forest products companies. Profits dropped as much as 40 percent for some large companies.[25]

By the summer of 1980, it became apparent that the 50 percent drop in housing starts had prompted the industry's worst slump in three decades. Lumber and plywood demand had fallen accordingly, leading to an unprecedented number of mill closings—particularly evident in the West, where 475 of that regions' 820 mills closed. Many fear these closings will be permanent. Even in the 1974–1975 recession, lumber production leveled off at 78 percent of capacity. Over 61,000 workers were idled in the mid-1980 economic crisis. The effect has been particularly harsh on small towns, where often a single mill provides 80 percent of the local jobs, and on small independent western manufacturers caught between the conflicting pressure of higher costs and lower prices.[26] While prices on lumber fell substantially, timber shortages drove up the price of federal timber (on federal lands), along with the sales of this timber to 74 percent over the 1978 levels. This increase in the price of timber on federal lands affects the immediately dependent industries, and through them exerts influence on other large sectors of the economy.

Even the larger integrated forest products companies closed lumber and plywood mills and shifted their hopes to the lighter lines on the paper side of the business. New patterns of integration became necessary for the industry in response to the crisis in timber supply. Curtailment of operation of timber-related sub-industries sharply diminished the raw inputs residuals derived from this initial process on which the paper industry depends for its own continued survival. In related developments, the wood pulp demand was tightened by the reduced sources of wood chips for pulp and paper mills. Finally, by July 1980, slack developed in the markets for coated paper, linerboard, and uncoated writing paper. Price drops in these formerly healthy product lines have caused many companies in the industry to rethink their ambitious spending plans, with companies such as Louisiana Pacific cutting back as much as 3 percent of its capital investment budget for the year. Kimberly-Clark, Boise Cascade, and Champion International made similar cuts.[27] The industry is expected to weather this recession better than the 1974–1975 recession, however, because of its greater reliance on internal capital. With average common equity as much as 65.4 percent of invested capital, the industry is considered to be only lightly leveraged. (Highly leveraged companies such as real estate and airlines, by contrast, are well above 59.7 percent industry average.) Similarly, the fixed-cost coverage ratio, or ability to pay its debt, is a very healthy 7 compared with the 5.5 all-industry coverage ratio. Finally, internal financing represents a 79.5 percent of the five-year cash flow for growth needs, which is more sound than the all-industry average of 74.2 percent.[28]

Thus, the product markets in this industry vary somewhat, but essentially all have experienced predictable downturns. The capital markets seen generally sufficient to fuel the industry's recovery as the GNP-inspired demand materializes. This industry has demonstrated good technological improvement and has faced repeated cycles of volatile market conditions. Such events, however, have tended to be slow-paced and easily managed. The public issues in the institutional environment reflect a very different level of uncertainty. Before examining these public affairs, let us consider some of the most dynamic technological issues facing the industry.

Technological Advances in Forest Management

New practices to increase the productive capacity of forests are being pursued by the forest products industry to meet long-range timber needs and to respond to the outlook for a 100 percent increase in demand for wood. The potential for increased wood production centers on establishing well-stocked stands of the desired mix which are under genetic quality control and are maintained as high-quality, disease-free forest growth. Tree improvement grows more important as the amount of land available for forests shrinks markedly. Urban growth has reduced forested areas in continental United States from an original 75 percent of total land coverage to 40 percent. In addition, destructive forms of uncontrollable tree diseases are on the rise. Of particularly alarming significance is the prevalence of fusiform rust, a fungus that attacks Southern pines, according to Robert Weir, director of North Carolina State University's Industry Cooperative Tree Improvement Program. In this disease the red oak is an alternate host, but the fungus, which deforms and kills the pine and renders the wood unusable, does nothing to the oak.

The maximum contribution and progress in U.S. timber production will probably result from a silvicultural management system that links the complex array of techniques developed by all specialists—including forest biologists, entomologists, and economists. The most promising new developments are in genetic improvement, fertility, and site preparation. Site preparation involves applying fertilizers and plant nutrition to maintain forest growing stock efficiently. A high rate in the survival and growth of newly planted seedlings and newly sown seed has been attributed to site preparation. Fast-growing stock requires expert coordination of the vast array of forestry techniques. Attention is thereby given to the soil fertility, soil drainage, site preparation, plantation arrangement, spacing, thinning schedules, harvesting methods in the conversion of overmature trees to young forests, control of insects and disease, and also genetic selectivity. Intensive regeneration of the stand in the improved forest, integrating chemical and mechanical timber-growing practices, enables it to outperform natural growth in unimproved forests.

The apparent potential of underdeveloped forest resources have inspired new interest in research. Expenditures for research were about $100 million in 1965 (under the Department of Agriculture) and were directed to immediate problems rather than long-range achievement. However, recent mergers of forest products firms into large corporate units with large timber holdings have led to extensive research investment, largely in the genetic improvement of trees and the production of trees of identical quality. Georgia-Pacific's university-run cooperative, for example, annually spends about ten times the 1965 amount and shares the information and results. Geneticists are working to grow forests of the future with seeds from superior trees or by grafting, and they hope to perpetuate valuable traits such as fast growth and resistance to insects and disease. It is also an objective of the industry to gain enough information from success in the laboratory to allow faster cutting of old-growth trees than would be possible if natural growth were relied on. An addition of 15 percent more wood to the Douglas fir is foreseen for the first generation; gains up to 20 percent have already been achieved in the first generation of genetically improved Southern pine. In California, Simpson Timber Company has been growing test-tube redwoods using tissue-culture techniques that embed tiny portions of the tree substance into a chemical medium contained in a test tube. This plantlet is later transferred to a nursery. Last year Weyerhaeuser invested $40 million in research laboratories near their Tacoma, Washington, headquarters, where eventually 800 people will work to further the concept of "high-yield forests" under controlled laboratory conditions.[29]

A new breed of tree is revolutionizing the forest products industry; it is called variously a "plus tree," an "improved tree," or a "super tree," and comes from forebears especially chosen for superior size, shape, and other factors. When these naturally superior trees are crossed with each other, they produce offspring that yield a greater volume and better wood than ordinary trees and, it is hoped, will be more resistant to disease. Bruce Zobel, founder of the first applied U.S. forestry genetic program at Texas A & M in 1951, reported a 10 percent improvement in yield and quality and expects up to 50 percent improvement in the future. Tree improvement is still in the early stage of development; and since trees take so long to mature, the true benefits of genetic work will not be realized until the turn of the century, when the new trees are harvested.

Genetic improvement is not an involved process. Once the superior tree is selected, small branches are grafted onto "rootstock" in carefully planted rows in experimental orchards. The resulting first-generation trees are, in effect, clones of the original superior tree. More important, they are the same age, start reproductive activity at the same time, and have exactly the same characteristics. After the process of matching the growing tissue, or the cambium layer, of trees was mastered, the rate of success of survival of the experimental series improved from 25 to 95 percent. The goal is to acquire an 80–90 percent resistance to disease in the worst areas; the present rate of resistance is 40 to 60 percent. Since cloned trees have the same age as the parent, they begin to produce both the male and female elements of fertilization within 3–7 years. (All loblolly pines produce both elements normally at age 25.) Pollen is collected from one family of the first-generation cloned trees and planted in cones of other families of cloned trees to produce seeds. Each protected clone placed in a scientifically selected area bears an average of 50 seeds, which begin growth when planted in nurseries. Grown in open land to hasten the process, the progeny reach sexual maturity in less than the normal 25 years. The best of these trees are then crossed again to produce the second generation of improved trees.

The loblolly species, a Southern pine and the Douglas fir in the Northwest are the species involved in most of the research. The goal is to reduce the average rotation age of the loblolly, which is generally harvested after 30–35 years, to about 5–7 years. Because the South outranks the Northwest as the nation's largest tree-growing region, and also because the loblolly accounts for about half of all southern pines and is the area's most prominent tree, its improvement is of significance to the industry.

Another important decision in forest management is matching species with soils; the choice is especially important in programs of artificial forest regeneration. Knowledge of species-soil relations and knowledge of the demands of the market determine the productivity of the total forest enterprise and provide the basis for sound forest-management decisions.

Growing trees in crops and applying agricultural methods to traditional forestry methods to improve and increase tree growth is another way of boosting forest yields. Various farming systems can be studied relative to the water balance under the plantations of trees, genetic improvement possible by nitrogen fixation, the economy of spacing trees, monitoring changes in solid nutrients, and other cultural management practices associated with agriculture.

Agro-forestry is a system of raising food crops and trees together. It is a productive system and ecologically sound, increasing both food and fuel production on marginal land. It could be used in the West and in poor farming areas. Agricultural scientists and forestry managers have begun to look into these alternative practices in place of monocropping and mechanized farming. This cooperative use of land keeps productive forests from being converted entirely to cropland. Since trees are adapted by their deep root systems to survive in situations in which annual crops would fail, many tree farmers are raising walnut and pecan nut crops on land used also for production of soybeans and corn in the South. Trees act to recycle nutrients when leaves decompose, they protect the soil and foliage, regulate microclimate, and prevent silting of streams.

"Biomass" plantations of fast-growing trees are being explored as an exclusive source of wood for fuel. Georgia-Pacific has established an experimental plantation to determine how quickly poplar seedlings reach usable size. It is hoped that a 20–30-foot tree can be gotten in seven years to be used for pulp wood and fuel. Other trees such as cottonwood and sycamore are also used for fuel wood, and there is a good energy potential in new-grown hardwoods. Massachusetts has formed a study commission, and several other states are conducting surveys, to consider appropriate guidelines for the wise use of forest resources as fuel-wood supplies. A demand for fuel wood is also coming from commercial electric-generating plants—wood has been found feasible for energy to be delivered at a 50-megawatt level. Over 100 industrial firms in the six-state New England region rely on wood today for at least part of their energy supplies, and the Burlington, Vermont, Electric Company now uses 100 tons of wood chips a day to generate 10 percent of its total electricity output. The demand for fuel-wood cost the northeastern forests about 2.85 million cords of wood, putting a strain on these forests before forestry officials have determined how much annual growth is available for such use. (Three cords of wood have the energy equivalent of 150 gallons of high-quality heating oil.) The U.S. Department of Energy has calculated that more than a million homes in the United States now use wood as their primary source of fuel, and that wood has provided half as much energy as is derived from nuclear power.[30] Mike Naylor, director of Deep-Portage Conservation Reservation, who is an environmental educator and biologist, says forest management for energy will be ecologically sound provided that we are conservative in our demands on wood as an energy source. He does see danger, however, in the new pelletizing process that compresses wood residues into heating pellets for automated home burning units. He fears in particular that forestry managers may take small immature trees as well as mature aspen, and end up leaving "cornfields" of trees with not much age-class dispersion—a detrimental effect on the wildlife habitat. With the proper balance of stand, ages, and cuts (under 20 acres), wood use to meet energy needs will have a beneficial effect on wildlife, according to Gordon Guillion, grouse expert with the University of Minnesota Forest Wildlife Project.[31]

The increased uses of wood and the use of waste wood for industrial purposes, may offer a tremendous opportunity for private woodland owners to realize greater profits than they can get from fuel wood. Future pressure from paper and chipboard plants, which rely on aspen stands, will also compete with fuel-wood users. The biggest users of wood for fuel are the forest products companies, who use solid waste and pulping wastes to generate 45 percent of their power needs. Wood fiber is continuing to prove itself a very adaptable resource and is being considered in much of the new technology. Examples are conversion of chips to oil, methane and hydrogen gas conversion in gasohol production, use as a feedstock in the chemical industry, and preparation of such basic chemicals as phenol and turpentine, and also a variety of drugs (for example, L-Dopa) for treating Parkinson's disease.

Summary

Our consideration of the industry's technological characteristics has helped to explain its size, location, and company structure. The readily transferable skills of cutting timber and making paper, along with plentiful raw materials (trees and water) encouraged the spread of this industry. Technological advancements joined the two great sections of this industry, wood products and paper products. The link between timber and paper eventually led to vertical integration within large companies. Technological advances in one sub-industry dramatically affect events in another. The shift in timber supply from the Northeast to the North Central states, and then to the Northwest and finally to the South greatly affected the economics and location of paper mills. New pulping technologies and the use of wood residuals in making paper have changed the use of various species of trees. Genetically improved strains of trees and improved forest management practices have further affected the planning and location of these sub-industries.

In the marketplace, competition across companies has been intense. Several thousand companies make up the lumber and timber side of the business, and several hundred the paper and packaging side. Most of the top twenty firms have fully integrated both sides of the industry, and they are very much in competition with one another. Their products are closely intertwined with almost every U.S. industry, particularly housing construction, food, and consumer products. The production of certain items, particularly in packaging, has shown a tendency towards overcapacity. Instead of giving way to substitute materials, the industry has succeeded in developing paper products that use new synthetic materials and has maximized its own position in the process. One of the many challenges in the distant future will be to develop the demand for fine paper after the long-heralded paperless office comes into being.

In this sketch of the development of the forest products industry we have seen the wide geographical dispersion, the very competitive structure, the centrality of this industry in the U.S. economy, and the more recent technological issues which characterize its traditional economic environment. The changes in these conditions have been substantial but not revolutionary. Thus, the various business relocations and technological developments have been gradual, market volatility has been predictable, and the key internal industry actors have been fairly stable. In the next chapter we shall consider the difference in the characteristics of this environment and of the industry's public affairs environment.

Endnotes

1. Ivor P. Morgan and Robert A. Leone, "The U.S. Timber Industry," Boston Industry Note 9-678-180, Intercollegiate Case Clearing House (Cambridge, Mass.: Harvard University Press, 1978).
2. Eugene Floyd, Richard Levitan, and Robert Leone, "The Pulp and Paper Industry in the United States," Boston Intercollegiate Case Clearing House, 9-678-186 (Cambridge, Mass.: Harvard University Press, 1978).
3. Benjamin Slatin, "Economic Structure of the Paper Industry," *Technical Association of the Pulp and Paper Industry Journal* 58 (July 1975).
4. Herbert Lambert, "Concern Focus on D.C., Survey Returns Indicate," *Forest Industries* (July 1979), pp. 30–31.
5. A. W. Nelson, in William A. Duerr, *Timber: Problems, Prospects, Policies* (Ames, Iowa: University of Iowa Press, 1973).
6. Samuel T. Dana, "Forestry Policies and Programs," in William A. Duerr, *Timber: Problems, Prospects, Policies* (Ames, Iowa: Iowa State University Press, 1973).
7. James D. Studley, United States Pulp and Paper Industry vs. Department of Commerce, Trade Promotion Survey No. 182 (1938).
8. Benjamin Slatin, "Economic Structure."
9. U.S. Bureau of the Census, *Annual Summary of Manufacturers* (1978).
10. Eugene Ford, Richard Levitan, and Robert A. Leone, "The Pulp and Paper Industry," Harvard Business School Reference Note, 9-678-186 (1978).
11. Ivor P. Morgan and Robert A. Leone, "The U.S. Timber Industry," Harvard Business School Reference Note, 9-678-180 (1978).
12. Lee Smith, "The Neglected Promise of Our Forests," *Fortune* (Nov. 5, 1979), pp. 111–124.
13. *Ibid.*
14. *Paper and Allied Products Data Sheet*, American Paper Institute, Economics Department (June 5, 1980).
15. Slatin, "Economic Structure," p. 59.
16. "Converters Secure Fuel Supply," *Pulp and Paper* (May 1971), p. 19.
17. Cited in Michael Harris, "The Boom in Wood Use: Promise and Peril," *American Forest* (September 1980), p. 43.
18. Kenneth Lowe, "North American Profile," *Pulp and Paper* (May 1979). Also Bill Sing, "Newsprint Customers are Edgy, But Paper Industry Sees Boom Ahead," *Los Angeles Times* (July 3, 1979), p. IV-1.
19. Benjamin Slatin, "Where Is Paper Usage Heading?" speech to Financial Analysts Federation (New York, June 12, 1978). Also Benjamin Slatin, "Economic Structure of the Paper Industry," *Tech. Assoc. of the Pulp and Paper Industry Journal*, no. 58 (July 1975).
20. Stephanie Pollitzer, "Financial and Fraction Capacity Data, North American Profile," *Pulp and Paper* (1979).
21. Elizabeth M. Fowler, "Big Paper Concerns Report Strong Gains," *New York Times* (October 17, 1980), p. D5. Also "Paper: The Big Story Is a Cost 'Squeeze,'" *Business Week* (January 14, 1980), pp. 88–89.
22. Willard A. Mies, "Paper Industry Costs Spending Plans for 1979," *Pulp and Paper* (July 1979), pp. 104–108.
23. "Paper's Risky Expansion Plans," *Business Week* (Nov. 19, 1979), pp. 160–161.

Also "Profits Stay Surprisingly Strong," *Business Week* (Nov. 19, 1979), p. 87; "Big Paper Concerns Report Strong Gains," *New York Times* (Oct. 17, 1979), p. D5; "Mead Corp. Executives See Recession But Feel Limited Effects So Far," *Wall Street Journal* (Nov. 26, 1979), p. 27.

24. "Lumber's Steep Prices Are Falling Like Timber," *Business Week* (Nov. 26, 1979).
25. "Profits that Mirror an Uncertain Economy," *Business Week* (April 28, 1980). Also "U.S. Paper Profits Down 4% in First Quarter," *Pulp and Paper* (June 1980).
26. "Lumber Industry in Steep Slump," *New York Times* (April 17, 1980), pp. D1–D2. Also Kathryn Christinson, "Northwest Timber Areas Hit by Housing Slump and Shortage of Trees." "It's Recession-Plus in the Forest," *Business Week* (June 2, 1980), pp. 98–99.
27. "G-P Cuts Budget—But Not Yet Afraid," *Pulp and Paper* (May 1980), p. 17. Also "Three Firms Defer Spending Plans," *Pulp and Paper* (June 1980), p. 21. "High Flying Paper Is Losing Its Lift," *Business Week* (July 7, 1980), p. 32.
28. "Short Term Debt Keeps Piling Up," *Business Week* (October 18, 1979), p. 76.
29. Steven Grover, "Pine Clones; Forest Companies Develop Superior Trees That Grow Faster and Resist Disease," *Wall Street Journal* (Oct. 2, 1980), p. 32.
30. As cited in Michael Harris, "The Boom in Wood Use: Promise and Peril," *American Forest* (September 1980).
31. As cited in Carol Bockman, "The Boom in Wood Use: Upper Great Lakes," *American Forest* (September 1980).

Chapter 7

PUBLIC ISSUES IN THE FOREST PRODUCTS INDUSTRY

From the perspective provided by the previous chapters, we can begin to understand the pervasive influence of the affairs of the forest products industry on society at large. It is the nation's largest private landowner, one of its largest employers, the dominant if not the central economic voice in thousands of mill towns across the country, the trustee of much of the nation's wildlife and natural beauty, a high-volume producer of vital supplies to virtually every other American industry, and the producer of a renewable resource of unique assets. Forest products companies therefore cannot help but confront many diverse stakeholders, who peer over the shoulders of management.

This chapter explores the range and depth of stakeholder claims on forest products companies. The purpose is not to analyze the accuracy of issues, but merely to document the multitude of external criteria. These stakeholders collectively dominate and significantly influence timber supply, forest management practices, land taxation, expenditures for pollution-abatement equipment, labor harmony, investor loyalty, and antitrust prosecution. In this system each stakeholder represents a complex and dynamic body of interests, exercising a measure of authority, and intent on securing specific goals. Combining forces to work in harmony, as multiple-interest groups, they increase their potential for affecting company strategy and operating policy; and at times they even pose challenges equal to the uncertainties of the marketplace. In response, the industry has to acknowledge diverse and competing demands, along with its concerns about production, from raw materials through marketing, and to formulate appropriate public policies.

Conservation versus Timber Supply

Forest ownership is considered an important asset to support the
financing of new equipment, and hence is monitored by the rating
services, such as Standard and Poor's, Moody's, and Dun &
Bradstreet. Historically, however, forest land has been bought to secure raw materials rather than to achieve cost savings or boost investor
confidence.[1] The historical migration of the industry from the Northeast to the Great Lakes states, to the Northwest, and now to the
South is explained by these timber purchases. Lumber experts claim
that timber demand is likely to rise 50 percent by the year 2000;
stumpage price increases over the past dozen years have greatly exceeded the general inflation rate.[2] In addition, favorable labor costs
and a vast transportation network offer the promise of closing the U.S.
$2.4 billion trade gap in forest products.[3] Further, it has been esti-
mated that by 2000 or sooner Americans may be getting 10 percent of
their energy from wood.[4]

The nation's forests now are harvested at a rate of 14 billion cubic
feet a year, while they grow at a rate of 22 billion cubic feet a year.
Some experts claim that, with proper technique, the forest in the United
States could yield as much as 60 trillion cubic feet annually.[5] In the
West, however, timber cutting has outpaced timber growth by 56
percent, leaving the next usable crop of trees 20 years in the future.
Part of this situation can be explained by federal policies of underusing
the old-growth timber. Although timber overcutting in the West has
exceeded the sustained yield and caused a shortage of timber in this
region, the industry claims this was necessary to remove old growth to
provide the proper environment for new trees. The industry attributes
the present age-class gap—created because removing old trees left
many underaged new trees—to this delay in harvesting mature trees.
Roughly a third of the nation's 740 million acres are considered commercial forest land.[6] While forest industries use about 30 percent of the
commercial forest land, they own only 14 percent of it.[7] Various companies have large landholdings, but only Weyerhaeuser approaches
self-sufficiency. Most companies in the West depend on the forest land
under public ownership, roughly three-quarters of the commercial
supply.

The Politics of Protection

Some of this land became protected with the creation of the Yellowstone, Yosemite, Sequoia, and Grant national parks, but most of it
was organized under the forest reserves acts of 1891 (26 Stat. 1905) and
1897 (30 Stat. 11, 34). The reservation of these 33 million forest acres

marked the birth of the National Forest System. The early conservationists who supported this legislation were most interested in curbing irresponsible forestry practices rather than in timber supplies.[9] In 1905, as this movement gained momentum, conservationist Gifford Pinchot with the support of the American Forestry Association secured the transfer of the forest reserves from the highly politicized Department of the Interior to the Department of Agriculture. He espoused management of the national forests for active use, the end of exploitation by land speculators, scientific natural-resource conservation principles, and the use of federal forest lands for the benefit of society and also economic progress. This advanced the early forest service practices that were directed toward forest protection, watershed management, mining, and livestock forage.[10]

The Weeks Act, in 1911, adding eastern forest land to the federal lands, designated distressed and cutover lands to be reserved for watershed and for recreation. In the 1920s the Forestry Service recognized the recreational assets of the forests as nontangible products and began a policy of promoting recreational use. Popular support led to the expansion of this program and the concern for preservation of recreation areas. The Multiple Use–Sustained Yield Act of 1960 (74 Stat. 215), to resolve the conflicting demands on public forest land, declared it the policy of the Congress that national forests would be established and administered for outdoor recreation, range timber, watershed, and wildlife and fish purposes in the combination that would best meet the needs of the American people.

Perhaps the sharpest controversy generated by this legislation has been caused by the definition of timber to be cut on public land. The Forest Service policy—called *even flow, sustained yield*—has sought to guarantee a perpetuity of harvests that do not impair the land's productivity. Much of the debate has focused on the definition of the "working circles," which constitute the allowable cut. The even-flow concept has come under similar harsh industry criticism in that it allows trees to mature and die because their replacements take so long to grow. In essence, this policy means that the volume of wood to be cut is limited by the volume that grows each year. It is frequently argued that this even-flow approach ignores overstocking of old-growth timber, which can be harvested without reduction in growth.[11]

A second controversial aspect of this 1960 regulation and the 1964 Wilderness Act has to do with the interpretation of "multiple use." The balance between timber production and other uses, perceived as conflicting, is the target of this furor. In simple terms, the debate centers on whether timber production has become a priority activity in federal forest management. Accentuated environmental concerns in the last decade, exemplified by the "forest for the people" movement, have made the public more aware of the forests' other amenities. The industry, troubled by declining harvest yields on private timberlands and increased demand for timber, is trying to establish support for logging as the affirmed use in natural forests. Much national forest land has been protected as wilderness in the National Wilderness Preservation System. Wilderness is the most restrictive designation Congress can give a unit of federal land.

To qualify for wilderness status, areas must be roadless, contain no permanent improvements or human habitation, and provide opportunities for unconfined recreation. Congress, using recommendations by the Administration, has the authority for final approval. Although wilderness areas are allocated largely by political decision, they have continued to gain stature as a precious resource whose diverse landscapes and ecosystems should be preserved for posterity. Biologists, who define as many as 500 basic ecosystems, and recreationists, who enjoy undeveloped areas, demand land-use options in wilderness policy.

Congress has included over 19 million acres of public land in the Wilderness Preservation System. The largest share is in the national forest lands (15.2 million acres) and is managed by the Forest Service. In 1977, the program known as the Roadless Area Review and Evaluation (RARE II) was initiated by the U.S. Forest Service, under the Multiple-Use Sustained Yield Act of 1960 and the National Forest Management Act of 1975. The purpose was to identify the remaining roadless lands on the 187 million acres of national forests (the total acreage of the National Forest System including Alaska), and to resolve the future management of these undeveloped areas. In this inventory, 62 million acres were identified as meeting the criteria for being roadless and undeveloped. In 1977, the Forest Service held seminars around the country to enable citizens to review suggested criteria for designating potential wilderness areas. The drafted environmental impact statement from RARE II sorted areas into wilderness, nonwilderness, and categories for further planning. The final decision recommended 15.4 million acres for wilderness designation; 36 million were allocated to nonwilderness uses; and 10.6 million were allocated to further planning. The areas to undergo further planning are to be preserved from development such as roads or dams. Oil and gas exploration is allowed under controlled conditions; there is no special protection against mining.

Environmentalists promptly challenged the final RARE II allocation decisions announced by President Carter on April 16, 1979; these recommended opening 36 million acres of undeveloped land for harvesting of timber, and permitted industrial exploitation of 10.6 acres in the category of further planning, pending future review. Public-interest and environmentalist groups vigorously disputed the environmental impact statement (EIS), claiming it was strongly slanted in favor of large nonwilderness designations. In addition they questioned the data on timber values and other resources, calling them out of date and invalid. Another deficiency noted was the failure to reflect the economic effect on taxpayers, especially the additional costs of maintaining nonwilderness use. Protection of wilderness was viewed as less of a financial burden on the public. The opponents decried the limited alternatives in the plan, and submitted an alternative proposal that would promote intensified management of currently developed areas to permit national forests to meet programmed harvests. Another criticism cited the 3.5-month review period for public comment as inadequate and also indicative of the Forest Service's failure to consider the full wilderness potential of the vast tracks of land.

The environmentalists challenged the plan and court action was instituted in California, where the environmental statement was claimed to be inadequate because it did not deal with areas individually. In early 1980, a federal court decision in California ruled in favor of this challenge, holding that the RARE II environmental impact statement failed to comply with the EPA as it related to the recommendations for nonwilderness lands, and that site-specific data were not considered.[12] The Sierra Club, meanwhile, has focused grassroots campaigns against commercial timber harvesting, and initiated a newsletter called "Sierra Club Forestry Bulletin."[13] Later that summer, the forest industry and the Forest Service began to develop their own responses.[14] The timber industry considered the RARE II allocations a triumph; it emphasized its view that wilderness studies have tied up valuable timber lands for too many years and urged immediate action accordingly. The industry also interpreted the Carter Administration's support as an effort to cut inflation through increasing sources for timber supply. The executive vice president of the Industrial Forestry Association, W. D. Hagenstein, exclaimed, "It appears that the President has responded to the logic that maintaining large volumes of over-mature forests which dominate western national forests and other federal lands, will actually reduce overall growth and future timber supplies."[15] The Sierra Club and the Wilderness Society have pledged to persist in their opposition around the country.[16] Ranking congressmen on the House Interior Committee such as Morris Udall (D., Arizona), John F. Seiberling (D., Ohio), and Philip Burton (D., Calif.) initiated a series of hearings in Texas and other states.

Efforts to pass wilderness legislation based on RARE II have taken the form of numerous bills introduced in Congress on a state by state basis. In every case the predominant issue is whether areas recommended for nonwilderness under RARE II should be returned to multiple-use management without permission for "release" from Congress. The past administration insisted it had the authority to administer the lands under existing law. The lumber industry is pressing Congress to resolve this controversy by legislating that RARE II nonwilderness areas are to be released from all future protection as wilderness. Meanwhile, on July 23, 1980, President Carter signed into law the creation of the 2.2-million-acre "River of No Return Wilderness" in central Ohio, the largest wilderness area in 49 states exceeded only by Alaskan wilderness. In addition, legislation passed by the House creating the 2.1-million-acre new National Forest Wilderness in California reflected broad environmental considerations not present in the original RARE II legislation. In the report accompanying the bill was a recommendation to the Forest Service to consider a new management designation, "conservation areas," for several areas that were not recommended for wilderness classification in the bill, and to "fine-tune" management beyond requirements in the National Forest Act. Protection for fragile areas and stream habitats, minimization of erosion, and provision for multiple-use activities including timber production were emphasized. Values were to be weighted, indicating "primary or dominant uses" permitted on various portions.

Conservation forces have managed to bring much legislative and litigative pressure on industry's practices in forest management. Especially notable is the success of the Sierra Club in persuading the Forest Service to agree to file environmental impact statements before signing timber-cutting contracts covering roadless areas. The Sierra Club also triumphed in a prolonged battle with industry to create the 58,000-acre Redwood National Park in 1968, and was later instrumental in the designation of 1.3 million acres as wilderness under the Endangered Wilderness Act of 1978.[17] These successes in legislation and in keeping more national forests from being opened for timber cutting caused a stalemate in corporate planning within forest products firms.

A study of testimony of national and regional organizations on selected federal forestry legislation that came before Congress during the period 1960–1979 was conducted by Dennis LeMaster, associate professor of forest economics and policy, Washington State University, and Terri Koester, a forester with International Paper Co., Oregon. On the premise that all interested parties in a pluralistic society must be heard for a democracy to function, the authors investigated how well this goal was achieved by organizations interested in forestry legislation at the national level, and how effective they were in persuading Congress to act in the public interest. Included in this study were 12 high-level proposals and 21 organizations grouped into four categories; conservation groups, timber-industry trade associations, professional societies, and "other organizations." It was found that conservation groups testified 67 percent of the time, and timber-industry trade associations 50 percent of the time. In addition to this finding that conservation groups testify more frequently on forestry legislation, it was also determined that this group's testimony seemed most persuasive in fulfilling their goals. The authors concluded that through active involvement, organizations contribute substantially to the federal legislative process with regard to forestry.[18]

Timber Harvesting and Public Affairs

Environmental groups, in addition to defending sustained-yield harvesting and protecting wilderness areas, are much concerned about clear-cutting, the length of the rotation period, water quality, fire, the diversity of plant and animal communities, the retention of old growth areas, intensive genetic and herbicidal manipulation, and the visual quality of forests.[19] They review pertinent episodes in forestry practices to substantiate the residual damage caused by destructive logging techniques. Sierra Club forester Gordon Robinson comments on past logging practices on the north coast of California:[20]

> *The resulting loss of soil and nutrients seriously lowers the growth capacity of the land. It endangers the future of our forest industries and may permanently undermine our whole economy through damage to watersheds. Nearby are areas that were logged twenty-five years ago in which skid trails are still bereft of vegetation and still rapidly eroding.*

Biologists charge that the industry has contributed to rapid water runoff, which causes flooding and erosion, thereby affecting the spawning ground of fish and soil nutrients necessary for future timber growth. Changes in the micro-environment accompanying clear-cutting can result in subsequent changes in species composition. Breaking the forest ground cover causes increase in rate of evaporation in proportion to the intensity of the harvest. Net environmental changes induced with added light, variable temperatures, and transpirational stress upset internal stabilizing mechanisms of forests and destroy their resistance to destructive influences.[21] Environmentalists charge also that because Western timber has been cut 56 percent over replacement, the industry is moving to the Southeast, and that it has neglected the long-range interests of the local forests and the economy dependent on them.

Similar voices echo charges of continued mismanagement around the country. A Ralph Nader report on the pulp and paper companies of Maine complained of the industry's hypocrisy concerning a commitment to forest growth:[22]

> *As paper industry spokesmen never tire of saying, the forest is a renewable resource. Unlike deposits of coal or iron ore, a stand of timber can regenerate after it has been cut. But championing renewability often disguises the fact that the paper companies do very little to manage the process of regeneration so that it will enhance the first quality.*

The report asserted that modern silvicultural techniques are often neglected in favor of uncontrolled clear-cutting, which leaves large flat-
tened tracts to grow back on their own. It found that company-
published claims of "assuring improved crops for tomorrow" through
"genetically improved seeds and seedlings" and proper preharvest cutting to remove defective trees are often sacrificed to pressure to cut
long-run investment costs. The principal author of the Nader study,
William Osborn, quoted company foresters who admitted the need for
improving the timber stand between clear cuts. He explained:[23]

> *These [cost] pressures force commercial foresters to make decisions that
> may go against their training. Frustration attends such decisions. A
> forester who has learned the value of timber stand improvements in
> forestry school will naturally resent the fact that he cannot apply his
> knowledge when he begins to work for a paper company. But speaking
> out against abusive cutting practices or parsimonious management may
> cost a man his job or his reputation.*

Company justification for clear-cutting regularly defends the practice
with ambiguous scientific praise of even-age management more than it
admits that the economic value is superior to selective cutting. A recent complaint against clear-cutting in Arkansas explained that the
widespread even-age approach ignores the wildlife needs for nesting
places in mature trees. The editor of *Arkansas Outdoors* explained:[24]

> *Current commercial forestry practice, however, uses what is known as
> "even-aged management," whereby stands of trees are all of one age. This
> technique is the most economical and cheapest to the company and con-
> sumer, since no one has to be paid to go out and mark trees of the right
> age to be cut. But it also precludes the necessary mixed-age trees required
> by the redheaded woodpecker.*

Similarly, in Oklahoma a featured series in the *Tulsa Tribune* enti-
tled "Wood and Wildlife: Room for Both?" noted that much of the
aesthetic value and wildlife security of Oklahoma's mountains has been
threatened by arbitrary clear-cutting of a large forest products company. While previously environmentalists had complained about soil
erosion, flooding, poor replanting, and the problems even-age growth
brings to wildlife, this series highlighted the recreational and wildlife
hazards of dense monoculture forests. Outdoor expert Bob Bledsoe
reported, "To survive, wildlife must have hardwood trees to provide
food and shelter. If there are no acorns, no hickory nuts, no hollow trees
for dens, there will be no squirrels, no raccoon, no deer, or wild
turkey."[25] Bledsoe went on to quote Keith Wright, a local conservationist: "If you like to hunt or fish, you can forget it down here. If you
enjoy watching the leaves turn in the fall, you better see it before
1997."[26] Wright added: "Down South in Georgia and Alabama, they've
got thousands and thousands of acres of pure pine forests. You can

walk in there any time and you know what you have? Nothing. Nothing at all. There are no birds. No animals . . . There's nothing in those woods to feed them or protect them. I don't want that to happen here."[27] The timber industry refutes these problems and contends that it is easier to hunt in a managed forest.

Forest Management Issues

Finally, conservationists have opposed the industry-endorsed National Forest Timber Conservation and Management Act of 1969, which would have created a "high-timber-yield fund" to support advanced agricultural practices in national forests. Termed the "Loggers Relief Act" by the Sierra Club, this proposal was defeated largely by joint efforts of several conservation groups.[28] In 1975 another successful challenge to intensive forest management practices led to a temporary freeze on clear-cutting and helped press for the passage of the National Forest Management Act of 1976. This act calls for an interdisciplinary committee of scientists to advise on drafting regulations. This act allows clear-cutting when it is considered the best method, but the act limits the size and dispersion of areas to be cut and protects areas adjacent to streams.[29]

Other current environmental concerns are the dangers of aerial acid spraying (which has been banned in some communities) and tropical herbicides. Of particular concern is exposure to dioxin in the herbicide 2,4,5-T, known to cause tumors and birth defects. Alarming levels of dioxin have been found in fish from a river polluted by Dow Chemical Company's discharges in the manufacture of 2,4,5-T, and concentrations are traced to forest-fire smoke. The EPA has temporarily banned this toxic substance.[30] A Crown Zellerbach executive complained that the loss of 2,4,5-T has approximately tripled the forest product company's cost of spraying, since less powerful substitutes must be used more frequently. In Maine, aerial spraying to kill the spruce budworm has raised a public outcry about the danger of these chemicals on wildlife.[31]

The Industry's Response

The forest products industry has responded to environmental concerns in several different ways. First it has tightened its relation with the Forest Service to maintain good rapport and as a precaution against recurrence of past disasters. The Forest Service continues to be more closely allied to environmental groups on some issues, and it differs with industry on other fronts also. This new relation is reflected both by limited industry support to Forest Service publications and by opposition to rumored relocation of the Forest Service to the Department of the Interior. (Such a move would symbolize a shift in interest from commercial goals to preservation.)[32] The industry believes that the shift to the Department of Interior, proposed by its then secretary, Cecil Andrus, and former President Carter, is doomed to failure, like similar proposals in the past. Furthermore, the industry contends, no convincing evidence of improvements is available to support the transfer of the service.

A second response may be to diminish federal decisions on land use. The Western Lands Distribution and Equalization Act, nicknamed the "Sagebrush Rebellion," was proposed in late 1979 by Senator Orrin Hatch (R., Utah) and other Western senators to assert state control over public land administered by the Bureau of Land Management. This bill claims both a historical and a constitutional justification, citing the retention of land by the federal government as an unfair condition of admission to the Union. They overlook the fact that the federal lands never did belong to the western states, which on entering the Union consummated irrevocable agreements disclaiming title to federal public lands within their borders. Lands of the West in the public domain were acquired by the national government through various means at the expense of all people in the nation. This bill would transfer some 544 million acres to the 13 western states. The spark for the Sagebrush Rebellion was the tighter land-use regulation under the 1976 Federal Land Policy and Management Act (FLPMA), which requires the secretary of the interior to prepare land use plans for all Bureau of Land Management (BLM) lands based on the principles of multiple use and sustained yield. Stiff criteria will determine which tracts of land will be designated suitable or unsuitable for mining or wilderness or available for disposal. Timber production is one of the six main uses cited in the act. Following procedures like those specified in RARE II (under FLPMA), the secretary over the next fifteen years is required to review all BLM roadless areas of 5000 acres or more for possible inclusion in the National Wilderness Preservation System. Interim criteria for managing the wilderness system areas proposed in January 1979 permit previous multiple-use activities, but any new clear-cutting, strip mining or permanent road building is banned. Most industry spokesmen think the criteria are too stiff, while environmentalists fear that temporary impairments may disqualify these areas from eventual wilderness designations. This bill will be a focus of attention in the 1980s. It will hamper national energy efforts and diffuse essential environmental programs and will be disastrous to western states and to all citizens who depend on the resources of public lands.[33]

The most dramatic industry response to the tightened western timber supply, however, has been the move to the South. Georgia-

Pacific, the nation's largest forest company, claims that it is experiencing difficulty in harvesting adequate lumber from the 775,000 acres it controls in the Northwest and is moving most of its operations to the 2 million acres the company owns in the South. This action included the relocation of the corporate headquarters to Atlanta from its present Portland, Oregon, location. Half of Tacoma-based Weyerhaeuser's timber lands and half of San Francisco-based Crown Zellerbach's are in the South. This mobility is not a luxury available to all. Timber industry companies dependent on federal timber (99 percent of the industry) say they do not have the option of moving and project the dismal prospect of shutting down several mills. On the other hand, international companies, they say, can acquire lands and shift emphasis. After the Wilderness Act was passed in 1964, Idaho-based Boise Cascade, recognizing the increased opportunities available and the long-range interests to be served by moving South, developed its Southern business. The company recently bought 130,000 acres in the Carolinas, making its Southern timber holdings one-third of its total lands. The South's share of U.S. pulp production has risen steadily over the past four decades to 65 percent of the country's total, while its share of the timber industry has risen from 22 percent in 1960 to 27 percent in 1978.[34] The importance of Southern wood for the future is perhaps best evidenced by the recent fierce bidding between International Paper and Weyerhaeuser, the world's two largest private timber firms, for ownership of 350,000 acres of timber land and cutting rights to 100,000 acres more. In Louisiana, in the late spring of 1979, International Paper won the competition with a bid of $1.10 million in preferred stock.[35]

Despite the jobs and money that this mobility is bringing to the South, local residents are not all embracing their new neighbors with open arms. An article, "GP Move May Not Be All Rosy," in the *Atlanta Constitution* suggests that traditional Southern hospitality may be muted in the suspicion of the potential harmful consequences of this move and the negative effect of the industry in other parts of the country.[36] There have been expressions of environmental concern for wildlife since the industry moved into the eastern timber lands, and some civic and government leaders fear a threat to community economic stability and are talking of federal regulation.[37]

State regulation already exists around the country. In the early part of the century, the Northeastern and North Central states acquired 21 million acres of commercial land for protection, with New York, Pennsylvania, Michigan, Minnesota, and Wisconsin passing the most restrictive policies. Zoning and slash-burning regulations are two types of local restrictions on private land designed to achieve conservation goals. Since the 1940s, some seventeen states have had their own forest practice acts, whose main purpose is to maintain a minimum stand of high-quality commercial trees, and to make sure that lands will be left in a timber-growing condition after logging. Oregon, in 1941, was the first state to enforce a rigid law prohibiting harvesting of immature trees. A similar law passed a few years later in Washington was ruled constitutional by the state supreme court. In New York, companies must agree to comply with the state's forest-practices act. Many states have passed incentive legislation to assist the nonindustrial landowner. Three examples of such programs exist in North Carolina, Texas, and Virginia. North Carolina's program requires active assistance by the state forest service to enable individual private owners to improve the productivity of the state's forest resources. In 1969 the state provided a $700,000 two-year grant for this program. The "aggregates" program instituted in Texas in 1964 provides for a local consultant to organize small, nonindustrial forest landowners for the purpose of developing improved forestry practices. A special funding program in Virginia assists landowners and enables them to gain greater productivity in management of pine lands. Various state laws on land use and environmental issues also affect forestry practices. Typical are the following laws passed in Pennsylvania within the last decade: Farmland and Forest Land Assessment Act, Open Space Acquisition Act, Pesticide Control Act, Clean Streams Act. In New Jersey several laws relating to forest land include the Pinelands Environmental Council Act, Green Acre Bond Act, New Jersey Natural Lands Trust, State Recreation and Conservation Land Acquisition Fund, and State Trails System. Local governments in all states have adopted a wide variety of environmental, conservation, and land-planning ordinances that affect use and preservation of timber land.

The federal government has helped the states in this effort with several pieces of legislation. The Weeks Act of 1911 authorized federal cooperation with individual states in projects relating to forest-fire control, watershed protection, and stream navigability. The Cooperative Farm Forestry Acts of 1937 and 1950 provide technical and educational resources to farmers. The Forest Pest Control Act of 1947 brought the federal government together with state governments in industry-government cooperation in this area. Other programs include the Soil Conservation Service, the Farmers Home Administration Service, the Extension Service of the Department of Agriculture, and the Federal Land Bank. The National Highway Beautification Act provided federal funds for buying a "scenic easement" in New Hampshire, which permits owners of the "Thirteen Mile Woods" to manage the area as a commercial forest in return for public access and developmental restrictions. A similar conservation easement has ensured the preservation of Acadia National Park in Maine.

Two states, New York and California, have wilderness systems as well regulated as the federal systems. In other states, wilderness areas are designated through an administrative rather than a legislative process, which permits modification under new administrations. Natural-area systems exist to preserve natural areas in 35 states that have no wilderness system. Federal preservation-oriented programs cooperate with state agencies to preserve vital ecosystems.[38]

A special target for state and federal regulation of private forest land has been private, small-forest owners, who own 59 percent of all commercial forest land in the United States. Over 70 percent of forests in the North and South are nonindustrial and privately owned. Thus the forest products industry is very dependent on these private sources, even though they are unreliable for future resources. Although production capacity of this land is very high, actual timber production is poor because owners fail to reforest after the sale of their timber. As a result, owners often convert their land to more lucrative uses with faster remuneration, such as development. Owners of less than 200 acres frequently err in thinking that they cannot practice intensive forest management.[39]

The growing financial burdens of municipal and state governments are forcing local public administrators to increase taxation of forest land. High ad valorem taxes add a powerful disincentive to private-forest timber growing. The common ad valorem tax is based on the value of the timber plus the value of the land. To calculate this tax, states use either cost, market prices, or future income flows expected from use of the land. One of the strongest complaints against this form of taxation is that it requires payments in the present on benefits that are not realized until the timber is sold in the future. Landowners feel that annual taxation on the value of timber that cannot be harvested for 40 years is unfair. In some states, timber growers have succeeded in gaining modification of this tax through such options as a differential assessment based on the present category of use of the land rather than on its market value. Alternative forms of taxation offer ad valorem tax exemptions based on the use of a specified number of forest-management practices, or applying the tax principle of yield, which delays payment of property taxes until the timber is harvested. Owners of timberland lobby for any one of such variations, depending on the nature of the land ownership and the purpose and speed of timber cutting.

Labor-Related Issues

We have seen how expectations and values of many distinct stakeholders greatly affect the location and volume of the timber supply available to forest products companies. Although the forests are a renewable resource, timber harvesting, forest-management practices, and cost structures of companies all directly affect many interest groups outside a company. Even after the raw materials are acquired, the forest products company faces a complex array of public issues associated with processing wood. Sawmills and paper mills are hazardous workplaces, generating toxic air and water pollutants. Availability of energy and the form of industry taxation greatly influence the type of investments these companies can make.

Looking first at labor issues, one sees a situation that appears arbitrary and discordant. Much of the logging, especially in the Northeast and South, is done by independent contractors. These loggers assume considerable risk in buying their own equipment, and they are frequently rewarded with low pay, hazardous work, sparse benefits, and isolation. William C. Osborn, in a Nader study-group report, referred to this situation as "pulpwood peonage."[40] These independent contractors lack many work benefits and the ability to organize. Nevertheless, they have tried to unite in the marketplace, the courts, and the legislature to improve their financial returns.

Many loggers employed by forest products companies, however, are represented by the International Woodworkers of America (IWA), an AFL-CIO union with roots in the activist International Workers of the World (IWW). This union represents 115,000 workers throughout the United States and Canada. In the West, the IWA along with the Lumber Production and Industrial Workers Union (LPIW) represent 80,000 workers. On the paper side of the industry, the AFL-CIO affiliated United Paper Workers International Union (UPIU) represents 300,000 workers nationally, and the independent Association of Western Pulp and Paper represents 21,000 workers in the western states.

Standard labor concerns with issues such as work conditions, wages, and job security all have a long history in the union, mostly of continuing controversy. The accident rate for serious injuries is 22 percent for the lumber industry, and far exceeds the U.S. average of 14.6 percent for all manufacturing industries. In just one typical year in California there were 5194 disability injuries and 21 fatalities in the lumber and wood products workforce. Falling timber, dangerous terrain, and malfunctioning chainsaws account for many of the work injuries in logging. A tremendous volume of noise in the sawmills leads to a high incidence of hearing loss, and the vibrations of woodworking machinery cause arthritis and circulatory complications. The wood dust from defiberization, pulverization, and mechanical cutting has been linked to various respiratory disorders, emphysema, and possibly susceptibility to leukemia. In sawmills, the cutting operations and transportation of material frequently lead to bruises, sprains, cuts, amputations and crushed limbs, and eye injuries. Fears articulated by unions also extend to various preservatives and glues considered to cause brain damage, tremors, blindness, and cancer of the lymph system. In recent years, labor unions have demanded health-research funds in their annual negotiation. Furthermore, OSHA and the federal court system have been tightening their scrutiny of the industry. Projected costs of just noise-abatement equipment compliance for the wood-processing industry amounts to $17.7 million, as opposed to $2.8 million for similar equipment in the rest of U.S. industry.[41]

Although current interest in the distinctly hazardous workplace is high, traditional concern with wage rates has dominated industrial relations since the turn of the century.[42] The industrial relations climate has been stormy over this time, with somewhat more tranquillity between the mid-1960s and mid-1970s.

The militancy of the timber union in the West was not matched in the wood-processing industry until the mid-1960s, with the founding of the independent Association of Western Pulp and Paper Workers (AWPPW). Despite relative youth and size, this union had been extraordinarily successful in its early campaigns. Its "whipsawing" pattern of negotiating has involved a strategy of targeting its demands first at mills most likely to cave in during a round of negotiations. They then move on to the next company, using the previous agreement as a springboard and adding further demands, repeating this pattern throughout the industry. In 1978, however, a snag developed in this strategy. After a normally successful first few months of negotiations between 10 union locals and 9 companies, the union drove right into a solid wall of corporate resistance. Twelve forest products companies refused to agree to the validity of the earlier labor agreements (21 percent wage increases over two years and substantial pension increases). An accumulation of a large inventory of timber products, added to a considerable overcapacity of necessary raw material in the paper side of the industry, afforded the impetus required to enable the companies to hold out. The union responded with an historic seven-month strike. Company unity and determination eventually prevailed; mills either were shut or were operated with skeleton crews of executive workers.[43]

The union is now trying to solidify union locals in preparation for a future showdown with management. The message is clear; both internal unity across locals and external unity across unions must combat the new management solidarity. Immediately after the union defeat, the rival West Coast forest products unions began to lay plans for more formal coordination, and the IWA and the LPIW began negotiating jointly to unify the bargaining of 80,000 western lumber workers from 150 operations of nine large forest products companies. These lumber

unions also began an effort to secure contracts that will expire simultaneously with the 1981 paper union contracts. The paper unions,
meanwhile, have targeted strong wage demands and have tried long
strikes (4–7 months) against individual companies.[44]

Another important objective of union activity is job security. In the
1950s and 1960s there was a shift in the workforce composition from
production workers to white-collar jobs. Intensive capital investment
has led to sharp workforce declines in the past ten years. Paper ship-
ments per employee more than doubled between 1965 and 1975. The
average volume of pulp and paper sales per employee has risen to
$48,000 in 1974 from $40,000 per employee in 1970. The sawmills and
lumber mills have experienced similar productivity increases and
workforce declines.[45] Such a trend toward increased capital intensity
and declining membership in unions has led the biggest paper union,
the United Paper-Workers International Union (300,000 members), to
hold merger talks with another capital-intensive industry's union, the
Chemical and Atomic Workers (160,000 members).[46]

The social effect of job dislocation has been recognized as substantial.[47] One industry researcher commented, "A delineation between
the personnel in a company organization and the community would
surely be superficial at best."[48] Mill closure means loss of primary
source of livelihood for many small towns, and loss of tax revenue; the
consequent economic ripple runs through the other local businesses
and institutions. Union officials in the West explain that poor land
management by companies and the economic downturn in general are
leading to widespread layoffs in the industry. For example, R. Dennis
Scott of the International Woodworkers of America commented, "The
big companies cut their own land too fast, putting us on the edge of a
timber gap, and now this housing thing comes along."[49] This union,
the IWA, has consequently lost 25 percent of its membership in 1979.
Oregon officials estimate that 75,000 forest products jobs disappeared
in the six months from November 1979 through April 1980. From
March to June of 1980 more than 475 of 820 mills were forced to close
or curtail production. In June 1980, the U.S. Bureau of Labor Statistics
reported that lumber unemployment was twice the national average.
While this industry affliction has hit the West the hardest, the southern
operation has suffered as well.[50] Such dislocation helps to fuel union
and community lobbying efforts for legislation that would require companies to give advance notice before closing plants and funds for employee severance pay and community economic assistance.[51]

With this desperate employment situation, it is easy to understand
labor union hostility to the perceived high volume of western lumber
exports to Japan. Softwood logs composed about 21 percent of the total
value of U.S. forest products exported in 1978, and this figure has been
increasing. Six percent of the annual U.S. softwood timber is exported

in log form. Raw logs rather than processed lumber are exported to Japan's highly fragmented lumber and construction industry, with its tiny sawmills cutting boards of the particular size appropriate for their use. As a principal lumber import nation, Japan has ordered only raw logs suitable for veneers and other wood products to be manufactured by specially designed equipment. The labor union's disapproval of exports of unfinished products and loss of jobs is explained in an editorial in the *International Woodworker*:[52]

> *It is less expensive to produce lumber and plywood in the Pacific Northwest than anywhere in the World, despite the relatively high rates. It is a comparative advantage which should be exploited. . . . But one of our [trading] partners chooses to maintain high employment levels at home while they place innumerable non-tariff barriers on American lumber to discourage its purchase. This is not fair trade in our minds. As it is now, a huge potential market is closed to American lumber so a friendly government can achieve a political goal while American workers are unemployed.*

In the 1960s, Congress, with the concurrence of both the industry and labor, passed legislation blocking the export of logs harvested from national forests. In 1973 and 1979 other attempts were made to regulate further the substitution of federal timber for wood exported by a company. Joining this effort were U.S. home builders and environmentalists, who were concerned about rising cost of timber and excessive harvesting. Although these groups fear the economic and social consequences of a diminished domestic timber supply, they are lobbying for stricter control over U.S. log exports and for compensation to the displaced.

Exporters of forest products counter that such exports (1) help the U.S. balance of payments, (2) provide employment for loggers, (3) yield revenue that can be directed towards domestic forest and equipment investment, and (4) are necessary for the highly specialized Japanese lumber industry, which must cut wood to sizes peculiar to Japanese construction methods, and which refuses to buy finished products.[53] It has been particularly difficult for the industry to deal with this issue because of the unusual alliance on each side of the issue and because of dissension within the industry. In addition, industry firmly holds that old-growth timber is better exported than left to rot in the forest.

Pollution Control

Public interests and corporate production interests confront each other in heated disputes on questions of environmental effect as the public learns of potentially harmful consequences. Environmental campaigns generate support from both local communities and national coalitions of interest groups. Previously we have discussed the influence of conservation forces on the acquisition of raw material and the influence of management through regulation of timber supplies from public lands used for commercial purposes, forest management practices, and timber harvesting methods. Many of the same interest groups share a common concern with pollution-control advocates about damage to our environment from industrial by-products in processes related to timber production. Public outrage over air and water pollution and the need for safe waste disposal of solids has forced modification in production processes in some lumber and paper mills. Current EPA regulations mandate advanced technological equipment for reducing pollution in air and water to minimum levels in compliance with established criteria. Requirements—put forth by OSHA and other licensing laws—for protecting the health of employees and safe working conditions now restrict mill location, construction, and operation.

Rivers, considered to be natural networks linking the forest and the mills, were often monopolized by the famous log drives. Although this river use has been banned in most states and curtailed in Maine, two rivers, the Kennebec and the Saint Croix (in Maine), continued in the early 1970s to carry logs. In this process dams and holding lakes store logs for as long as eight months; wet storage is often an integral part of production. Degradation of waterways resulted from organic solubles leached out of the logs, and from massive wastewater discharges from pulp and paper mills containing tons of dissolved organic compounds, hundreds of pounds of suspended solids material, oil, and other substances toxic to aquatic life. In a recent report, the U.S. Army Corps of Engineers declared that the "pulpwood blankets" that cover the waters and sunken logs embedded in the bottom silt of these two rivers pose hazards to navigation and make fishing impossible. The Environmental Protection Agency in 1971 concluded that the rotting bark debris alters the natural substrata and contributes to severe biological deterioration and elimination of aquatic life.

In addition, the large quantity of water required for processing wood in the mills contributes to the extensive pollution problem. Water is used for debarking, for separating the fibers from the lignin that binds them, for washing digester chemicals from the pulp, and for carrying the wood fiber in a concentration of one part fiber to ninety-nine parts water through the Fourdrinier wire, the first stage of a paper-making machine. William Osborn, writing in 1975, described some of the consequences of this process in Maine at that time.[54]

Every day Maine's sixteen mills pour wastes that rob the rivers of oxygen, clog them with solid mulch, and give them a ripe smell. The pollution has destroyed valuable fisheries, forced industries and municipalities to seek

new water supplies, depreciated property values, and discouraged rec-
reational use of rivers.

Generally companies did nothing about water pollution until local regulations in a particular community or state required that they use
available pollution-abatement equipment. Similarly, legislative enforcement was necessary to prod many of the forest products companies into correcting air pollution. Hydrogen sulfide and methylmer-
captan are the most common mill odors, resembling rotten eggs and
decaying cabbage.[55] The particulate matter and sulfur dioxide emitted
by the pulp and paper mills as by-products of production cause adverse
health effects even at low levels of concentration in ambient air. These
contaminants, besides reducing visibility in an area, also damage property. Several progressive firms, however, have completed required
conversions, and significantly reduced odorous emissions and pollutants by not straining the capacity of their mills beyond 100 percent.

Despite a history of reckless pollution, the industry has come to
recognize its responsibility for dealing with the negative externalities of
its operations. In 1943 the industry formed an organization that is now
designated the National Council of the Paper Industry for Air and
Stream Improvement. During that period, several states responded to
growing community apprehension and in the 1940s and 1950s created
commissions for controlling water pollution. In 1965 on the national
level, Congress acknowledged the vulnerability of our water resources
and passed the Water Quality Act; it empowered the federal government to (1) clear up interstate streams and (2) distribute construction
grants for municipal plants for treating sewage. The Clear Water Act of
1972 required mills to use the best practical technology currently available (BCT) and by 1983, the best available technology (BAT). The
ultimate goal was to have zero pollution discharge by 1985. The Clean
Air Acts of 1967 and 1970 set maximum levels for the pollution of
ambient air, including contamination by such by-products as sulfur
dioxide and particulate matter. States are obligated to develop plans for
acting on pollution abatement at the source. If a state is deficient in
meeting federal guidelines, the EPA can intervene and dictate appropriate plans.

The cumulative cost of compliance with these pollution control regulations from the mid-1960s to the mid-1970s has been estimated by
the industry to have run as high as $3 billion. Expenditures on equip-
ment between 1972 and 1975 of $6 billion a year represented a full
third of the industry's total capital spending.[56] The Department of
Commerce found that in 1979 the industry planned to spend $296
million on pollution control, a 24 percent increase over the previous
year. This increase in expenditure was allocated as follows: 35 percent
for both air-pollution control ($142 million) and solid-waste control ($42

million) and 9 percent for water-pollution control ($112 million). These increases are substantially greater than the 6 percent increase in environmental spending by U.S. business overall. Environmental expenses for public utilities and for petroleum and chemical companies, however, exceed such expenses for the forest products industry.[57] Both the congressional legislation and administrative regulations establishing new standards for industry to meet are under constant reevaluation and modification, and they require sustained monitoring.

The congressional maze and the challenges of special-interest groups add to the complexity of interpreting detailed legislative mandates. This convoluted process is illustrated in a record of the infighting over the clean-air regulations. The intensely debated 1977 amendments to the Clean Air Act of 1970 extend some compliance deadlines, provide strict penalties for noncompliance, strengthen a joint, federal-state regulatory system, and resolve growth-related provisions. The industry is concerned about effects on economic growth, the use of land and energy resources, and adjustments that cost billions of dollars to meet. Environmentalists see this law as eliminating tons of pollution from the atmosphere and controlling the rate of industrial growth.

The 1977 amendments call for EPA to review and revise the *primary standards* (to protect human health) and the stricter *secondary* standards (to protect public welfare) for seven principal air pollutants. The law is a compromise and sets up a classification that identifies "maximum allowable increases" in sulfur dioxide and particulates. Air quality in Class I areas, including national parks and large wilderness areas, are to remain unchanged. Some modification is sustained for Class II areas (all other clear areas). Class III areas (which are to be designated by the states) may show greater increases.

New polluters in any serious degree must provide a preconstruction evaluation of the effect of emissions on clear areas. Many industries became eligible for review by the change of the term *allowable* to *potential* emissions of 100 tons or more of pollutants a year (in the amended version). *Potential* is defined as the level of emissions generated without control equipment, and *allowable* refers to those emissions after elements of control are in place. However, existing plants may bypass review for expansion projects if they reduce pollution from other sources of the site. To permit growth in an area of high pollution, an "offset policy" mandates that the area assume the responsibility for cutting back emissions from existing sources. A big issue is that the standard for sulfur dioxide emission will require the new coal-fired plants to be built by 1990 to conform with the stipulation in the law to use the *best available technology (BAT)* to clean up emissions. The EPA is referring to flue gas desulfurization, which uses scrubbers to remove damaging compounds in coal smoke. Plants that convert from oil to coal must clean up 85 percent of their sulfur dioxide emissions on a daily basis. Industry points to high inflationary consequences, but EPA maintains that the performance standard would raise utility construction cost by only 2 percent. A "partial scrubbing" option was proposed by industry to permit plants burning low-sulfur coal to exceed the 85 percent reduction level so they would need less control equipment.

The 1977 amended Clean Air Act extends the state compliance deadline to 1982 with strong sanctions for noncompliance, such as suspension of authority to operate and cutoffs of federal funds. *State implementation plans* (SIPs) are also required to include areawide transportation controls, for instance, preferential lanes on freeways for buses and carpools to promote mass transportation and to reduce pollution from car exhaust. The EPA has begun to direct attention towards acid rain resulting from airborne sulfur dioxides and nitrogen oxides, which has been observed in 12 states since its effects were discovered in 1974; acid rain is related to damage of soil and crops, retardation of forest growth, and fish-kills in lakes and streams. Scientists now associate sulfur-bearing winds with damage to forests. The forest products industry fears more stringent controls on boiler emissions under programs to eliminate acid rain.[58] Heavy fines proposed by the EPA will restrict any competitive edge to be gained in ignoring capital investment for equipment to abate pollution.[59]

Projected 1984 goals for controlling water pollution may cost the industry an added $2 billion without appreciable improvement in water quality to the desired "fishable and swimmable" levels. Despite strong federal laws, progress in restoring the chemical, physical and biological integrity of the nation's waters has been only limited. The Federal Water Pollution Control Act of 1972 set deadlines for industries and state and local government to meet federal standards for clean water. By 1977, about 80 percent of industrial discharges were within the requirements. A great multibillion-dollar program was initiated by Congress to fund planning and construction of facilities for treating sewage. Only a third of the projects have been completed and only 40 percent met 1977 deadlines. Very little change has been reported in levels of five major pollutants. The problem is that Section 208 of the Water Quality Act, which requires regional or state planning agencies to identify and propose solutions to their water-pollution problems, is just getting started. Another problem is that difficulties have arisen in dealing with sources of pollution that have no one point—runoff from forest practices, mines, farms, and city streets. Although these are important factors in polluting groundwater experts point to still more severe threats from surface and subsurface disposal of industrial wastes used in manufacturing operations, oil drilling, and forest-related industries. The EPA has identified 133,000 sites where harmful disposal has been made.

Section 208 of the Water Quality Act is a new approach to controlling pollution, and it focuses more on prevention and nonstructural alternatives than on the traditional methods of treating waste. This statute describes plans for controlling pollutants, and coordinates planning with building of treatment works; it also ensures that commercial discharges receive pretreatment. The law classifies streams and rivers according to water quality. Water-quality standards (with goals of "fishable, swimmable" water by 1983) define the maximum amounts of pollutants the state will allow to be discharged into state waters; thus the water uses designated for each body of water can be upheld. Effluent limitations set the degree of reduction of a pollutant that can be got from various levels of technology. Waste-load allocations identify the total pollutants from point sources and nonpoint sources that can enter a waterway without violating state quality standards. The National Pollutant Discharge Elimination System (NPDES) applies to permits for "point source" pollution, including industry, municipal treatment facilities, and certain forestry, mining, and fishing operations. Since water is being used in greater quantities than what rainfall or other sources can replenish, industries that consume large volumes, like the forest industries, bear responsibility for predicted shortages of water in the future.

Increasing amounts of solid waste, new federal restrictions on open dumping and landfill siting, and decreasing available land around the country have made disposal of solid waste an important environmental concern. The Resource Conservation and Recovery Act (1976) provides a "cradle to grave" regulatory system for proper treatment, storage, and disposal of hazardous wastes. This act outlaws open dumps, and the disposal of hazardous wastes in sanitary landfills. It also sets criteria for constructing proper disposal facilities. The act requires that lagoons for wastewater from mills be relined (at an average cost of $20 million each, or $200,000 for a 100-acre lagoon). The industry proposes an alternative classification that would not lump purchasers of dangerous chemicals with producers of wood products, so the latter would not have to bear the high costs of hazardous waste spills for which they bear no responsibility.[60] New federal regulations that went into effect in November 1980 are designed to bring consistency to the maze of inadequate and conflicting state laws. The rules will eliminate jurisdictional loopholes that in the past allowed offenders to evade responsibility by tracking waste from one state to another. Waste generators, haulers, and disposal facilities will be held responsible for safe disposal in licensed sites. The EPA estimates that 25,000 new permits will have to be granted during the next five years for storage, disposal, or treatment sites to accommodate the large amounts of wastes generated.

Residents in communities in which it is proposed to establish such sites, are contesting the plans. The scarcity of available sites seems to be a greater problem than the $25,000 dollar-a-day fine for illegal dumping.

The commitment of the American people to environmental goals emphasizes the urgency of protecting the environment and also recognition of the costs of cleaning up and trading off. Over the years, legislative decisions for environmentalist positions have been difficult to secure; increasingly powerful pressures to dilute, delay, and circumvent legislation have had to be overcome. Appeals to Congress from representatives of municipalities, from the auto industry, and from the utilities to modify policies on standards for air quality and regulation of auto emission brought about hearings on these regulations by the House Subcommittee on Public Health and the Environment and the Senate Subcommittee on Air and Water Pollution.

Arguments from industry to weaken the Clean Air Acts were tied to rising energy costs, fuel shortages, and employment layoffs. Coal industry spokesmen were particularly vocal in protesting limitations in coal use that may result, and also predicted a shortage of low-sulfur fuels. Manufacturers charged that removing lead from gasoline will waste a million barrels of oil a day. To head off problems, EPA granted seven emission variances to power plants who are unable to get low-sulfur oil. Environmentalists, countering charges that pollution control equipment wastes electricity, held that electric-power generation is inefficient in that 70 percent of the energy used to produce electricity is lost in generation and transmission. Automakers were granted relief when EPA delayed compliance with nitrogen oxide emission standards to 1990. Industrial polluters continue to pit clean air advocates against workers who fear job loss as a result of strict standards. Environmentalists argue for proof that the shutdowns are due to these laws.

The Sierra Club has asked the public to note that the price tag on controlling air pollution in 1977 was $2.5 billion as opposed to an estimated $12.8 billion of potential damage to health, buildings, and crops from sulfur oxides and particulates. Defending stringent carbon monoxide levels, EPA asserted that quality standards were promulgated to protect the largest number of people, including those most susceptible to air pollution. Groups such as the Center for Science in the Public Interest, the Environmental Defense Fund, and the Public Interest Campaign fought to get lead-free gasoline, pointing to the irreversible damage this dangerous substance deposited in air through auto exhausts causes in young children.[61]

Intransigence on the state level in compliance with clean air laws is exemplified by action of the EPA on August 1979 to halt a large new industrial construction in California until the legislature adopted a program to inspect cars annually for faulty smog devices. An editorial in the *Los Angeles Times* stated that action on 45 similar applications may result in cutting off billions of dollars in federal funds for highways and for waste-treatment plants.[62] An editorial in the *Arizona Republic*, August 30, 1979, referred to Arizona's compliance with the clean air act (because the state's urban air quality needed improvement and protection) and labeled Californians' resistance as "stupid in considering their autos above the law."[63] Chambers of commerce and developers of land around urban areas fear that regulations ignore tradeoffs between environmental and socioeconomic conservationists. Representatives of such industries as copper, utilities, and the National Coal Association disputed the intention of Congress to establish air-quality goals that are more strict in clean-air regions than national primary and secondary standards and supported the procedure of allowing states to determine "significant deterioration case by case." The Sierra Club urged more stringent interpretation, citing serious park and forest deterioration "from a haze of pollution blanketing the Southwest." Gus Spaeth, a member of the president's Council on Environmental Quality, in a discussion about environmental priorities in the 1980 budget, rejected the idea that it costs a lot to deal with cleaning up pollution. He referred to a recent study by Data Resources, Inc., which concluded that air and water programs contributed only slightly each year to the annual increase in the consumer price index (0.1–0.2 percent) each year for the period 1980–1986.[64] The effect of environmental regulation on the whole economy was considered more beneficial than harmful. The benefits mentioned were reduced demand for health services, more agricultural output, more forest output, and long-term conservation of soil and forest resources, which should hold down prices on housing and other necessities.

Besides conservation groups, the EPA, state and local governments, numerous federal agencies like the U.S. Fish and Wildlife Commission, and also the Bureau of Land Management, the Forest Service, congressional committees, industry, labor, and consumers all participate on a regular basis in legislative developments affecting the environment. The U.S. Justice Department has recently created a new post of deputy assistant attorney general in the department's enlarged Land and Natural Resources Division. This action reflects the extent to which courts have been involved in the environmental decisions.[65]

Energy and Transportation

Although energy and transportation issues represent important production concerns to forest products companies, they are not peculiar to this industry. The forest products industry is the largest user of residual oil in the country and the third largest user of all fuels, and it also supplies 10 percent of the total freight revenues of U.S. railroads.[66] Generally, the industry has aligned itself with other business groups lobbying for decontrol of crude oil and natural gas. Several who speak for the forest products industry have joined speakers for other industries in objecting to many aspects of the Department of Energy (DOE) regulations, under the Powerplant Industrial Fuel Use Act of 1978. (These regulations prohibit the use of oil and natural gas at particular industrial sites.) Some suggest that the industry also resents DOE intrusion under the National Energy Conservation Policy Act of 1978, a mandatory program that requires the fifty most energy-intensive companies in the nation's ten most energy-intensive industries to report their conservation progress. Companies feel that they can better maintain confidential material by working through trade associations.

Energy issues are illustrated at the state level by the controversy on the rate base that exists between the prevailing, and industry-favored, "embedded cost of service" and the consumer-preferred marginal-cost pricing on inverted rates. This decontrol philosophy has predictably strengthened industry support for deregulating railroads and truck companies.

Another special energy resource in this industry is "cogeneration," the rechanneling of steam for heating and for generating electricity; This process has been encouraged by the Crude Oil Windfall Profits Tax Act of 1979. A section of this act allows a 10 percent investment tax credit for expanding "cogeneration" capacity. Already the pulp and paper industry accounts for 40 percent of the electricity produced by cogeneration in the country.[67]

Such regulations affect competitors differentially, as forest products companies vary in the ways their operations have expanded into adjoining industries. For example, Georgia-Pacific's operations expanded into energy, while Boise Cascade has expanded operations into transportation. In the South and West, gas and coal are common, while oil prevails in the East.

Financial Considerations

Several integral financial issues such as information disclosure, accounting standards, taxation, insurance premiums, and merger activity pertain especially to the forest products industry. The personal values of executives have much to do with corporate positions on issues like broadening corporate governance, the accounting and antibribery provision of the Foreign Corrupt Practices Act, and proxy disclosure sales. Several companies in the industry have opposed regulations for expanding disclosure down the product line. Generally the industry has tended to resist the growth of reporting rules. Many activist groups and members of the academic community, however, have campaigned for including nonfinancial subjects in financial reports—namely, employment practices, environmental activities, and consumer and safety matters. Forest products companies would have a particularly difficult reporting burden in that many aspects of their business are turbulent and confusing.

The industry is also concerned about another set of disclosure obligations. The Financial Accounting Standards Board (FASB) has issued many new guidelines for financial reporting, covering, for example, inflation accounting, foreign currency translation, capitalization of interest costs, and contingency reserves. Forest products companies often take the position that such rules do not assist managers or investors and that they diminish the industry's ability to raise capital by exaggerating the erratic nature of industry earnings. Since the industry is so changeable, it is easy to understand such resistance to plans that would introduce further uncertainty.

As we have seen, taxes are important to the industry. Large forest products companies are interested in the proposed act for recovering capital cost; this would reduce the timetable allowable for writing off investment in plant and equipment.[68] The American Paper Institute has suggested that this legislation might add almost a billion dollars a year to the industry's cash flow. Some economists question whether it would really be an incentive to investment, and small businesses tend to see it as a giveaway to large companies. Lastly, government officials see this measure as a sharp loss in funds to the government.

Merger and acquisition, another category of financial topics, has special significance to the forest products industry. The main growth of most of the giant integrated concerns has taken place through acquisition rather than internal development. In recent years, however, these same companies have themselves become prey for larger companies outside the industry. Companies such as ITT, Time, Inc., Texaco, and Mobil have become large owners in forest products. Merger rumors have periodically included Scott Paper Company (until a recent major stock purchase by Branscam Ltd.) and several other paper companies. Oil and other natural-resource companies are frequently suspected to be potential buyers.

The 1979 Mead-Occidental battle is a good recent example of the takeover threats. Mead, itself the purchaser of over 40 companies and the seventh largest company in the industry, now found the tables turned. Through stockholder and director loyalty, Mead management triumphed in a long stormy battle with Occidental Petroleum.[69] Mead's asset base and profitability made the company look very attractive.

This appetite for forest products companies has remained strong. Two other giants, Diamond International and Hammermill, were hit with unfriendly takeover attempts in the spring of 1980. Cavenham U.S.A., Inc., subsidiary of English financier Sir James Goldsmith's Generale Occidentale S.A., began a violently contested proxy fight for control of Diamond International and for the Hammermill Paper Company.[70] New York arbitrager Carl C. Ichan began a similar battle. Hammermill had become one of the leading paper companies through its own acquisition of 30 paper-related firms. Its appeal, like the appeal of many other companies in this industry, is the low stock price. Profit changes and undervalued timber land often cause these market prices to trail far behind book price. At the time of the Ichan overtures, Hammermill stock was selling at $24 a share, while its book value was roughly $37 a share. One analyst, Margarette Suhl commented, "Paper companies in general have been attractive takeover possibilities in the last year or so because their assets are much higher than what's on the books."[71] It is suspected that Ichan would reap the profits of this undervalued stock by liquidating the enterprise. The threat of predatory dismemberment is a fear throughout the industry. This may be why a survey by *Institutional Investor* rated the paper industry as one of the outstanding industries in the practice of investor relations.[72]

The Marketing Perspective

Various interest groups, including labor, environmentalists, local communities, and small lumber companies oppose U.S. log exports, thereby claiming a stake in the way forest products companies market their products. These companies are not allowed to sell timber from national forests to other countries, and further restrictions are being proposed to control the substitution of public timber for exported private timber.

The industry has also been closely watching other developments in international trade. The 1979 Tokyo round of multilateral trade agreements led to substantial tariff reduction (more than 50 percent) for the U.S. paper products of U.S. trading partners.[73] The industry is now anxious to see that these agreements are properly monitored and enforced. The difficulty in enforcement arises from the complexity of the agreements as well as from the competition for government attention among the industries involved. Appropriately, forest products companies are anxious to limit protectionist pressures at home and thereby to avoid retaliatory acts that could damage entry to new European markets. Many believe that some reorganization of government departments would further these goals.

The industry is also anxious to avoid outside influence on product standardization. The Federal Trade Commission (FTC) has proposed the creation of mandatory standards to guarantee the quality and dimensions of certified products. The industry generally does not think that government, consumers, or industry would benefit from what is seen as a derailing of voluntary standards. The industry has argued that the federal government should be involved in standards but that mandated standards would inhibit invention and variety.

Company pricing practices have engendered even greater government involvement in corporate activity in two ways. First, several companies (Scott, Hammermill, Crown Zellerbach, and Union Camp) exceeded the President's price increase guidelines according to the Council on Ways and Price Stability.[74] The second collision with public institutions was the injurious antitrust prosecution of the 1970s, which has cost the companies in the industry well over half a billion dollars in company fines alone. (Some companies have already paid as much as $60 million). The proceedings have incalculably damaged corporate public image, credibility with officials, trust of customers, employee morale, and the lives of families and convicted, jailed executives.

Twelve lawsuits have been brought in the following sub-industries: plywood, paper labels, folding cartons, consumer boxes, corregated containers, and fine papers. In the proceedings for folding cartons, which the U.S. Justice Department characterized as the largest since the infamous 1960 electrical-contracting conspiracy on fixing prices, 20 companies and 47 executives were convicted of fixing prices.[76] Fifteen executives were sentenced to prison and others were fined. Individuals have paid $300,000 in fines, $275,000 in civil fines, and $186 million to customers (generally large consumer-products companies) in a class-action civil suit. In addition, the carton producers had to agree to antitrust compliance programs and sharply restricted communication across companies.[77] The even larger $300 million civil lawsuit against the corrugated container firms was the largest ever in a private antitrust suit.[78]

Besides these suits, there have been federal grand jury investigations in Philadelphia, California, and Cleveland, as well as FTC litigation against unfair discounting of prices. Also resulting was the need for more precise and consequently more expensive antitrust legislation (from the standpoint of the government as well as the industry).[79] The so-called Illinois Brick law would have countered a recent Supreme Court decision and allow the ultimate consumer, even as an indirect purchaser, the right to recover antitrust damages.

Research suggests that forest products producers may be more susceptible to fixing prices for several reasons that are antithetical to economists' notion of an oligopolistic collusion. Many sub-industries have a very crowded market and mature products, and profits have been elusive for some time. Furthermore, forest products are, by their nature, often not much differentiated among companies. On top of these pressures has been strong competitive pressure to consummate further acquisition. Acquisition-fueled growth, in turn, has led to cultural collisions between acquired companies and their parents. Some managers had been socialized to certain norms of business practice that conflicted sharply with new company policy. In addition, company personnel practices (training programs and performance appraisals) generally had worked at cross purposes with codes of ethics and programs for legal compliance by encouraging profits at any cost. The formal structure of the organization often did not clarify authority for setting prices, nor did it limit involvement in trade associations. Lastly, these companies never focused the various internal perspectives on problems from the external environment. Each level of management in the corporation tended to have a markedly different understanding of the outside world.[80]

Conclusions

The technological, market, and institutional sectors of the business environment have each had a pronounced influence on the development and contribution of forest products companies. This industry does not face the technological turbulence of many other industries such as communications, electronics, or transportation, nor does it have to deal with the marketplace uncertainty of agriculture, retailing, or banking. For forest products companies, much of the real drama arises from public issues that these companies, as important social institutions, must manage.

In neither technology nor the market are the important events sudden and surprising. The fundamental technology of Leif Ericson's loggers, Paul Bunyan, and the ancient Chinese and Arab papermakers has been dramatically improved, but the changes have been gradual and the stages have remained remarkably stable. New products have appeared, and substitute construction and packaging products have become widely used. Through wild growth by acquisition and substantial improvements in transportation, the competitive structure is becoming more national and international than local. Yet changes have still been gradual, and the GNP remains a powerful predictor of demand.

In the remaining institutional sector, public affairs are far less certain. In each of the functional areas of the forest products business, companies must reckon with a complex and changing scenario. Corporate actions involving raw materials (timber supply), production (primary and secondary conversion), financial affairs, and marketing all directly or indirectly affect many segments of the community. The voices of the community are represented by public interest and environmentalist groups, shareowners, employees, plant communities, labor unions, municipal and state governments, federal agencies, and the judiciary. These groups are the forces that confer social legitimacy on a corporation. While their expectations may at times be unreasonable or contradictory, they have at least as much power as management in determining the continued life of an enterprise. Their expectations therefore must at least be considered.

Looking briefly at each of the functional areas, we have seen that the supply of *raw materials* is very much affected by (1) the release of public (national and state) forest land for commercial use; (2) legislation (such as taxation and zoning) that promotes the commercial forest potential of private land; and (3) regulation of forest management practices, including the size of clear-cutting lots, monoculture, soil conservation, fire control, wildlife management, and herbicide and insecticide spraying. Environmental issues also resurface as constraints on *production*. Production-related public issues thus include (1) serious air and stream pollution; (2) brittle labor relations (from hazardous conditions, salaries, mill closings); (3) energy legislation (involving biomass fuel, hydro power, and steam cogeneration); and (4) transportation. *Financial* matters are very much affected by taxation (of forest land, plant, and capital equipment), reporting (disclosure requirements, and complex nonfinancial reporting on land use and employment practices), and intense merger threats (because of greatly undervalued stocks). Finally, company *marketing* activities are restrained by limits on log exports, possible product standardization, and strict penalties for fixing prices.

Through this wide-ranging and lengthy exposure to public affairs, the forest products industry has developed an outstanding degree of sophistication in managing public affairs issues. The three chief national trade associations—the American Forest Institute (public relations activities), the National Forest Products Association (general representative of lumber and wood products companies), and the American Paper Institute (general representative of paper and packaging companies)—have shown sensitivity to environmental and other public affairs for over 40 years. Both the NFPA and the API have economists, policy analysts, and lobbyists working separately on a wide range of public affairs. Joint committees meet regularly and frequently to coordinate their views in a single industry voice on certain issues. These organizations communicate with the member companies through company representatives on committees, rotating officers from the companies, and various newsletters and bulletins. The API's 300-page *Public Affairs Leadership Manual* stands out as a special and impressive trade group effort to educate and assist its members in developing their own programs of public affairs.

Although the industry has a good sense of public image, it could improve. A recent survey conducted by Yankelovich, Shelley, and White for the American Forest Institute found that the public's perception of the forest products industry as socially responsible has seriously eroded. In 1978, 29 percent of the public felt that the industry has done a "good job" of behaving in a socially responsible manner; in 1979 this figure dropped to 21 percent. The industry thus slipped from the top to the middle of a group of twenty leading industries; broadcasting companies, banks, telephone companies, airlines, food companies, and drug companies were seen as superior performers.

Similarly, this study found a sharp reversal in the upward trend in the public's perception of the industry as a conserver of natural resources; its "good job" rating plunged from 34 to 26 percent. In fact, 46 percent of the public thinks that both forest products and oil have done a "poor job" in conserving natural resources. Both government officials (61 percent) and the media (48 percent) see the industry as exerting "undue influence" on government—a rating equaled only by the oil industry. Eighty percent of the public disagree with industry perceptions, believing that the primary purpose of national forests is to provide habitat for wildlife. Eighty percent of the public also feel that the federal government has allowed too much harvesting. Almost half the government officials surveyed believed that clear-cutting forests is subject to widespread abuse. The industry is generally seen as complying fairly well with pollution laws, but the public has maintained a strong interest in control of litter, ranking it right in behind inflation, energy, and pollution, and along with taxes, on a list of domestic issues for which corrective action has been suggested.[81] This has implications for solid waste and recycling legislation.

Thus, substantial gaps between how the public views things and the interests of industry remain. A survey focused on various interest groups and agencies might well suggest an even wider gap in expectations. Even more important are industry-level actions and the aggregate image of the industry projects for the relations between individual firms and particular stakeholders. While many of the public issues facing forest products companies are common to firms across the industry, the outcome of public negotiations may reflect a firm's specific fortunes as much as a cross-company shared fate. Many public issues exist at the firm level. Regulatory agencies, for example, take enforcement action against individual firms for noncompliance. Individual mills or firms must deal with local taxation and licensing authorities. The union locals in the industry are far more powerful than national leaders in labor disputes. Although company holdings are distributed unevenly across the states, the dramatic growth in regulation affects the internal operation of all plants and mills with equal vigor. Thus, company-specific pressures are evident.

Furthermore, even the industrywide issues affect individual firms differently. Interest in log exports or land taxation have a lot to do with a particular company's land-ownership profile. Similarly, forest product companies find different sorts of energy legislation attractive, depending on their biomass fuel potential, their generation of steam, and the oil reserve, gas reserve, and hydropower potential of their properties. Even the effects of regulation controlling air and water pollution depend on a company's product line, location, effluent systems, and antitrust compliance. Lastly, shareholder loyalty can be realistically nurtured only at the firm level.

As the forest products industry has grown from fragmented regional clusters into a well-integrated national system, the latitude of managerial discretion has become tempered by the increasing influence of public agents on the use of public resources. Market growth, technological development, and changing public expectations over the past century have caused corporate social behavior to shift through three phases. The original policy of unbridled resource exploitation shifted to prudent resource management, and now has shifted to a policy of mediating management and public interests. Accordingly, managerial prerogative has been eroded in each of the functional areas of the enterprise. The nature of these institutional responsibilities also cuts vertically through an industry's position, company strategy, and daily plant-level activities. Successful negotiation of management's interests and public interests requires both attentive listening and appropriate responses at each of these levels and across each of the functional areas. Public affairs are isolated from other business priorities not by the nature of the issues but by the training and perspective of the actors.

Endnotes

1. Norman Douglas Hungerford, "An Analysis of Forest Land Ownership on the United States Pulp and Paper Industry," Ph.D. dissertation, State University College of Forestry at Syracuse University (1969).
2. "Woodman, Don't Spare That Tree," *Newsweek* (June 25, 1979), p. 69.
3. Lee Smith, "The Neglected Promise of Our Forests," *Fortune* (Nov. 5, 1979), pp. 111–124.
4. Kathleen K. Wiegner, "America's Green Gold," *Forbes* (December 24, 1979), pp. 40–46.
5. William A. Duerr, *Timber: Problems, Prospects, Policies* (Ames: University of Iowa Press, 1973). Also Smith, "Neglected Promise."
6. Duerr, *Timber*.
7. Benjamin Slatin, "Economic Structure of the Paper Industry," *Technical Association of the Pulp and Paper Industry Journal*, 58 (July 1975).

8. A. J. Vaux, "Timber Resource Prospects," in Duerr, *Timber*.

9. Ralph R. Widner, "Supply and Consumers," in Duerr, *Timber*.

10. Samuel T. Dana, "Forestry Policies and Programs," in Duerr, *Timber*.

11. Smith, "Neglected Promise," Ivan P. Morgan and Robert A. Leone, in "The U.S. Timber Industry," Boston Industry Note 9-678-180, Intercollegiate Case Clearing House (Cambridge, Mass.: Harvard University Press, 1978). Also Weigner, "Green Gold"; *Newsweek*, "Woodman."

12. Luke Popovich, "Timber—A Supply Stock Problem," *Pulp and Paper* (June 1980), p. 41.

13. "Protecting Our Forests," *Sierra Club Forestry Bulletin*, No. 1 (Nov. 1979).

14. Luke Popovich, "Ah, Wilderness," *Pulp and Paper* (June 1979), p. 5. Also, "Agency Chief Outlines Approach to National Forest Management," *Forest Industries* (Oct. 1979), p. 28. Also "RARE II Wilderness Not Enough For State," *Forest Industries* (September 1979), p. 19; Luke Popovich, "Stakes Are Huge in California Lawsuit," *Forest Industries* (Oct. 1979), p. 9; Herbert Lambert, "Wilderness . . . Half a Tank Away," *Forest Industries* (October 1979), p. 4; "California Wins Ruling to Protect Wilderness Area," *Wall Street Journal* (January 11, 1980), p. 3. Merrill Sheik and William J. Cook, "The Alaskan Lands Battle," *Newsweek* (August 4, 1980), p. 50–51.

15. "Carter Ups Timber Sales Goal," *Pulp and Paper* (August 1979), p. 25.

16. Luke Popovich, "January 4—Beginning of the End?" *Forest Industries* (Feb. 1979), p. 4.

17. "Redwood Victory," *New York Times* (Oct. 11, 1968). Also Prakash, Sethi, "Georgia-Pacific Corporation," *Up Against the Corporate Wall* (New York: 1977).

18. "Dennis C. LeMaster and Terri S. Koester, "The Persuaders," *American Forests* (Oct. 1980).

19. *Ibid.*

20. Gordon Robinson, "The Loggers' Rape of Our National Forests," *Business and Society Review*, 30 (Summer 1979), p. 44.

21. John T. Curtis, "Modification of Grassland and Forest by Man," *Man's Impact on Environment*, Thomas R. Ketwiler (New York: McGraw-Hill, 1971).

22. William C. Osborn, *The Paper Plantation* (New York: Viking Press, 1974), pp. 184–185.

23. *Ibid.*

24. Brad Kennedy, "Protecting Wildlife," *New York Times* (January 13, 1980), p. C-23.

25. Bob Bledsoe, "Kiamichi Dilemma: What Price Progress?" *Tulsa Tribune* (Jan. 28, 1980), p. 1A–8A.

26. *Ibid.*

27. Bob Bledsoe, "Wildlife Protection Goal of His Campaign," *Tulsa Tribune* (Jan. 29, 1980), p. 8A.

28. Widner, "Supply," p. 40.

29. "Silvicultural Practices," *Sierra Club Forestry Bulletin*, no. 1 (Nov. 19, 1979).

30. "Fallout from Agent Orange Days a Herbicide," *Business Week* (March 24, 1980), p. 114. Also "California Standard Unit Settle Weed-Killer Dispute," *Wall Street Journal* (May 11, 1979), p. 3. Also Bernard Weinraub, "Pentagon Disputed on Exposure of GIs to Herbicide in Vietnam," *New York Times* (Nov. 22, 1979), p. 1.

31. *Environmental Impact Statement by the U.S. Department of Agriculture to the Council on Environmental Quality on 1973 Cooperative Spruce Budworm Control*

Project (April 12, 1973). Also "Paper Concern to Pay Damages to Gardeners Because of Herbicides," *New York Times* (Sept. 16, 1979), p. 8A.

32. Luke Popovich, "Whither Will Go RARE II Reorganization?" *Forest Industries* (Jan. 1979), pp. 9, 13.

33. Richard Pardo, "Washington Lookout," *American Forests*, 85 (Dec. 1979), pp. 9–10.

34. Pamela G. Hollie, "Northwest Timbermen Go South," *New York Times* (June 13, 1979), pp. D1 and D18.

35. Robert H. Cole, "Bodcaw Bought for $160 million," *New York Times* (May 9, 1979), p. 3.

36. Sheila Tefft, "GP Move May Not Be All Rosey," *Atlanta Constitution* (Jan 24, 1979).

37. A. W. Nelson, in William A. Duerr, *Timber: Problems, Prospects, Policies* (Ames: University of Iowa Press, 1973), p. 54.

38. George D. Davis, Coordinator U.S. Forest Service (RARE II Region), *American Forests* (August, 1980).

39. Morgan and Leone, "U.S. Timber," p. 11.

40. Osborn, *Paper Plantation.*

41. "Worst Advice Issued on Wood Dust Production," *International Woodworker* (Jan. 31, 1979), 44, p. 1. Also, "Wood Preservatives—Hazards and Precautions," *Workers Compensation Board News* (May–June 1976), pp. 4–5; John Gregg, "Chain Saw Vibration," *International Woodworker* (May 26, 1978), pp. 1–3; Verna Ledger, "The Great Unknown—Are We Guinea Pigs?" *Western Canadian Lumber Worker* (March 1979), pp. 1–2; Morris Davis, "Hazards of Logging and Sawmill Operations," *Monitor*, Labor Occupational Health Program, Univ. of California, Berkeley (June–July 1976), pp. 4–5.

42. "Wage and Benefit Gains," *Pacific Northwest Lumber and Wood Products Industry, 1915–1976* (Portland, OR International Woodworkers of America, 1977).

43. Anthony Bianco, "What's Next for the Rebel Paper Union," *Willamette Week* (June 15, 1979). Also, "Long West Coast Paper Strike Ends," *Pulp and Paper* (June 1979), p. 12.

44. "Joint Northwest Bargaining Planned," *Pulp and Paper* (June 1980), p. 19. Also "UPIW More Vocal on Guidelines," *Pulp and Paper* (June 1979), p. 9; "Potlach, Union End 7-month Strike," *Pulp and Paper* (June 1980), p. 19; "ICZ, IP Settle: Two Mills Still Out," *Pulp and Paper* (Feb. 1980), p. 19.

45. "Productivity and Average Hourly Earnings in the Paper Industry, 1965–1975," *Employment and Earnings*, American Paper Institute (1976). Also Eugene Floyd, Richard Levitan, and Robert Leone, "The Pulp and Paper Industry in the United States," Boston Intercollegiate Case Clearing House, 9-678-186 (Cambridge, Mass.: Harvard University Press, 1978); Charles Wolf and Jean Volley, "Mechanization Bringing Broad Changes in Makeup of Labor Force in Logging," *Forest Industries* (Sept. 1976).

46. "UPIW Talks Merged With OCAW," *Pulp and Paper* (June 1980), p. 19.

47. "Community Unemployment Impact from Anticipated Pulp Paper Mill Closures," Report to Economic Development Administration, U.S. Dept. of Commerce (Oct. 1972).

48. Hungerford, "Analysis of Forest Land Ownership," p. 139.

49. Kathryn Christinson, "Northwest Timber Areas Hit by Housing Slump and Shortage of Trees," *Wall Street Journal* (October 12, 1980), p. 1.

50. "It's Recession Plus in the Forest," *Business Week* (June 2, 1980), pp. 98–99. Also "Lumber Industry in Steep Slump," *New York Times* (April 17, 1980), p. D1.

51. Victor S. Kamder, "When Corporations Get Up and Leave Town," *New York Times* (June 10, 1980), p. D16.

52. "Victims Desure Benefits," *International Woodworker*, 9 (August 1979), p. 1.

53. Dave Pease, "Log Exports: Dilemma with NO Solutions," *Forest Industries* (Oct. 1979), p. 7. Also Rolf D. Gerlum, "Questions and Answers about Log Exports," *Portland Magazine*, No. 6 (Nov. 1979), pp. 39–41.

54. Osborn, *Paper Plantation*, pp. 37–38.

55. Osborn, *Paper Plantation*, p. 103.

56. "Pollution Expense," *Pulp and Paper*, No. 50 (May 1976), pp. 92–94.

57. "Pollution Spending on the Rise," *Pulp and Paper* (August 1979), p. 27.

58. "EPA Beginning to Look at Acid Rain," *Pulp and Paper* (June 1980), p. 29.

59. "EPA Proposes Added Air Penalties," *Pulp and Paper* (May 1979), p. 25.

60. Luke Popovich, "Haste, Too Makes Waste," *Pulp and Paper* (July 1979), p. 35. Also Luke Popovich, "Hazards of the Superfund," *Pulp and Paper* (August 1979), p. 22.

61. *Clean Air: Costs and Trade-offs*, League of Women Voters, 167 (1978). Also "The Environmental Revolution," *National Voter*, 30, 1 (1980).

62. Claire Spiegel, "New Industrial Construction in State Banned," *Los Angeles Times* (August 25, 1979), p. 1.

63. Editorial, "Cost of Defiance," *Arizona Republic* (Aug. 30, 1979), p. A6.

64. Cited in "Environmental Regulations: Cost or Benefit," *National Voter*, 39, League of Women Voters (Nov. 1, 1980).

65. "U.S. Moves to Enforce Laws on Pollution," *Wall Street Journal* (Oct. 3, 1979), p. 21.

66. Slatin, "Economic Structure," p. 59.

67. Luke Popovich, "Windfall Energy Savings," *Pulp and Paper* (May 1980), p. 33.

68. "Business for Depression Tax Changes," *Washington Report* (Oct. 1, 1979), p. 9.

69. "Mead Corp. Says Holders Are Opposed to Occidental's Offer," *Wall Street Journal* (Oct. 17, 1978), p. 16. Also Agis Salpukis, "Born Again Mead Paper Leads Revival," *New York Times* (March 18, 1979), p. F7.

70. Robert J. Cole, "Battle for Diamond Intensified" (May 12, 1980), p. D1. Also "Cavenhan Unit Bids Diamond," *Pulp and Paper* (June 1980), p. 8.

71. "The Hammermill Tug-of-War," *Business Day* (May 1, 1980), p. D1. Also "Hammermill Takes Proxy Vote," *Pulp and Paper* (June 1980), p. 6; "Hammermill Readies its Icahn Defenses," *Business Week* (May 5, 1980), p. 48.

72. Laurie Heisler, "Making It in Investor Relations," *Institutional Investor* (March 1980), pp. 27–40.

73. "Paper Industry a Winner at Gatt."

74. "COWPS Closely Watching Paper," *Pulp and Paper* (June 1979), p. 24.

75. Jean A. Briggs, "For Whom Does the Bell Toll," *Forbes* (June 25, 1979), pp. 33–35.

76. Morris S. Thompson, "Aids of Box-Making Concerns Sentenced to Prison, Fined, in Price Fixing Case," *Wall Street Journal* (Dec. 1, 1976), p. 4.

77. "Carton Makers Settle Suit," *Pulp and Paper* (August 1979), p. 19. Also "Carton Producers Clear Plan to Settle Price Fixing Suit," *Wall Street Journal* (June 29, 1979), p. 21.

78. "Acquittals in Corrugated Case But Civil Settlement Costly," *Pulp and Paper* (June 1979), p. 1, 7.

79. Edward Cowan "Bill Backing Anti-trust Suits Gains," *New York Times* (May 9, 1979), p. D1. Also "Grand Jury Probe Concluded," *Pulp and Paper* (August 1979), p. 19; "When Lawyers Dictate the Limits of Marketing," *Business Week* (July 14, 1980), p. 76.

80. Jeffrey Sonnenfeld and Paul R. Lawrence, "Why Do Companies Succumb to Price Fixing?" *Harvard Business Review*, 56 (July–August 1978), pp. 145–157.

81. Yankelovich, Skelly, and White, *Public Policy Pressures on the Forest Products Industry*, prepared for the American Forest Institute (1979).

Chapter 8

DEPARTMENTS AS RECEPTORS

The portrait of public affairs complexity in the forest products industry shows merely a sample of the various influential constituents with whom industry executives must interact. A company's ability to hear and understand the nature of the claims of each set of constituents is related to the company's structure for receiving and processing that information. Further, the sensitivity of this structure to external stakeholder groups varies by company.

Before investigating company differences in receptivity, we first looked at differences among departments as receptors across the total sample. Executives tend to view the world through a bias from their own particular functions. Membership in a particular department influences one's commitment to public affairs. The overall corporate sensory structure is important for encouraging a wide view of the public affairs landscape. Lack of a proper structure may lead to overemphasis of various departmental perspectives and hence blur company vision. The potential of a department either as an information receptor or as an information blinder can best be understood by inspecting the dominant orientation of the executives in each department. We shall look at ten departments, with particular focus on eight, each of which makes up at least 5 percent of the total sample. They are, in order of size, general management (18 percent), government relations (18 percent), human resources (15 percent), public relations (13 percent), engineering (10 percent), finance (9 percent), legal (7 percent), and public affairs (5 percent).

Interaction with Stakeholders

It is possible to imagine each of these departments with substantial responsibility for interaction with constituents. For example, general management might be expected to represent the company to outside

127

groups with interests that cut broadly across the company, such as trade associations, legislators, and local officials. Government relations, with primary responsibility for lobbying and political analysis, would be very heavily involved with legislators and regulators. Human resource executives would have good reason to become heavily involved with labor unions and regulators (OSHA, Dept. of Labor, EEOC, IRS, ERISA). It would be expected that public relations, as the corporate mouthpiece, would be in close contact with the press, with civic groups, and with harsh external critics (for example, environmentalists and labor unions). Engineering executives might have substantial contact with professional associations, outside experts (advisors), and regulators (EPA, OSHA). The finance department might also be involved with regulators (SEC, IRS, and the like) as well as the investment community. The legal department might get involved with a diverse set of regulators over interpretations of guidelines, and over licenses and permits, and also with unions over labor disputes.

Interaction Time

While the actual reported time involvement with stakeholder groups was substantial in every department, there were significant differences among the departments; Table 8-1 indicates the allotment. For example, while general-management executives reported that interactions with stakeholders accounted for as much as roughly a quarter of the average work week (12 hours), government-affairs executives claimed that such activities account for over three quarters of the average work week (34 hours). Glancing down the second column of Table 8-1, ("Interaction Time with Stakeholders") one sees clearly that the other departments relating to public affairs, such as public relations and legal, also spent more time interacting with stakeholders than the other departments.

More insight on this sharp difference between the use of time in public affairs versus non-public affairs departments is illustrated pictorially in Figure 8-1 and statistically in Table 8-2. While it would be expected that executives for public affairs would spend more time in public activities than executives not directly concerned with public affairs, this classification by stakeholder groups is revealing in its detail. Most outstanding in this analysis is the sharpness of the differentiation between public affairs executives and non–public affairs executives relative to the first several stakeholder groups. The five stakeholder groups (industry associations, state legislators, the U.S. Congress, environmentalists, and the press) are significantly more prominent in the schedules of executives concerned with public affairs than in the schedules of other executives ($p < .001$). Primary responsibility for

Table 8-1 Departmental Receptivity

	Percentage of Sample	Interaction Time with Stakeholders (ave. no. hr. in public affairs contact)[a]	Breadth (no. of outside contacts)[a]	Appreciation (information)[b]	Attention (total boundary spanning)[c]	Listenership (information flow rate)[d]
Government relations	18	33.81	15.81	2.17	24.04	1.06
Public affairs	5	32.14	15.43	1.92	22.86	1.05
Public relations	13	24.28	10.83	4.36	22.00	0.95
Legal	7	16.40	12.90	7.87	20.40	1.37
Engineering/environment	10	15.86	8.43	13.64	19.36	0.97
Planning	2	14.00	10.00	8.69	19.50	1.37
Human resources	15	13.29	7.76	10.84	18.45	1.25
General management	18	11.92	8.61	12.82	21.08	1.12
Finance	9	10.83	7.42	8.72	19.36	1.01
Line officials	4	7.20	5.20	16.81	16.60	1.12
Total Sample Mean		19.22	10.53	8.05	20.39	1.09
F (value)		5.3	3.64	2.52	4.16	2.03
df (degrees of freedom)		(9,137)	(9,138)	(9,113)	(9,138)	(9,115)
Significance		$p < .001$	$p < .01$	$p < .05$	$p < .001$	$p = 0$

[a] Average per executive within department.
[b] Units equal the information value of stakeholder contacts divided by the time in such interactions.
[c] Units equal the sum of average boundary spanning ratings within a department, ranging from 6 (not at all) to 30 (a great deal).
[d] Ratio of information inflow to information outflow.

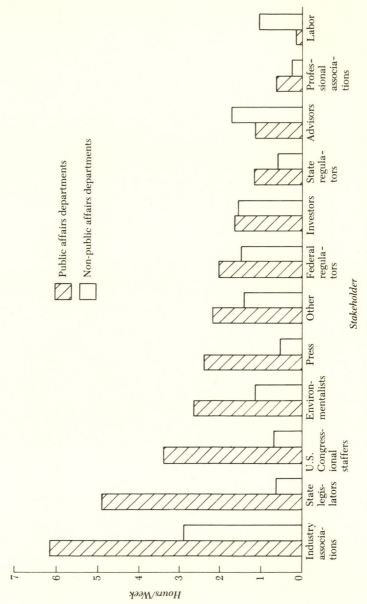

Figure 8-1 Interaction Time with Stakeholders. (See Table 8-1 for comparative statistics.)

Table 8-2 Interaction Time with Stakeholders by Departments

Stakeholder Group (Ordered by public affairs interaction time)	Public Affairs (hr./wk.)	Non–Public Affairs (hr./wk.)	Significance[a] (F value)
Industry associations	6.18	2.95	10.60[b]
State legislators	4.95	0.62	40.00[b]
U.S. Congress	3.45	0.63	21.00[b]
Environmentalists	2.68	1.15	11.90[b]
Press	2.33	0.49	12.70[b]
Other (such as local and civic)	2.07	1.23	NS
Federal regulators	1.98	1.26	NS
Investment community	1.57	1.41	NS
State regulators	1.12	0.56	NS
Advisors (such as consultants and institutes)	1.02	1.62	5.05[c]
Professional associations	0.62	0.22	6.53[c]
Labor	0.13	1.09	NS
TOTAL	28.07	12.67	30.80[b]
	N = 60	N = 81	

NOTE: Public affairs departments include legal, public relations, and government affairs departments, and the public affairs departments per se. Non-public affairs departments include general management, line operations, finance, planning, engineering, and human resources departments.
[a] Degrees of freedom (1,139). [b] $p < .001$ [c] $p < .05$.

interacting with regulatory bodies and the investment community is far more blurred, and the involvement with advisors and labor unions may even be greater for executives in non–public affairs. It is possible that the first five stakeholder groups involve activities in which the company is more involved in an effort to maintain its image as well as to respond to more general external challenges. The other activities, however, may represent more specialized, technical interaction, where functional expertise becomes vital. Thus non–public affairs departments would tend to get more involved in more specific interaction with stakeholders.

This possibility is supported in Figure 8-2*a* and Figure 8-2*b*. First, in Figure 8-2*a*, we see that stakeholders who are concerned with specific issues (for instance the investment community and labor and professional associations) do not have much to do with individual public affairs department. This is not true across non–public affairs departments. Figure 8-2*b* suggests that non–public affairs departments may specialize in a particular stakeholder group or two (for example, engineering executives may specialize in regulators, human resource executives in labor unions, and finance executives in the investment community).

Two final observations on stakeholder interaction with departments comment on both the departments and the stakeholder groups. First, whether a department has overt, broad responsibility for public affairs or not, interactions with stakeholders represents an important time commitment. Executives from each department acknowledge important outside constituents. Second, it is interesting to note the relative lack of attention given to state regulators and labor unions. Either the industry feels that the interests of these groups are easy to understand or else these groups have far less power than other stakeholder groups. Neither conclusion seems justified from our earlier analysis.

There is no reason to believe that the amounts of time a department spends in interaction with stakeholders is an index to the quality of information reception. Various stakeholders may be overlooked while others are overemphasized. Furthermore, this time spent in interacting with stakeholders may be for buffering rather than getting information. Studying the time involvement is helpful in understanding the bias inherent in executive roles. Because the types of stakeholder contact are so different for the various groups, the internal perspectives on public issues are likely to be diverse. Thus, some departments are technically specialized in public affairs and others are oriented towards involvement in politics and communications. Whether such differences are vital inputs from diverse receptors or uncritical restatement of a departmental bias depends on the unit receptivity as defined in the model we have proposed (Chapter 4).

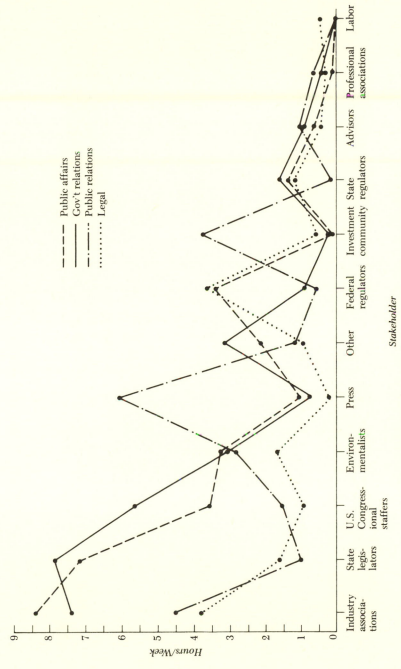

Stakeholder

Figure 8-2a Public Affairs Departments: Interaction with Stakeholders.

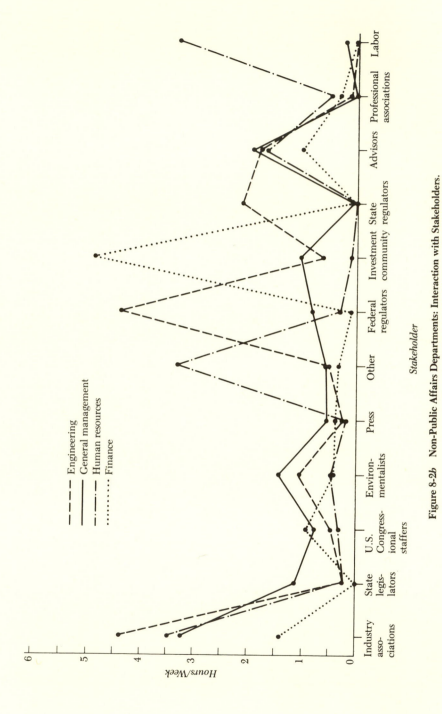

Figure 8-2b   Non-Public Affairs Departments: Interaction with Stakeholders.

Breadth of Interaction

The first of the receptivity dimensions, *breadth*, refers to the distribution of potential sources.* A further inspection of the profiles of interaction with stakeholders for each department (Figures 8-2a and 8-2b) suggests that some departments have a wide array of channels to the outside and others have a few, significant channels. In an actual count of the number of stakeholder channels for each department (interaction of 1 hr./week or greater), the differences among departments turn out to be significant ($F = 3.64$, $df = 9,138$, $p < .001$). The scores for each department appear in Table 8-1 and are presented pictorially in Figure 8-3. These data show the public affairs departments with far more channels to the outside. Non–public affairs departments also make a good showing.

Appreciation

Thus far we have seen that public affairs executives, compared with other executives, spend more time with outside stakeholders and interact with a wide variety of stakeholders. It would be erroneous, however, to conclude that these departments necessarily receive more information from the outside as a consequence of these interactions. In fact, an examination of the use of time with stakeholders as an information source suggests just the opposite conclusion.

Thus, outside stakeholders as information sources measure lower for public affairs departments than for non–public affairs departments. This is demonstrated in Table 8-1 and Figure 8-4. These departments were compared by a score for the "appreciation" of the information potential of time spent on public affairs. This is calculated by dividing the aggregated reported value of various outside sources (listed on the questionnaire) by the time spent in interaction with such sources. The non–public affairs departments clearly surpassed the public affairs departments in willingness to appreciate the information value of time spent with outside stakeholders (see Figure 8-4). Since Figures 8-3, receptor breadth, and 8-4, appreciation, are essentially inverses, it is not surprising to find department scores in these two areas negatively correlated ($r = -.52$, $p < .001$). Therefore, although executives in general management, human resources, engineering, and finance spend less time dealing with outsiders, what time they do spend tends to be in gathering information.

It is an important aside to this discussion of information sources that

---

* This was measured by averaging the number of different outside sources with which a particular executive spent at least an hour a week.

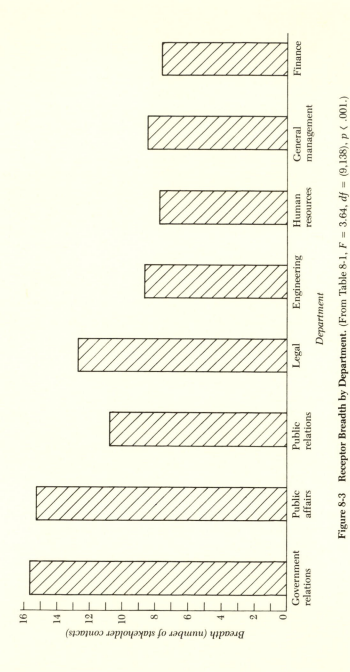

Figure 8-3   Receptor Breadth by Department. (From Table 8-1, $F = 3.64$, $df = (9,138)$, $p < .001$.)

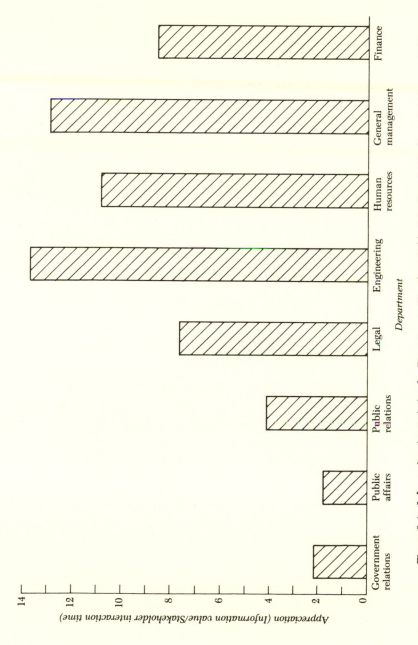

Figure 8-4 Information Appreciation by Department. (Based on Table 8-1, $F = 2.57$, $df = (9,113)$, $p < .05$.)

Table 8-3   Rank Order of Value of Information Sources

Rank Order	Information Sources	Average Rating (1 = low, 5 = high)
1	Within the company	4.021
2	Trade associations	3.246
3	*Wall Street Journal*	3.207
4	Trade contacts	2.761
5	*Business Week*	2.619
6	Professional press	2.556
7	Broadcasting	2.546
8	Government contacts	2.526
9	Popular press	2.481
10	Business research organizations	2.478
11	Books	2.256
12	*Fortune*	2.234
13	Government publications	2.328
14	Trade press	2.321
15	*Forbes*	2.210
16	Consultants	2.197
17	*New York Times*	2.09
18	*Duns*	2.007
19	Public interest groups	1.985
20	Environmentalist publications	1.978
21	*Harvard Business Review*	1.884
22	Investor community	1.733
23	Environmental contacts	1.706
24	Labor contacts	1.453
25	Labor publications	1.380

these sources could be classified either by stakeholder group or by closeness of contact. The departments did not differ significantly in either of these two categories, but the findings support such distinction. Thus in the first classification, the sources were positively related by stakeholder interest (ranging from $r = .30$ to .50, $p < .01$, two-tailed). Examples of such groupings are trade associations and the trade press, environmental publications and direct contact with environmentalists, and direct contact with government officials and government publications).

The second grouping, while still not significantly different across departments, unveiled an interesting characteristic about gathering information on public affairs. Regardless of departmental affiliation, executives tended to prefer impersonal information media rather than direct sources. Two rough source clusters seemed evident in that several popular and professional press sources such as the *New York Times*, the *Harvard Business Review*, trade publications, and the broadcast media were inversely related to sources such as the use of trade associations, trade contacts, internal sources, and environmentalist contacts ($r = -.13$ to $-.18$, $p < .005$, two-tailed). Within each of these clusters, we found positive relations ($r = .56$ and $r = .33$, for primary and secondary sources respectively, $p < .005$, two-tailed). Table 8-3 shows this ranking of preferred sources. The values on this list are widely distributed and a comparison of the values of the top third of the list with values in the bottom third suggest that the general order is significant ($F = 20.9$, $df = 130$, $p < .001$, two-tailed). This list shows strong preference for indirect (impersonal) sources of information.

Attention

The next two receptor dimensions were constructed from an analysis of department descriptions of the purpose of their boundary spanning. It is clear from the data in Table 8-1 that the amount of time spent in spanning the boundary with public affairs was more highly valued by executives in government relations, public relations, and general management. Thus, these departments gave greater *attention* to public issues ($F = 4.16$, $df = 130$, $p < .001$).

Further insight can be gained through the detailed analysis in Table 8-4. First we see that the lawyers tended to lag behind the other public affairs departments in the intensity in which they engaged in each of the boundary-spanning categories. The lawyers seemed less inclined to cross the company boundary on their own initiative. Second, the non-public affairs departments excel only in activity, called transacting, with market-relevant resources. This distinctly different set of findings for "transacting" versus the other boundary-spanning activities is consistent, then, with the matrix correlating the boundary spanning role. This matrix showed a moderate correlation with pairs of the first five dimensions in boundary spanning ($r = .60$ on the average, $p < .001$), but a lack of significant relation to transacting.

Listenership

The general outward focus manifested by the *attention* scores of public affairs departments can be further analyzed by examining the information flow from the outside to the inside. While executives may devote much attention to public affairs, their attention could be directed towards receiving information (listening) or sending information (projection). The relative magnitude of the listening activities can be ascer-

Table 8–4   Boundary Spanning by Department

Department	Representing	Protecting	Monitoring	Scanning	Transmitting	Transacting
Legal	2.90	3.50	3.80	3.70	3.90	2.60
Finance	3.92	3.00	3.08	3.33	3.00	2.73
Planning	4.00	2.00	3.50	4.56	3.00	2.56
General management	3.35	3.42	3.86	3.57	3.46	4.06
Government relations	4.27	4.42	4.64	4.42	4.50	1.73
Line	2.80	2.80	3.00	3.20	2.00	2.80
Public relations	4.61	3.72	3.83	4.00	3.88	1.89
Human resources	2.95	3.15	3.45	3.75	3.40	1.75
Technical	3.14	3.71	3.06	3.64	3.50	2.36
Public affairs	4.13	3.86	4.29	4.14	4.14	2.29
F value	5.81	3.14	5.49	2.31	4.18	6.86
df (degrees of freedom)	(9,130)	(1,130)	(9,136)	(9,130)	(9,129)	(9,129)
Significance	$p < .001$	$p = .002$	$p < .001$	$p = .019$	$p < .001$	$p < .001$

NOTE: The numbers reflect average department ratings in the dimensions defined by the column headings. The ratings were made on a scale from 1 (not at all) to 5 (a great deal).

tained by comparing listening to projection. Thus the ratio of receiving information to projecting information is a helpful index. A low figure would indicate that the unit in question functioned more as a corporate orator than a listener. The scores on this variable, as presented in Table 8-1, suggested that public affairs executives (except for lawyers) tended to be worse listeners than non–public affairs executives ($F = 2.03$, $df = 9,130$; $p < .05$). Those charged with understanding public constituencies may have a very one-sided comprehension of key issues.

Conclusions

Several interesting departmental differences within the sample were uncovered in this discussion. Departments were compared by (1) the time spent in contact with outsiders, (2) the breadth of contact with different outsiders, (3) the appreciation of outsiders as information sources, and (4) two qualities of departments' boundary-spanning efforts—underlying conscious attention to the outside and readiness to listen to signals. Certain general characteristics of stakeholder contact and information sources apply across the departmental level of the sample. For example, most departments put time into trade association activities and with legislators, while state regulators, unions, and professional associations were given relatively little time. Executives strongly prefer impersonal sources. Finally, substantial differences exist in the perspectives of departments within the surveyed companies.

This reporting should not, however, obscure the observation that activities on public affairs were far from incidental to any type of executive. No department allotted less than 25 percent of the average work week to interactions with stakeholders. Each department maintained contact with at least seven stakeholder groups. Finally, every department reported that it recognized more than a fair amount of responsibility for boundary-spanning activities.

Some of the sharpest differences appeared between public affairs departments (government affairs, public affairs, legal, and public relations), and non–public relations departments (general management, human resources, engineering, and finance). Public affairs executives tended to spend far more time in interaction with outside stakeholder groups and maintained contact with many more outside constituents. Furthermore, these executives recognized a greater responsibility for public affairs.

Non–public affairs executives were more issue-specific in their interacting with stakeholders. They also were more likely to acquire information from their efforts for two reasons. First, non–public affairs executives valued their time with stakeholders more highly as a source of information. Second, non–public affairs executives tended to see their role more as a listener than as a disseminator.

This differentiation seems to bring company executives into contact with public issues for different reasons and in different ways. Public affairs executives as protectors of the institutional boundary may have a more general interest in stakeholder challenges. Non–public affairs executives, however, have different functional concerns (for example, marketing, operations, and engineering), and hence may be more interested in the resolution of only the particular issues that interfere with these concerns. A company should want strong performance in receiving both types of stimuli. Qualities such as a broad view of the public environment as well as the ability to listen carefully to specialized challenges should not be mutually exclusive qualities even if company departments are not generally equally strong in these areas. In the forest products industry, effective management of public affairs cannot be anchored strictly with the trade associations and the general press at the expense of attention to regulators, unions, and other interest groups.

Thus, in the language of the model proposed (Chapter 4), we have demonstrated that various company departments, like specialized sensory receptors, act to detect different signals from the environment. Biased readings of the environment are understandable from the differences in executive training, stakeholder exposure, and organizational responsibilities among departments. This sort of differentiation may capitalize on internal expertise but if this information remains in the receptor units, companywide perceptions of the outside are fragmentary and distorted. This information must eventually be centrally coordinated, as in the human sensory system.

Chapter 9

STRUCTURAL SENSITIVITY OF
THE COMPANIES

A companywide system is needed for receiving and processing information about public affairs. Forest products companies are immersed in a stormy sea of external critics. Each company must navigate its own passage through these waters. Some public issues affect a whole industry and some are specific to a firm. Interpretation of the issues, however, is not necessarily consistent within a firm. Executive vantages are systematically biased by departmental activities. Thus, each company's perception of public affairs and responsiveness thereto is affected by the company's structural sensitivity to the environment; a particular department must not distort its vision. Accordingly, let us examine the structural sensitivity of each company of our study as measured through three proposed features: departmental *receptivity*, public affairs *influence*, and internal *integration*.

Departmental Receptivity

Interacting with Stakeholders

Our proposed perceptual model for involvement in public affairs outlines five qualities obviously needed for *receptivity*: (1) the *breadth* of outside contacts, (2) the *appreciation* of the information potential of outside contacts, (3) the *attention* given to spanning the boundary to public affairs, (4) the emphasis on *listenership*, and (5) the *depth* of involvement in issues. Beyond these five qualities are the deliberate efforts company executives make toward receptivity. These deliberate efforts can be measured by the time executives reportedly spend in stakeholder interactions. Because our findings indicated that there is not much association between such time allotments and receptivity, we

143

shall hold this measurement of the quantity of interaction time apart from the dimensions of receptivity, the quality of this interaction time.

In looking at time spent in interaction, as diagrammed in Figure 9-1, we can surmise that the companies with a high interaction, such as Northwest Forests, Pacific Timber, and U.S. Paper, consistently give substantial effort to activities across stakeholder groups. The companies investing less effort in such activities showed some evidence of more specific use of time (like American Forests' commitment to the investment community or New York Paper's commitment to environmentalists). Pacific Timber executives devoted substantially more time to these interactions and New York Paper spent far less time ($p < .01$ on pairwise comparisons). One of the most dramatic aspects of this diagram, however, is the tremendous amount of time Northwest Paper devoted to interaction with public affairs. As you can also see by inspecting the actual numbers for contact time, in almost every type of outside contact, Northwest Forests ranks at the top. It is true that the sample from Northwest Forests was somewhat underrepresented by general management (13 percent in this company versus an average of 22 percent in the total sample). This company's interaction with stakeholders, however, remained strong even when company comparisons that eliminated general management responses were made. Therefore, the differences were not due to overrepresentation of executives for public affairs. In the full sample, for instance, they spent triple the time of any other company in contact with labor unions; and when we inspect just staff groups, we find that they spend five to ten times as many hours as any other company. Only American Forests exceeded Northwest Forests in contact time with the investment community. Similarly, only Pacific Timber exceeded the amount of time that Northwest Forests spent with environmentalists.

This extreme difference in the companies is best viewed in the figures on total time spent in such activity. Whether we consider either the entire set of respondents (Table 9-1a) or the set limited to staff members (Table 9-1b), Northwest Forests executives reported spending roughly 30 hours a week in public affairs contact. This is approximately a third more than the second-highest group, Pacific Timber, and fully twice as much as the lowest companies. Furthermore, the two least active companies, New York Paper and American Forests, were quite far below the other four.

Despite the control for interference in the response rate by general management, one might still be concerned about the overrepresentation of public affairs executives in Northwest Forests and U.S. Paper (67 and 62 percent, respectively, with a sample mean of 43 percent). The information in Table 9-1c, however, may mollify such concern. There was no significant difference in the interaction times for public

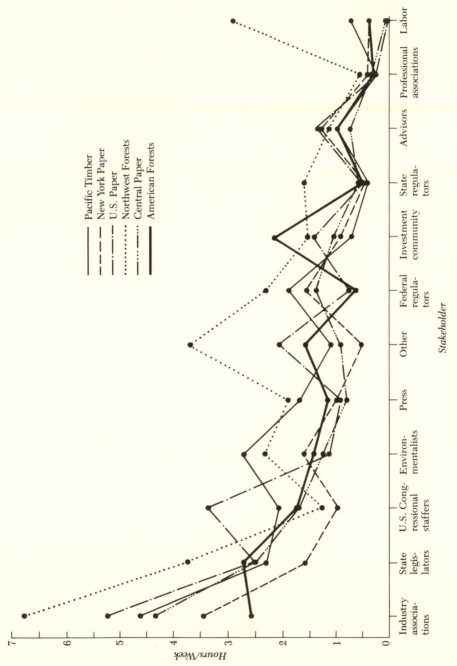

Figure 9-1 Company-Stakeholder Interaction Profiles.

Table 9-1a   Interaction Time with Stakeholders by the Entire Firm

	Pacific Timber	New York Paper	Central Paper	Northwest Forests	American Forests	U.S. Paper
Investment community	0.63	1.11	1.17	1.93	2.35	1.52
Professional associations	0.26	0.39	0.33	0.60	0.36	0.57
Industry associations	4.63	3.46	4.30	6.67	2.57	5.38
U.S. Congress	2.00	0.93	1.74	1.20	1.74	3.48
State legislators	2.37	1.61	2.56	3.73	2.61	2.52
Federal regulators	2.04	1.75	1.56	2.67	0.78	0.81
State regulators	.56	0.61	0.74	2.07	0.65	0.67
Environmentalists	2.74	1.71	1.33	2.40	1.43	1.29
Advisors	1.26	1.60	1.00	1.47	1.26	1.67
Press	1.70	1.04	0.74	2.13	1.35	1.05
Labor	0.81	0.39	0.15	3.20	0.39	0.10
Other	1.26	0.57	1.04	3.93	1.70	2.29
TOTAL	19.87	15.18	17.19	29.53	16.83	21.71

NOTE: Contact units are in hours per week.

Table 9-1b Interaction Time with Stakeholders by Staff Groups

	Pacific Timber	New York Paper	Central Paper	Northwest Forests	American Forests	U.S. Paper
Investment community	0.65	0.86	2.00	1.92	2.78	1.56
Professional associations	0.35	0.52	0.47	0.69	0.39	0.67
Industry associations	5.85	3.90	5.68	6.15	2.83	4.83
U.S. Congress	2.55	1.00	2.32	1.38	2.11	3.72
State legislators	2.75	1.67	3.16	4.31	3.11	2.61
Federal regulators	2.60	1.95	1.74	2.62	0.78	0.94
State regulators	0.75	0.67	0.95	2.38	0.83	0.50
Environmentalists	3.05	1.19	1.53	2.69	1.56	1.00
Advisors	1.35	1.43	1.00	1.39	1.11	1.61
Press	2.00	1.19	0.89	2.46	1.61	1.17
Labor	0.85	0.38	0.05	3.69	0.50	0.00
Other	1.70	0.76	1.20	4.15	1.84	2.61
TOTAL	23.90	15.62	21.26	31.00	19.11	21.44

Table 9-1c   Company Stakeholder Interaction Time by Department (hours per week)

Company	Public Affairs Executives	Non–Public Affairs Executives	Significance[a] (F value)
Pacific Timber	36.82	8.23	21.42[d]
New York Paper	17.00	14.32	.17
Central Paper	28.22	11.67	6.55[b]
Northwest Forests	28.10	32.40	.25
American Forests	29.44	8.71	9.39[c]
U.S. Paper	27.17	13.63	3.32
TOTAL SAMPLE	28.07	12.67	30.30[d]
Significance (F value)	.95	3.83	
	(1,60)	(1,34)	
	NS	NS	

NOTE: Public affairs departments include legal, public affairs, government relations, and public relations departments. Non–public affairs departments include general management, finance, line operations, engineering, and human resources departments.
[a] $df = (1,140)$, [b] $p < .05$, [c] $p < .01$, [d] $p < .001$.

affairs executives across the companies. There were very significant differences in these times across non–public affairs executives ($F = 3.83$, $df = 1,79$, $p < .001$). Therefore the company-stakeholder interaction times are not likely to have been caused by response patterns. Non–public affairs people at both Northwest Forests and U.S. Paper spent far more time interacting with the public. It is quite striking that while the public affairs executives (legal, public relations, government relations) in Northwest Forests spend only an average amount of time for such departments in interaction with public affairs, non–public affairs executives spend anywhere from two to four times as much in such activity ($p < .001$, two-tailed on pairwise t comparisons). This further corroborates the observation that there is something different in the way Northwest Forests manages its relation to public affairs.

These data suggest a poor differentiation or separation of responsibility across departments. Figures 9-2a and 9-2b suggest that this lack of differentiation is apparent also at New York Paper and U.S. Paper. Pacific Timber, on the other hand, seemed extremely well differentiated by time use, followed by American Forests and Central Paper. Perhaps poor differentiation exists when public affairs are seen as a primary responsibility of non–public affairs executives, or when the public affairs executives are not trusted, or finally when the whole company tends to get involved in reacting to crises.

Thus there may be three important characteristics indicated in this time allocation. First, it is possible that three companies, Pacific Timber, Northwest Forests, and U.S. Paper, spend much more time in

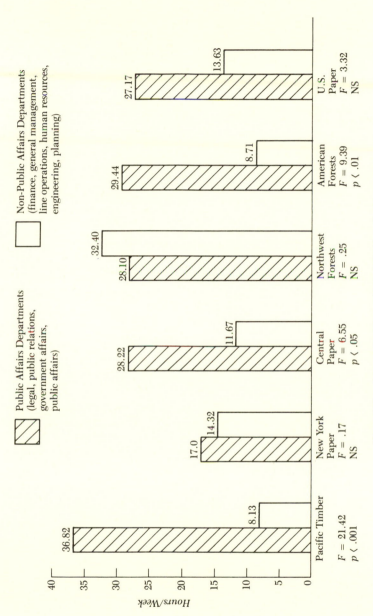

Figure 9-2a Interaction Time with Stakeholders (by Company).

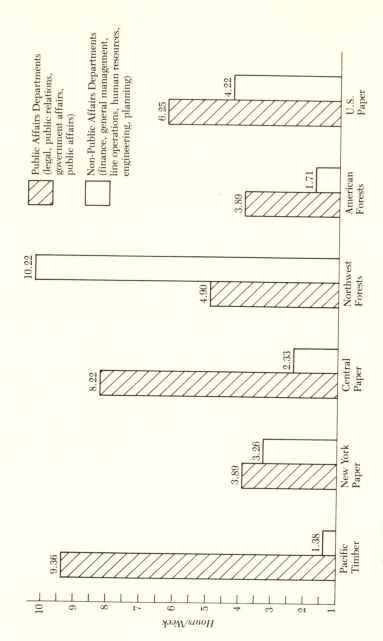

Figure 9-2b Interaction Time Spent in Industry Trade Associations (by Company). ($F = 2.76$; $p < .005$.)

interaction with stakeholders. Second, it seemed likely that throughout the company, Northwest Timber is highly oriented towards interaction with stakeholders. Finally, it seemed probable that public affairs executives are well differentiated from non–public affairs executives in this activity in Pacific Timber and American Forests.

This differentiation between public affairs and non–public affairs departments may enhance a company's receptivity in that through the differentiation of tasks, there is greater clarity of executive roles, and hence the opportunity for systematically tracking much information. A different possibility is that more receptive companies can afford the luxury of specialization. Less receptive companies have waited so long that the issues now threaten many company officials.

Breadth of Contact

The above three sets of inferences on interaction are supported by the first receptivity measure, breadth of contact. By scoring each company for the number of different stakeholders with which it maintained contact (more than 1 hour a week of contact), rather than the number of hours, we see distinctions like those in the last chapter's discussion of departmental differences. This information on the number of outside contacts (breadth), as it appears in Table 9-2, separated the companies into high and low groups. Further, this table demonstrated that executives in both public affairs and non–public affairs maintained equally large numbers of outside contacts. Finally, Pacific Timber and American Forests showed the greatest differentiation in such activities be-

Table 9-2 Breadth by Company, Measured by Average Number of Stakeholder Contacts Per Company

Company	Entire Sample	Public Affairs Executives	Non–Public Affairs Executives
Pacific Timber (PT)	10.52	16.91	6.13
New York Paper (NYP)	9.68	11.89	8.63
Central Paper (CP)	9.37	13.33	7.39
Northwest Forests (NF)	16.47	16.50	16.40
American Forests (AF)	7.96	11.00	6.00
U.S. Paper (USP)	11.76	12.92	10.13
High Group = 12.35 (PT, NF, USP)	$F = 2.06$ $df = (5,137)$ $p < .05$	$F = 0.71$ $df = (5,54)$ NS	$F = 2.85$ $df = (5,74)$ $p < .02$
Low Group = 9.06 (NYP, CP, AF)			

NOTE: Public affairs include legal, public relations, government relations, and public affairs groups. Non–public affairs include engineering, finance, line operations, general management groups.

tween public affairs and non–public affairs executives. This last analysis, then, suggests that the three inferences about stakeholder contact are not consequences of idiosyncratic involvements with any particular stakeholder groups.

Before we leave this discussion of interaction with stakeholders, similarities should be drawn between the present company comparisons and the comparisons of departments made in the previous chapter. The greatest amount of time was dedicated to trade associations (4–6 hours per week). A moderate amount was spent with environmentalists, and state and federal legislators. Comparatively little time—generally less than an hour a week—was spent with labor officials, state regulators, and professional associations. In view of the challenges faced by the industry, an important question might be how much the glamor or the convenience of the interaction along with the potential impact of the outside group affects the time allocation. State officials and labor union leaders may represent less pleasant but equally critical relations.

Appreciating the Value of Source Information

The next measure of receptivity looked more at how quality of information from stakeholder groups was perceived. Just as the departments favored impersonal sources to personal sources, so did each of the companies (see Chapter 7). Outside sources, in general, were rated as "somewhat" valuable (3 on a 1–5 scale) across companies. When the value of information from outside sources is divided by the time spent in contact with these sources, we can sense how a company tends to value its time spent in external contact. Companies with a high score tend to value such contact as a source of learning. They may then see stakeholders more as partners than passive audiences. Through Table 9-3 we learn that those companies spending more time with outside sources may not necessarily use that time to develop potential information sources. Rather, that time may perhaps be used to set up channels for one-way communication from the firm outward. In particular, both Northwest Forests and U.S. Paper seem to downgrade the information value of their most important interactions with stakeholders, while Pacific Timber had both high interaction scores and high estimates of the information potential of such activity. Public affairs departments (legal, government relations, public relations) generally tend to rate the value of their interaction time the lowest, regardless of company. The difference between the high- and low-scoring companies here seemed to be in the evaluations made by non–public affairs executives. An interesting further observation about Northwest Forests is that although their non–public affairs executives are involved 4–8 times as much as their counterparts in other companies, they do not value

Table 9-3 Information Source Potential of Stakeholder Contact Time (Appreciation)

| | | | | | Departments | | | |
Company	Total Company	Legal	Finance	General Mgmt	Gov't Relations	Public Relations	Human Resources	Engineering/ Environmental
Pacific Timber	10.40	6.33	15.25	14.66	1.78	2.27	19.12	2.59
New York Paper	10.21	3.70	10.01	5.13	3.57	7.02	3.78	26.28
Central Paper	7.36	14.50	3.22	7.64	1.48	8.50	9.32	9.30
Northwest Forests	1.91	1.73	...	2.35	1.57	2.33	2.35	...
American Forests	10.36	5.18	7.50	26.88	2.29	2.83	20.07	2.54
U.S. Paper	.486	23.50	4.00	1.74	1.86	3.24	8.04	6.50

High Group = 12.35
(PT, AF, NYP) = 10.32

$F = 2.43$
$df = 137$

Low Group
(USP, NWF, CP) = 5.34

$p < .02$

NOTE: Planning, line, and public affairs departments were dropped for lack of data from four companies on this variable. The numbers reflect the information value of the monthly hours spent in such interactions.

Table 9-4 Boundary Spanning by Company

Company	Attention (Total Boundary Spanning)[a]	Listenership (Information Inflow)[b]	Listenership (Information Inflow Staff Only)	Monitoring (Staff Only)
Pacific Timber	22.23	8.08	8.42	4.11
New York Paper	19.18	6.68	6.67	3.19
Central Paper	19.27	7.11	7.42	3.58
Northwest Forests	21.67	8.00	8.23	4.00
American Forests	21.86	7.74	8.11	4.11
U.S. Paper	22.10	7.94	7.78	3.94
F	2.19	2.40	3.40	2.30
df	(5,134)	(5,134)	(5,107)	(5,107)
Two-tailed significance	$p < .05$	$p < .05$	$p < .01$	$p < .05$

[a] Attention equals the sum of company self-ratings on all boundary-spanning activity.
[b] Listenership equals the sum of company self-ratings along "scanning" and "monitoring" scales.

Table 9-5 Company Information Inflow by Department

Company	Legal	Finance	General Management	Government Relations	Public Relations	Human Resources	Engineering
Pacific Timber	9.00	8.50	7.14	10.00	9.00	8.25	5.50
New York Paper	7.50	4.50	7.40	8.50	6.33	6.75	6.75
Central Paper	8.00	6.33	6.00	9.50	7.00	7.33	6.50
Northwest Forests	6.00	...	6.50	9.75	9.00	6.00	8.00
American Forests	10.00	7.00	6.40	8.60	9.00	7.75	6.65
U.S. Paper	4.00	9.00	9.50	9.00	6.67	6.63	8.00

$F = 2.05$
$df = (47,92)$
$p < .002$

highly the information potential of their time allocation to public affairs. It is possible that non–public affairs executives in this company are involved through response to environmental events rather than through gathering information in advance.

Attention and Listening

The next two measures of receptivity relate more to the overt purpose of executives within a department than to manifest attitudes and behavior. The most conscious level of this information flow can be assessed through the set of questions on intended boundary-spanning concepts. Intended purpose was measured by examining how executives assessed themselves on spanning boundaries. The six boundary-spanning activities (representing, scanning, monitoring, protecting, transmitting, and transacting) did not have significantly different values individually until the company comparisons were limited to staff executives. Like the findings on stakeholder contact time, these findings reported far greater monitoring of public affairs for Pacific Timber, American Forests, Northwest Forests, and U.S. Paper than for either New York Paper or Central Paper ($F = 2.3$, $p < .05$). This same grouping of the companies was indicated by the company scores on total boundary-spanning activity, "attention," as presented in Table 9-4. In one measure of reported information flow across firm boundaries, "listenership," the influx of information (scanning plus monitoring) also followed this split among the companies, with highest values attributed to Pacific Timber, Northwest Forests, American Forests, and U.S. Paper. This analysis holds for the entire set of respondents ($F = 2.4$, $df = 5,134$, $p < .04$), and staff executives alone ($F = 3.4$, $df = 5,107$, $p < .001$). Little insight is gained through comparing the companies by department, however, except that the listenership scores for public relations executives in the higher-listenership companies were far higher than in low-listenership companies (see Table 9-5).

Depth of Involvement

A final measure of receptivity, "depth," or length of issue involvement, found Pacific Timber and U.S. Paper to be involved in issues for a significantly longer period (6 months to a year), 1–2 months longer than each of the other companies except American Forests (from $t = 2.05$, $df = 39$, $p < .025$, two-tailed, to $t = 2.73$, $df = 39$, $p < .005$) for comparison with Northwest Forests and New York Paper. This implies a more superficial background on issues at Northwest Forests, New York Paper, and Central Paper. Once again, then, there is little likelihood of any information enrichment from Northwest Forests' great commitment of company effort.

Public Affairs Influence

Moving from receptivity to the other dimensions of structural sensitivity—influence and integration—we see that once again Pacific Timber appears in the high group and Northwest Forests in the low group. Table 9-6 presents the total of the seven aspects of internal organization that public affairs influence (time and attention of chief executive, time and attention of board of directors, annual planning, personal progress, performance appraisals, career paths, management training programs). Here American Forests and U.S. Paper scored even higher than Pacific Timber (third place, $f = 4.13$, $p < .01$). Public issues were distinctly less important in Northwest Forests and Central Paper. The second column of Table 9-6 indicates that this greater influence of public affairs in American Forests, U.S. Paper, and Pacific Timber is expressed. The companies also exhibited significant differences on each of three individual areas showing influence: (1) the time and attention of the CEO, (2) the time and attention of the Board, and (3) personal progress (see Table 9-4). These particular dimensions of influence were presented because inspection of the data for the total sample suggested a preference for informal dimensions within the companies.

Only American Forests was consistently represented in the high group across these dimensions of influence. U.S. Paper slipped from the high-influence group to the low-influence group relative to the time and attention of the chief executive. Pacific Timber slipped from the high-influence group to the low-influence group relative to the time and attention of the board of directors. Overall, however, American Forests, U.S. Paper, and Pacific Timber displayed a more influential role for public affairs.

None of the companies rated public affairs as more important than other functional areas of the business (general management, line operations, human resources, finance, engineering, control, or planning).

Internal Integration

In the measure of companywide integration, the last dimension of structural sensitivity, Pacific Timber and U.S. Paper again rate high. Integration is most appropriately measured by using temporary coordinating teams and permanent committees. In Table 9-7 are the very

Table 9-6 Internal Influence of Public Affairs

Company	Total Influence[a]	Non-Public Affairs Executives	Time and Attention of Chief Executive	Time and Attention of Board	Respondent's Personal Career
Pacific Timber	19.50	18.53	3.82	2.70	3.33
New York Paper	19.07	17.95	3.89	3.25	2.65
Central Paper	18.15	17.65	3.42	2.60	2.96
Northwest Forests	16.53	17.00	3.80	2.10	3.00
American Forests	21.62	22.15	4.89	3.10	3.59
U.S. Paper	21.48	21.50	3.48	3.10	3.80
$F =$	4.13	2.46	4.14	5.12	2.52
$df =$	(5,137)	(5,71)	(5,137)	(5,137)	(5,137)
Two-tailed significance	$p < .01$	$p < .05$	$p < .05$	$p < .001$	$p < .03$

[a] Total of 7 dimensions.

Table 9-7 Companywide Integration

Company	Task Force Frequency[a] (1 to 5)	Degree of Establishment of Steering Committee[b]	Total Integration[c]
Pacific Timber	3.78	4.48	8.26
New York Paper	3.18	3.82	7.00
Central Paper	2.82	2.00	4.82
Northwest Forests	2.53	1.93	4.46
American Forests	2.95	1.90	4.85
U.S. Paper	3.14	3.62	6.76
$F =$	6.55	2.18	2.43
$df =$	(5,138)	(5,138)	(5,138)
Significance (two tailed)	$p < .001$	$p < .025$	$p < .001$

[a] 1 (very infrequently) to 5 (very frequently).
[b] 1 (poorly established) to 5 (well established).
[c] Sum of scores on task force frequency and establishment of steering committee.

significant company comparisons of how often temporary task forces (teams) are used to deal with public affairs ($F = 6.55$, $df = 137$, $p <$ .001). Sharp differences between the companies existed also in permanent top-level steering committees ($F = 2.18$, $df = 137$, $p < .005$). Pacific Timber, New York Paper, and U.S. Paper were by far the highest in each of these measures. There was a positive correlation between these two dimensions of integration ($F = .37$, $p < .001$). Neither of these items showed ratings that varied significantly by department. Furthermore, classification by department and company indicated that these scores were consistent throughout each company. Therefore, we should expect the best coordination of concepts and action at Pacific Timber, New York Paper, and U.S. Paper.

Conclusions

We have observed the differences between companies in amount of time spent with stakeholders. None of the comparisons gave us much insight into the quality of company structure as a perceptual system. Rather than tally amounts of time or numbers of bodies devoted to public affairs we applied a model which suggested that gathering vital information and processing the items require a certain structure that is alert to public affairs. The quality of a company's *receptivity* was assessed for *breadth* of contact, capacity for *appreciating* the information potential of interaction with stakeholders, amount of *attention* directed towards crossing the firm's boundary to the outside, readiness to *listen* rather than buffer, and *depth* of involvement with issues. Those features represent systemic qualities of gathering information rather than physical structures. Certain companies were found to be particularly receptive to external information. The company that claimed to allocate almost three-fourths of its work week to interaction with stakeholders, Northwest Forests, appeared to be the poorest receptor of information about public affairs.

The companies differed in strength of the transmission lines through which this information about public affairs travels in the direction of influencing company politics and practices. Finally, coordination of information may vary by the strength of the integrating bodies in the company that pull together diverse talents and sources.

While the success of the companies varied in each of these dimensions, one company, Pacific Paper, as you can see in Table 9-8, had a distinctly more permeable boundary, and another company, Northwest Forests, had a distinctly more resistant boundary. From these findings, our model predicts more accommodating perceptions, greater internal perceptual consensus, and greater responsiveness ratings for

Table 9-8 Structural Sensitivity: Summary

Company			Reception			Integration	Influence
	Breadth (no. of outsiders)	Appreciation (information/time value)	Attention (total boundary spanning)	Listenership (scanning, monitoring)	Depth (involvement time)	Coordinating Activities (task forces, steering committees)	Significance in 7 Dimensions of Power in Overall System
Pacific Timber	high	high	high	high	high	high	high
New York Paper	low	high	low	low	low	high	low
Central Paper	low	low	low	low	low	low	low
Northwest Forests	high	low	medium	high	low	low	low
American Forests	low	high	medium	high	medium	low	high
U.S. Paper	high	low	high	low	high	high	high

Pacific Timber and U.S. Paper. We also predict that American Forests would not share more accommodating perceptions of the outside but would be viewed as more responsive. This company's overall sensitivity may be diminished by its low integration, which should hurt the internal consensus.

Nevertheless, we conclude that the companies with more sensitive structures are Pacific Timber, U.S. Paper, and American Forests, and the companies with less sensitive structures are Northwest Forests, Central Paper, and New York Paper. Before examining the internal perceptions and external performance ratings, however, we shall try to enrich the numerical descriptions presented by the researcher's field observations and interviews at each of these companies.

Chapter 10

CULTURAL SENSITIVITY TO PUBLIC AFFAIRS

Thus far, we have created a language of analysis derived from a theoretical model. We have applied the language as a fundamental tool for describing the flow of public affairs uniformly within six companies. As psychologists have cautioned us, an interpretation of the world is necessarily constrained by the limits of our language. The implied assumptions built into the language of the present study are that each company's behavior is the sum total of the components of structural sensitivity. These components were pictured as the static machinery that drives responsiveness, a dynamic company process. Thus our variables were described and measured much as the output of conveyer belt machinery is measured—to judge the assembly line. In this assembly line, equipment is replaced and assembly worker attitudes and actions vary. Similarly, in an organization, such variables as those measured by our questionnaires and inferential statistics do not tell the whole story. In gathering data on the industry and the companies, we found that certain qualities of the *character* of each of these companies could never emerge from use of such limited diagnostic tools. Each of these companies had a very different history of community interaction, product lines, financial performance, and sets of ideological values. With more quantitative data then, we can try to portray the heritage and norms that may be clues to the "cultural" rather than the "structural" sensitivity to public affairs.

The suspicion that such a cultural sensitivity existed came from signals that flashed during the data collection. The companies varied in their enthusiasm for the research. For example, Table 10-1 shows that Pacific Timber, New York Paper, and Central Paper had substantially higher response rates than Northwest Forests, American Forests, and U.S. Paper. The executives in these companies of higher response rate

163

Table 10-1 Cultural Indices from the Company Surveys

| Company | Total Response Rate (%) | Public Affairs Executives (%)[a] | Average Tenure (Length of Service) | | | | | |
| | | | Entire Company[b] (years) | | | Staff[c] (years) | | |
			Company Tenure	Department Tenure	Government Tenure	Company Tenure	Department Tenure	Government Tenure
Pacific Timber	90	40	16.78	7.84	2.41	14.10	7.40	3.25
New York Paper	93	31	17.18	7.11	.25	17.19	7.67	.33
Central Paper	90	32	17.00	8.15	.48	16.79	9.42	.58
Northwest Forests	50	67	13.67	8.67	1.07	13.00	8.23	1.23
American Forests	77	39	11.48	4.65	1.87	9.67	4.61	2.34
U.S. Paper	70	62	8.95	3.81	5.24	8.22	3.50	6.11
$F =$			3.01	3.62	5.84	3.01	2.87	4.29
$df =$			(5,103)	(5,103)	(1,103)	(5,103)	(5,103)	(5,103)
Significance			$p < .05$	$p < .01$	$p < .001$	$p < .05$	$p < .05$	$p < .001$

[a] Percentage of company respondents from public affairs departments (legal, public relations, government affairs).

[b] All executives from each company.

[c] Staff (all executives except those from line operations and general management).

also seemed to have significantly longer service in the company. These data apparently contradicted the findings expressed in Chapter 9. As before, the behavior of Pacific Timber and the behavior of Northwest Forests represented polar opposites, the other four companies appeared to reverse their relative positions. According to the data in Chapter 9, U.S. Paper and American Forests seemed more structurally sensitive. Now however, these companies seemed to have traded places with Central Paper and New York Paper. Therefore the possibility may exist of another dimension of sensitivity to the outside.

Cultural sensitivity was assessed through three different perspectives of the organization. These were:

1. *Reputation*, according to a general outsider.
2. *Establishing contact*, the experience of the particular researcher.
3. *Executive themes*, the attitudes and experience offered by company executives.

Reputation was assessed through several sources directed to the public. They included such leading business periodicals as *Business Week, Fortune, Forbes,* and the *Wall Street Journal.* Those periodicals revealed operating and marketing objectives, which may make up goals related to public affairs. Next, company literature was used to understand the image a company was promoting; style of expression, empathy towards outsiders, and the like were assessed. Finally, leaders of dominant stakeholder groups were interviewed for general impressions. This group included six persons from the American Paper Institute, three from the National Forest Products Association, two from the Wilderness Foundation, three from the Sierra Club, and two from the Wilderness Society; an analyst from each of six investment banking firms; four executives from a proxy-soliciting firm; four journalists; four federal regulators; six regional regulators, three top labor union officials, and two officials from an industry association on public affairs. Company founding, market success, financial strength, interaction with public affairs, and manifest commitment to cultural values were the issues raised in these open-ended interviews.

The category "establishing contact" considered the quality of the researcher-company relation throughout the research. It was thought that the treatment given the researcher might indicate the company's graciousness in receiving outsiders. The types of data reviewed were (1) the speed of company response to the initial solicitation letter, (2) the helpfulness of the company in arranging schedules for the field trips, (3) the response rate and speed of returns on the questionnaire survey.

Lastly, the third perspective, "executive themes," focused on the values, objectives, and operating style that were perceived during on-site field interviews with executives in each company. The officials interviewed generally included the chief executive, two or three senior line officials, vice presidents of affairs in the government, public relations, legal, environmental and financial fields, and also two or three executives in each of the public affairs departments (legal, public relations, government, and environment).

Each company was judged by these three perspectives. To protect the identities of company executives and stakeholders, references and citations to individual names and publication titles have been omitted.

Pacific Timber

Reputation

In more than a century as a prominent forest products concern, Pacific Timber has been a leading landowner, researcher, and image advertiser. Pacific Timber, like the rest of the industry, reported strong performance in 1978, the year ending before the interviews. Long one of the leaders in sales and earnings, the company continued to grow at rates equal to or in excess of the highest-growth company of stature in the industry; its profitability tapered off in 1980 and declined during the first quarter of 1981. A key characteristic of its relative financial health is the buffering from market instability that the company has enjoyed. The stabilizing influence of large blocks of founding-family stock along with other loyal long-term owners and self-sufficiency from a substantial timber supply have afforded management the opportunity to look beyond immediate short-term pressures.

Perhaps because of this internal stability and long-term business focus, this company's strong social commitment has become a fundamental assumption of most of the specific stakeholder groups as well as of the general public. Surveys conducted by independent pollsters have found this company to more readily come to the minds of industry stakeholders and the general public. The public's ready recall of this company, when asked to name a forest products company, has made the company's name almost synonymous with the industry. Company communications are considered very reliable sources of information, virtually on a par with publications of the U.S. Forest Service. The company is generally viewed as ethical, law-abiding, and environmentally responsible. The investment community and local officials have spoken most favorably about the company. Environmentalists, however, differ markedly and were often sharply critical of the company. A well-respected conservationist magazine complimented Pacific Timber and offered some backhand praise to Pacific Timber, calling it the "best of the SOBs." Several environmentalists took strong exception to this praise and suggested countering adjectives, such as *hypocritical* and *insincere.* These critics pointed to such practices as extensive clear-cutting with little regard for either scenic beauty or mixed-species forests. In addition, there were also a few examples of poor environment-company interaction that were well circulated around the environmental network, threatening to poison rapport more widely.

Nevertheless, Pacific Timber was praised by top officials of most environmental organizations, who offered comments such as:

[*Pacific Timber*] *is exceptionally good in the industry.*

They [*Pacific Timber*] *are very supportive of the State Forest Practice Acts and are leaders in regulation.*

They [*Pacific Timber*] *really try for the best forest land management.*

A lot of these companies have kneejerk reactions against anything environmentalists suggest. [*Pacific Timber*] *is curious and interested to hear our perceptions of herbicide and pesticide issues, however, because they feel they might learn something from our critique. The kneejerk companies assume we're totally antichemical and want to go back to the Stone Age.* [*Pacific Timber*], *however, doesn't stereotype what we're doing. . . . They're inquisitive.*

Similarly, mixed reviews were offered by labor officials. They claimed that once the companies had begun to band together, disagreements were frequent, but that historically Pacific Timber had been a fair bargaining partner. Frequent mention was made of company success in changing over a mill from one operation to another rather than closing it, as economists might suggest. Trade association officials were far more flattering, stating that Pacific Timber was far ahead in its contribution to the industry throughout its unwavering commitment to research and development as well as through keen sensitivity to local communities. One trade association leader said, "Beyond their spending, their attitudes are just different. They're willing to bend more and even admit when they're wrong."

Beyond relying on the effect of company history to promulgate certain traditionally valued company beliefs, senior management depended on two additional internal mechanisms. The mechanisms were (1) an elaborate statement and set of activities to promote the desired ethics of business conduct, and (2) a sophisticated system for managing public affairs. The public affairs department was designed to coordinate these two sets of activities.

The first of these institutions promoted company ethics through films, detailed brochures, group sessions, a business committee for whistle-blowing and clarification, and finally the attention of the chief executive. The films include lectures and dramatizations that consider ethical dilemmas in fixing prices, relations with government, conflicts of interest, and the like. The brochure treats these topics as well as product quality, confidentiality, company records and property, and inside information, and others. While not so specific as the documentation now used at a few other companies in the industry, it is a detailed guide that presents responsibility as individual instead of in the chain of command. A very broad view of outside partners is indicated in this material: "The company cannot and will not compromise the trust and respect afforded us by shareholders, customers, government officials and the general public."

Managers are given a complete guidebook on meetings, which explains how to design and conduct discussions on this material with employees. They are also given documentation on the diverse composition of the committee on business conduct, which oversees these standards and to which there is easy access. This program is coordinated through a vice president, who is assigned to this activity as a primary responsibility. He prepared, for example, extensive surveys on attitudes, with questionnaires anonymously completed, to show the spread of employee belief in the sincerity of company statements of ethics. Finally, the chief executive followed up on these rules by periodic, internally directed comments on successes and failures in company publications. For example, the chief executive harshly reprimanded rule violators in a newsletter, stating:

> *There are people operating in each of the industries in which we compete whom, frankly, I wouldn't touch with a 10-foot pole. I don't want any of our employees to seek out such people, or even to associate with them in any way.*

In a similarly directed statement, the chief executive emphasized the preeminence of ethical standards over market success:

> *If I came to lack any confidence in the ability of any of our businesses to meet our growth goals in any way but full compliance with the letter and spirit of the law and our own internal business conduct policies and guidelines, we will get rid of that business. We have done it before and will have no compunction about doing it again.*

They had eliminated one of their businesses following its moderate involvement in a serious conspiracy in fixing prices. Senior management concluded that Pacific Timber had inadvertently acquired an unethical culture along with the purchase of a forwardly integrated company and promptly disposed of it. While a casual reading of ethical proclamations of companies can lead to blurring in the reader's mind, the careful reader must note the uncharacteristically forceful expression and unique system for company followthrough in Pacific Timber's decrees.

The second big effort in social policy involved an extensive apparatus for managing public affairs. Executives responsible for business divisions and executives responsible for geographic regions were encouraged, through senior management directives, to focus on key stakeholder groups. The existence of such documentation was not only unique, but the list of twelve stakeholder groups was far more extensive than the list of audiences recognized by any of the other companies. The list included federal government officials, state and local government officials, legislators at all levels, media, environmentalists, recreationalists, the financial community, employees, labor leaders, and others. This list in itself suggests a possible greater appreciation of the diverse expectations of each group. The material on public affairs stated, "Each public has a different viewpoint, each a different context, each a different level of involvement issue by issue." Understanding their distinct values was strongly emphasized. Other companies, in their eagerness to clarify their own message, tended to blur distinctions. Stakeholders, it was pointed out, are regular people with normally complex lives and reasonable expectations.

Pursuing this philosophical perspective on the segment of the public who promote the various issues was the issue-management system itself. The goals of this program were (1) *to identify* current important issues on which the company must take a stand, (2) *to communicate* this position on big issues to key managers, and (3) *to identify and monitor* developing issues. Four categories were used to define current issues which were seen as (1) affecting Pacific Timber particularly, (2) affecting the industry, (3) affecting American business, and (4) affecting U.S. society. These categories were used to allocate company resources such as executive time, research attention, formulation of strategy, and the efforts in industry associations. Essentially, the company focused on the first two categories, the company and the industry.

A 12-member steering committee for managing issues met monthly to assess interests and develop the company position. This steering committee was headed by the senior vice president for public affairs; it included the chief executive, the senior vice presidents of operations and the business divisions, and also vice presidents of staff divisions—in finance, human resources, communications, law, and government relations. Regional vice presidents also rotated through as temporary members. As issues were identified, managers for these issues were assigned. These people tended to be regional, business, or staff vice presidents from departments or divisions intimately affected by the issue. A broad task force of appropriate top-level representatives of other affected departments and divisions was appointed. Roughly a dozen issues were under analysis at the time of this study. A director of public affairs helped to provide the task forces needed background in research and communications resources, while another director of public affairs coordinated company actions with activities of the industry association to ensure consistent positions on these issues.

Executives were informed of how to best interact with the company's department for public affairs. This department was unique in the industry in its breadth. The vice president of public relations and advertising as well as the vice presidents of legal affairs, and of government affairs, and officers in charge of industry affairs and environmental compliance all reported to a senior vice president of public affairs. These sub-departments were sized comparably to their counterparts in other companies (for example, 10 governmental affairs officials, 13 officials in public relations and advertising). On the regional level, the corporate public affairs department had indirect coordination with 13 managers for public affairs throughout the company. This regional level was different from other companies in that (1) it contained roughly twice as many regions, (2) it reported to regional vice presidents with integrated responsibilities across business divisions, and (3) the public affairs managers had integrated responsibilities across public affairs areas, not being charged with a specific public relations function or a specific government issue.

Establishing Contact

Despite the enthusiastic support of the senior executive in this analysis of public affairs, the company was a bit reluctant to be compared with others in the industry. Several executives explained that much of what they themselves were able to achieve was a function of their special history, and that the present management of its competitors were trying equally hard under their own special company realities. Furthermore, conscious of problems such as strikes, prosecution for fixing prices, and environmental compliance, the company resisted any appearance of bragging. Nevertheless, the chief executive agreed to the researcher's request four months after the original appeal.

Once the company gave its consent to the study, company commitment was very good. The researcher was given a private interview location across from the chief executive's office. Executive schedules were carefully coordinated to allow for a wide cross section of staff, regional, and business division executives. The company gave each executive an advance copy of the researcher's solicitation letter explaining the research as well as copies of the researcher's previous related publications. The follow-up questionnaires were later distributed by the senior vice president of public affairs. A high percentage (90 percent) of the questionnaires were returned to the researcher. These questionnaires were also returned very promptly (all returned within one month after distribution).

Executive Themes

The company's modern headquarters was a three-story building that blended into the forest in which it was set. The interior was an open design with chest-high office dividers and a virtual internal forest of tall plants. Employees dressed more casually than those in other companies (for example, sport coats instead of three-piece suits). The interviews were congenial and matched this casual atmosphere.

One of the most striking features of these interviews was the respect for the expectations of outside groups. For example, a financial executive explained that the company had benefited by pulling in executives with interests beyond the industry. He stated:

> *Industry insiders can often come to resent every outside critic as the enemy. This leads to a lack of a capacity to see the problem from the other guy's perspective. Insiders may all scream that we're capitulating to the other side, but you have to know what responsibilities you have to renew your license from the public to operate.*

A technical director of environmental compliance added that such understanding involves some tolerance and curiosity:

> *We must be careful not to take a hard line against outside critics and instead recognize that there are important unanswered questions. You need more than a vicious PR fight. People are asking sincere questions. People are turned off by constant kneejerk reactions that produce self-serving rhetoric.*

A public relations executive indicated the great effort that the company had undertaken to maintain contact with a broad range of stakeholders and also the effort to poll these groups on how successful they perceived the company in its effort at contact. He explained "What we're trying to do is build a bank account of respect."

Several executives complained that the short-term perspectives of the investment community can make achieving this sensitivity to stakeholders difficult. The chief executive commented, "There is no way some of our social investments will give a flashy, fast payoff. We're trying to do something more fundamental."

Even more surprising was the uniform praise stakeholders had for Pacific Timber's formal mechanism for treating issues, in view of the apparently informal company style. Several executives explained that the improved focus on key issues cut down company infighting for public affairs resources such as lobbying time and reduced the likelihood of confusing, apparently contradictory actions. A government affairs officer explained:

> *Sometimes business vice presidents tend to get us to take on every ideological issue from common situs picketing to something like the Chrysler bailout. Other companies still do this and this affects the industry association. We can now steer clear of this drain of effort and credibility.*

A company lawyer similarly commented:

> *It was incredible how much we spent on every industry association with no idea what the net impact was, let alone the contradiction. This has been resolved through the sorting out of priorities.*

A senior vice president concurred, stating:

> *We used to get choked by a list as long as your arm. Now we decide what we can leave to the trade associations and what we can best do on our own. Some issues are so global that you're wasting your time.*

The vice president of public affairs agreed, stating that this systematic way of employing resources increased the clout of the company:

> *We were able to cut back when we were too involved and amplify the really big concerns.*

He added that fewer issues were now likely to slip through the cracks:

> *We used to be a little too active. Sometimes we had, in effect, overlapping issues managers on general industry problems, while important company problems weren't addressed at all.*

In addition to valuing this improved concentration of company resources, executives across all departments complimented this structure for helping to keep line and staff working as a team on problems. Some public affairs executives said that it allowed line management to buy into the plans and contribute to them. Furthermore, an operations executive pointed out, "Line involvement adds some expertise and creates a level of awareness that better permeates the organization." A public affairs official stated in summary that this coordination provided both "internal authority to present policies to the business divisions as well as the external clout the company has when it speaks with one loud message voice instead of four or five garbled ones."

The chief executive cautioned that this rosy picture is misleading, however, in that problems occur from delays. "Analysis paralysis," was cited, and also problems in improving external communication at the local level and in truly tracking nascent issues. The company's rejection of futurists as "too distant and irrelevant" has diminished the ease of picturing the issue scenario five years from now.

Both internal company executives and outside stakeholder representatives have observed that this company is philosophically different from many others in the industry. It has been suggested that long-term shareholder support, vast timber acreage, and a century-old family heritage of public responsibility have helped contribute to a cherished tradition of sensitivity to public complaints. In addition, however, company insiders stressed the importance of the structure for managing public affairs that coordinated this commitment. Finally, both inside executives and outside executives acknowledged that neither the cultural sensitivity nor the structural sensitivity was flawless. While stakeholders were rarely seen as intruders, there were examples of clumsy or periodically hostile interaction. Similarly, the structure seemed to manage existing issues well but did not seem to scan for developing issues. In particular, various issues such as impending labor relations problems were far less well understood. Overall, however, the efforts and accomplishments well exceed those at the companies described in the following profiles.

New York Paper

Reputation

The origins of this 80-year old concern are in the paper side of the industry. It grew through the melting together of twenty family operations. New York Paper has frequently been viewed as a laggard in financial performance; yet it performed well in 1979 and set a record for the first quarter in 1980. Its return on sales and on equity were a bit below average for the industry.

Over the years the company has had its share of problems in public affairs. It has been one of those hit hardest for price fixing, and for difficulty with Indian land claims. In addition, it has created health hazards through spraying operations, caused water pollution problems, and suffered from labor strikes. Nevertheless, it is not hard to find people who have a kind word to say about New York Paper. One trade association leader commented, "They're damn nice people, but their management has had to take a low profile on controversial issues to avoid offending the handful of families that controlled the company's ownership." Another trade official stated, "They are well liked but not too effective as lobbyists. They're liked because their lobbyists become so focused on issues such as certain taxation provisions that they wind up serving more as issue specialists for the industry than issue generalists for the company." Despite chronic problems with fixing prices, the company has impressed courts by its sincerity in long-standing efforts at legal compliance. Even a manager convicted of fixing prices conceded that, as the dominant force in the region, the company had little to gain from the conspiracy. He explained how a "moderate price floor was the statesmanship responsibility to keep smaller mom and pop operations in business." This company was also one of the pioneers in efforts to educate the public about responsible forest management in films, television and magazine advertisements, and school materials. Much of the effort was, of course, directly intended to boost the company's image, yet a lot of the material did not focus on the company in particular. It began working with the states early in the environmental movement and frequently relied on local legal firms to represent company interests.

Recently, rather than combat local opposition to building plans in the Great Lakes region, the company crossed over to Canada. It has also recently decided to keep its corporate headquarters in the present home city to maintain community commitment. While each company of the foremost companies in the industry have published promotion materials that try to portray outstanding corporate citizenship, New York Paper's material stands out in that it does not define this citizenship by philanthropy. Instead, the mixture of short-term goals and long-term social commitments is stressed. The company states, for example, "Regardless of economic demands, ecological awareness is fundamental to our actions. . . . The corporation sees itself as part of its community in all of its operations, whether in a single town, a major city, or an entire county." The emphasis on corporate values may truly reflect more image management than honest commitment, but at least it reaches for a richer concept of social responsibility than other companies that stress either the contribution of company products or public gifts.

Establishing Contact

New York Paper was the first company to respond to the letter soliciting participation in this research. Before the researcher could make the phone call that was supposed to follow the letter, the chief executive officer telephoned on his own, with the intention of declining. This CEO had received much industry recognition for his activities in public affairs and had recently taken over the reins from his predecessor in a smooth transition of authority. He was aware of previous company cooperation on another project with this same researcher and was pleased with that project. He felt, however, that this particular research endeavor was "too ethereal" for company interests. Reflecting aloud, however, he conceded that the company perhaps could learn to operate more effectively; and reversing his original position, he agreed to participate. This company subsequently had the highest response rate (95 percent), and all the questionnaires were returned within a month of their receipt.

Executive Themes

New York Paper's headquarters were far less glamorous than those of most of the other companies. Similarly, the conversations with top executives tended to have fewer frills and salesmanship. Instead, the executives honestly considered the gap between company goals and successes. Rather than blame their failures on a hostile environment, they willingly reflected on their own actions. One senior general management official commented that the company had recently learned that "regardless of political party or philosophy, three-fourths of the time a congressman will listen to company position and respect well-thought-out arguments." This executive, however, felt that there was little reason to fight solitary battles since there were "damn few company-specific issues." A divisional executive vice president, for example, commented:

> *OSHA is not as vicious as it was thought to be and the FTC has become far more responsive. Even unions have grown up a lot. They better understand the need for productivity and have also helped in government relations.*

Such stakeholder tolerance was far more the exception than the rule across companies. The officer for public affairs explained that the company's tax specialization was not accidental, just a planned contribution to the industry. He explained that New York Paper relied on a specific company for wilderness issues, another for energy, a third company for transportation issues, and so on. He went on to say that trade association relations were unsatisfactory due to inappropriate regional biases. He felt that while a widespread sensitivity to government affairs was important, ". . . not many people around here are trained in public affairs. We have lots of people making political decisions routinely, but they don't know it. They accept it without a lot of ranting and raving about government abuses." This senior official for public affairs explained that thus far, this sensitivity had been achieved through internal communication of issues.

Another executive for public affairs explained this approach in more detail. He stated that the company tended to focus on a few key issues instead of having a broad outlook:

> *The public affairs network in this company is not yet a formalized mechanism, but we're working towards that. The eight or nine central public relations people along with eight or nine government affairs people select and prioritize the issues for the company to follow. They don't do it in a*

vacuum but they solicit the concerns out in the field as well as in central management.

A public relations officer described the department's role as:

. . . *a service function to government affairs. Once the issue is zeroed in on and the position developed, we decide who to communicate with. We will frequently get assistance from financial and legal people. Our employees are our most important audience. If you don't inform your own team members, how can you expect outsiders to understand you? If employees don't stand up for an issue, why should a congressman care? Employees make or break legislation.*

Thus we see evidence of an appreciation of the various stakeholder roles.

In this communications effort, the people in the department for governmental affairs produce several publications, such as a monthly newsletter about federal affairs, monthly newsletters from each of five regions, and more detailed background papers on issues. The public relations department produces many in-house films, a monthly companywide magazine, a regular weekly digest of public issues and trends for management personnel, and a very sophisticated monthly magazine on communication at plant levels. This magazine explains how to set up good relations with the community through involvement with the civic associations, organize plant open houses, maintain nonhostile press relations, and provide detailed descriptions of teamwork between company officials with labor unions and trade groups and community groups to develop legislation. Finally the public relations officials in the company's business division work with company officials in developing meetings for divisional vice presidents for public affairs and planning plant newsletters. A divisional vice president rated this communicating effort as only moderately effective:

We inform them well but then we consistently refuse managers the time to think and act on long-term rather than short-term issues. In the old days he had time to reflect on his statistics, but now information travels so fast and the pressure to look intelligent is so strong, there is no time for a broad view. Having government affairs specialists at least makes it easier. A manager doesn't have to rely on fast seat-of-the-pants judgment alone.

A general manager similarly complained that without an appropriate structure, senior management has "gotten too involved in details rather than the big issues." Another senior vice president complained that the communications effort coordinated thoughts more than actions. While executives responsible for human resources, engineering, and finances have managed to separate responsibilities well, there has been some historical antagonism between the legal department and the department for public affairs. For example, the public affairs department went out and hired outside counsel to help resolve Indian land claims without consulting the legal department. On another occasion, the legal department and the engineering department were called to one of the Great Lakes states to assist in proceedings for construction permits. Various government engineers were involved but the public affairs department was left out. On such occasions the neglected departments have "raised all kinds of hell at being left out."

In essence, this company has worked to establish a set of organizational values. The company's long establishment and good efforts at communication have helped promote these values. When the company officials were convicted of antitrust violations, actions conflicting with the well-communicated corporate standard of business conduct, a senior executive pounded his fist on the table in exasperation and shouted that the convicted executives "just didn't listen or were plain stupid." In that instance, formal pressures for higher prices applied by growth targets, performance appraisals, and other such features inadvertently contradicted the desired informal company values. This conflict between cultural values and formal inducements to perform may have permeated New York Paper's interaction with public affairs.

Central Paper

Reputation

Despite its origin from the linking of many joint ventures, executive succession has been remarkably smooth and tenure has run quite high at Central Paper. It is widely recognized as a company that gracefully transformed itself from a loose, informal, family-dominated corporation to a professionally managed, diversified company. The 150-year-old company became a dominant force in the industry just after the turn of the century, but its growth, fueled by acquisitions, did not begin until the first generation of professional managers came in the late 1950s and 1960s. In the early 1970s the company suffered from overexpansion, but it decentralized and improved product focus within profit centers. A landmark seven-week retreat for several hundred senior executives helped set the climate for change over a decade ago.

While the stock is considered to have been periodically undervalued, experts in the financial community widely acclaim the company's performance. It has been rated near the top in return on equity. *Value Line* has praised the clear focus of the Central Paper community, judging that it "isn't the same company it was a decade ago."

The company has received even more unanimous praise for its commitment. The chief executive was regularly identified by the chief executives of other big forest products companies, and also by trade association officials, as the prime force behind the industry's strong emphasis on public affairs and its involvement therein. The strength and breadth of the board of directors has frequently been cited in the foremost business publications. In particular, this company has been among a small number of major U.S. firms that have been pioneers with board committees on social responsibility. The company has had one of the most thorough antitrust compliance programs—with expense-account audits, mock interrogations, and simulated grand jury proceedings. For a decade, Central Paper has maintained a close communication with shareholders. This relationship may have contributed to the ownership loyalty during a recent challenge for takeover. Finally, state regulators have commented on the company's apparent honesty in reporting environmental mishaps. Recently, *Institutional Investor* identified this company's investor-relations programs as one of the best in the country.

Other manifestations of this company's philosophy of respect for the social obligations of the enterprise can be found in many company publications. One original piece is the "Guidelines for Proper Business Practices" where Golden Rule proclamations (for example, "It is only by dealing honestly and fairly in all things that real success is attainable") set the tune for far more specific guidelines for each business function. For example, the guidelines for general business conduct state:

> *The company recognizes that its policies and actions may also impact on other individuals and groups who have only an indirect relationship with the company. [Central Paper] employees must be sensitive to these impacts.*

This same sensitivity to the various legitimate roles by key public affairs actors is demonstrated throughout the more functionally specific guidelines. For example, the public affairs guidebook states:

> *Government personnel should be treated as peers, having neither unlimited authority because they are "government" nor to be looked down on because they are public servants.*

Despite this long-standing ethical commitment, the company has just recently begun to introduce the latest management techniques for managing public affairs.

Establishing Contact

Central Paper's chief executive was among the first to respond to the letter soliciting company support. The interviews were arranged through the chief executive's office. The company was exceptionally hospitable and gracious to the researcher, as evidenced by such gracious gestures as carefully coordinating schedules for interviews with executives, and providing transportation and food. In addition, company officials went out of their way to provide the researcher with unbiased background material and general non–company publications on industry issues. Finally, company executives returned 90 percent of the questionnaires to the researcher.

The interviews were held in the company's strikingly attractive five-year-old office building, which was a cornerstone of the city's urban redevelopment.

Executive Themes

The senior management group was very conscious of the internal culture that had developed over the company's history. Virtually every vice president referred to the once "clubby atmosphere" and the still manifested "historical values" of Central Paper. The chief executive began his description of the company's commitment to social responsibility by explaining that every corporation is, like a family, a product of its heritage. Several executives characterized the company's individual culture as "more liberal" than the rest of the industry. The chief executive suggested that the company has tried to stress a respect for a less autocratic form of public policy. He stated that in the past decade:

> . . . *everything that institutions do today is visible and subject to concerns, criticisms, and public scrutiny. . . . autocratic behavior in the U.S. has been gradually eroded. . . . a system that has become increasingly pluralistic must recognize that "vested" or "single-interest" groups must be expected to optimize their interests—or else we do not have a free society.*

The implications he drew for the company were essentially that there was an obligation to understand rather than resent the various stakeholders. Furthermore, he explained, this company had an obligation to become an active participant in exchange with the public.

Such sensitivity to public affairs was expressed by both government affairs and public relations officers, who identified similar external audiences in noncritical terms. Of even greater significance were the sentiments of other senior staff vice presidents. Financial executives seemed keenly sensitive to the importance of relations with state and local officials; this held in developing tax policies or in the value of good shareholder relations. Instead of the common "we versus they" attitude of industry personnel, executives at Central Paper identified five legitimate overlapping categories affected by company policies: (1) unions, (2) non-union employee groupings—age, minorities, and the like, (3) regulatory officials, (4) broad social-interest groups, and (5) narrow special-interest audiences—retired employees, community groups, and the like. Company lawyers similarly looked beyond the courtroom to constituents such as local communities, government officials, shareholders, and unions. These executives, regardless of department, spoke of the need to go beyond objective rationality to understand the emotional aspect of such issues as cutting trees and safe use of chemicals.

Despite this long-term cultural commitment to social issues, however, the company has organized for it only recently. Much of the company's appreciation of public affairs was described as "a response to the spirit of Earth Day and the late 1960s." The department of public relations, for example, was about as big as the average in the industry, with seven professionals at the corporate headquarters and an indirect responsibility for fourteen field units. The department for government relations had six full-time professionals (two in Washington) with indirect responsibility for the coordinating seven representatives for affairs in state government. The corporate legal department of three lawyers was far below the norm for the industry because of the continual reliance on outside counsel and the employment of attorneys independently by other departments. The environmental compliance unit (20 professionals), and the finance department (investor relations unit), and a separate tax department were exceptional in their involvement in public affairs.

These departments had recently (in the late 1970s) strengthened and clarified their individual contributions. In particular the department for government affairs had just begun to pilot new programs in managing issues and in establishing relations between managers and legislators. Literature from the departments of public relations and government affairs had been upgraded. Finally, these departments had recently begun to coordinate their efforts in public affairs through task forces. Operating units were not formally represented on these task forces. Executives differed on the receptivity and significance of task force meetings as well as on the appropriate membership and agenda.

Since the key parts of the structure for managing public affairs was so new, executives were more critical of the company's performance than of its cultural values. One staff vice president complained that there was a lack of coordination in making contact with stakeholders:

> *You can't have everyone out there playing his own tune; you need an orchestra leader. We have very inconsistent dealings with communities. We love them when we need them, and then leave them. Our mill managers are too busy fixing boilers to get to know the key local officials. I've tried to demonstrate at least the financial value of sharing information and interests by serving in community organizations.*

Another senior vice president complained:

There is no master plan. The government affairs and public relations people generally follow their own agenda. I can't pick up a notebook anywhere and find out where we stand on an issue. We've talked about doing this but we haven't yet.

One senior executive confessed to having just learned that his own subordinates so carefully guarded their turf that "they would stonewall cooperation with other departments." A top public affairs vice president conceded that this problem had been recognized:

Our problem was that we had no message at all, rather than conflicting messages. We didn't know what [Central Paper's] position was on an issue, but this should be changing.

Several other executives said that while coordination and clarification would help, the company still had to change its time frame of orientation to the analysis of public affairs. One senior executive complained,

We need to take the specialists further, we have a couple of phobias like being very afraid to poll constituents, and have folks follow up on these issues.

A similar self-criticism noted:

We don't research issues far enough in advance. It is important for us to learn to build a fact background, learn to influence the public consensus builders.

A public affairs vice president agreed and commented that, "We should be further out than what Congress is doing tomorrow, particularly since some of these issues have been around for a long while." He insisted, however, that this was a result of a lack of resources and not a lack of interests. Now that the company had strengthened its sensory mechanisms, he expected that the company would be more prepared in advance.

Thus, Central Paper appeared to be a company that has smoothly reoriented itself over the past century by first consolidating management and then embarking on a high-growth strategy in vertical integration; this was followed by diversification, and then slower growth. Now that the company has identified its marketplace constituents clearly, it is belatedly organizing itself to interact most effectively with its public constituents. Throughout this period, however deficient its structural sensitivity to public affairs, Central Paper's culture has promoted a strong ethical commitment to honesty in stakeholder dealings and an independent company tack. The chief executive himself explained:

Our history of strong beliefs from the top can be tough to maintain even with no acquisitions. Yet, with our acquisition policy it's even more difficult. . . . We had to go in with the old management still in place. Managing a lot of newly acquired divisions is like trying to raise adopted kids.

Northwest Forests

Reputation

Northwest Forests has recently weathered some stormy political infighting between past and present chief executives. Continued top-level changes at the time of the study guarantee that the following description no longer accurately reflects this company's stature in public affairs. While interviews with environmentalists, labor union officials, regulators, and most other stakeholder representatives indicated hostility towards this company, its financial performance was considered outstanding. In the year of the study, sales rose over the preceding year with one of the highest returns on sales, and earnings rose almost 20 percent. This was accomplished despite conservative accounting practices (deferred-investment tax credits, lease capitalization, and LIFO inventory assessments). In the first quarter of 1980, however, earnings slipped dramatically from the previous year. Investment services such as *Value Line* and forest products newsletters by Goldman, Sachs and by Piper, Jaffray, and Hopwood praised Northwest Forests as not only one of the industry giants in sales but as consistently one of the most profitable in the industry. This company was founded in the 1920s, but through thirty years of explosive growth it changed from a moderate-size producer to one of the leading companies in the industry.

Stakeholders claim that this growth was at the expense of any sensitivity to the company's environment. One newspaper characterized the company's image as "a public relations nightmare" and claimed that the company had "managed to antagonize virtually the entire state." By the 1950s it had firmly acquired the reputation of a "cut and run" operation, as newly acquired timberlands were rapidly harvested to repay the loans required for such purchases. These controversial land purchases and the massive forest clearance came at a time when much of the rest of the industry had already become committed to more conservation-minded reforestation programs. To protect this cutting, the company got involved in fierce tax-legislation battles with local competitors. Since that time, the company's reputation has been further tarnished around the country. The National Park Service, environmentalists, and the national press attacked the company for violating a congressional timber-cutting moratorium to protect 300-year-old redwoods. Regulatory problems have included a 20 percent spinoff of their operations in an agreement with the Federal Trade Commission on antitrust charges, price-fixing prosecutions (along with the rest of the industry) and charges from the Securities and Exchange Commission of stock manipulation. Their latest ripples in public affairs were caused by the sudden announcement that the company intended to vacate its large 11-year-old headquarters and move to another region in the country.

The company did little to respond to its growing difficulties relative to public affairs except to fight back harder. One environmentalist leader commented, "This company has always played it rougher and tougher in my experience. . . . [Northwest Forests] has showed nothing but contempt for us and our value system." A longtime local journalist from the company's hometown commented that Northwest Forests "is the most secretive of the SOBs." An investment analyst complained that Northwest Forests "is nasty as hell to deal with if they don't receive favorable ratings." Even some trade association representatives found reason to say that this company has an inherent hostility towards outsiders. One trade association lobbyist complained that Northwest Forests will "fight whatever the issue is, all the way, taking a hard-setting conservative stance no matter how it may hurt the issue stands and general congressional relations." Another trade lobbyist complained, "They aggravated every labor lobbyist in town on the common situs issue when we needed them. They hate to compromise." A local regulator noted their lack of involvement in community affairs and commerce and concluded that this was consistent with their environmental stance. He explained:

> [Northwest Forests] established a reputation that they don't give a damn about anything or anybody on the outside. It doesn't matter whether it is true or not, but through cut and run operations and community isolation, they are not viewed as good corporate citizens.

Despite such poor relations, it should be pointed out that the company's record in environmental compliance and technological invention is generally strong. Environmental violations, of course, are largely determined by the precise location and nature of one's operations.

Establishing Contact

With this background of hostility, the company officials surprisingly were either indifferent or actually congenial to the research on public affairs. Original organizational entry was cloudy, and so was subsequent research contact. This was the only company of the twenty largest companies in the industry in which both the president and the chairman refused to respond to repeated overtures through the mail, follow-up phone calls, and personal visits by the researcher. Contact was finally established after six weeks of no response. The researcher left word that he would be in the vicinity of the corporate headquarters and would pay a visit to check on the status of the request for company participation. The chairman was then telephoned again from a pay phone alongside a noisy construction spot across the street from corporate headquarters. He answered his own phone and denied ever receiving any information about the study. He abruptly but politely declined, stating, "It sounds very interesting, but we're too busy to get involved now. Thank you," and hung up. The researcher had barely finished a second line of description about the study and suspected that the chairman had assumed that the project was seeking company funding or a good deal of executive time.

To clarify this possible misunderstanding, the researcher crossed the street and entered the corporate headquarters. He rode up the elevator to the executive suite with an executive going to a meeting on that floor. The thirtieth-floor suite was protected by a plexiglass shield with a receptionist on the other side. She recognized the researcher's fellow elevator passenger, a company official, and opened the door for him. After crossing through, the researcher interrupted her request for identification by asking for the chairman's secretary. The researcher then simply walked off to that corner suite with a photostat of the last solicitation letter in hand. The chairman's secretary exclaimed, "My, that's a coincidence. We were just looking for your request letter; it's not logged as having been received in June." The researcher produced his copy and said, "Well, that's okay, I'll just deliver it while I'm here." Over her protests, the researcher walked into the chief executive's office, introduced himself, apologized for the intrusion and passed over the solicitation. The chairman laughed, saying "How the hell did you get in here?" He read it over and suggested that the vice president of public affairs might help. This person was quite helpful and assisted in arranging other executive interviews. Meetings with the executives were very cordial, although the response to the questionnaire survey was only 50 percent at this company and the response time was slow (3 months).

Executive Themes

The various departments for public affairs were not housed near each other and each reported separately to top management. There was no formal coordination between departments such as public relations, government affairs, and legal affairs. The corporate staff for government affairs was one of the largest in the industry, with 16 full-time professionals in two locations. The public relations staff was composed of nine full-time professionals in corporate headquarters with dotted line authority to officials in large facilities. The public affairs departments were not formally coordinated, thus the legal, public relations, and government relations departments staked out their own turf. The public relations and personnel vice presidents did not have offices in the executive suite. A public affairs area vice president explained,

> *We are pretty loosely structured. The officers in town get together for Monday morning breakfasts and they serve as the catalyst for certain issues. We could be more formalized in issue management. But things just seem to happen. We attend to them as they occur.*

Another public affairs vice president agreed and described the company as a relaxed place to work:

> *We're all a bunch of friends around here. Our offices are all close. Each department knows what their responsibilities are, an issue is either in the courts, a legislature, or the papers. We can each determine our own priorities. We do not operate by committee. We believe in giving a person a job to do. I develop programs depending on what I see needs to be done.*

A lobbyist explained, "I know about the issues; only if I have a speech problem do I go to PR." Another vice president explained,

> *You've got to stay loose. Some companies have too structured a program. You have to stay loose. This also helps us stay lean. Some other companies in this industry are just too bold around bureaucrats. We let our trade associations hammer out priorities. That's why we pay our dues.*

A vice president of operations agreed with this reliance on industry associations:

> *The anticipating stage of public issues is in the state level and national level trade associations. They pull a lot of issues together and have the stuff to react. In public affairs, your competition is your best friend. His problems are your problems and your problems are his.*

A company lobbyist had a different view of priority setting. "You generally just know where the company will come down on a certain issue. With that in mind, I can act to set priorities in that I can also judge the payback on certain issues. If I can get some fast action, I'll take that issue right away."

This emphasis on informal coordination and reliance on industry trade associations was not universally praised by company officials. A top-level general management official stated:

> *You know, we have a lot of officers that are out in the region and just aren't around for these informal chats. Even around the headquarters, lots of decisions are made by some executives whom a few of us call the three horsemen.*

An operations vice president focused on the significance of a lack of formal coordination to line managers:

> *A lot of my managers aren't sure where to go when they have a problem. They hear presentations by attorneys or government affairs people, and so on, but they still don't know where to go and don't bother with a lot of things.*

As a result, he stated, "Everyone is a little reluctant to grab the ball. If the issue is banging at the window, then someone will react."

These problems were acknowledged to varying degrees by public affairs officials. A government relations officer said:

> *We go around to quarterly meetings of management groups. I found you don't hear equally from all the divisions. But like any company, some divisions maintain closer relations with government affairs divisions. Of course, it's true that that doesn't mean that the ones you don't hear from don't have any problems.*

A public affairs vice president tied the loose structure to a lack of forethought:

> *We often wish things were more structured. Our staff people are set up only to help the line. We don't have the corporate voice of other companies. We're so decentralized, we spend a lot of time running around after disasters. The general attitude is "don't fix something until it's broken."*

He went on to say that not only did the company fail to act in advance of problems but different units acted in contradictory ways:

> *A general manager of a plan will call us for help on little problems, but they are free to tell a county commissioner to go to hell, despite how that may affect other company units. We can only lobby on the inside. The mentality of local people often doesn't mesh with corporate goals.*

Several executives cited internal company inconsistencies, in which different regional representatives would get national attention for conflicting views on issues such as clear-cutting or insecticide use. Some complained, while others boasted, of the lack of a clear company policy on important issues.

An executive vice president acknowledged that this disorganization had proved costly:

> *We should think much more about what is coming. We've frequently fought when we should have listened. If we had corrected certain water systems when we clearly saw the public sentiment, it would have been cheaper had we delayed. We're equipped, for we have a general awareness of public affairs issues to handle catastrophic happenings such as a recent boiler explosion, but we don't coordinate our personnel.*

The fight mentality was still present in the company as the following comments echoed in the interviews:

> *This Endangered Species Act is just nonsense. We'll just have to learn to live without a lot of species. What's the difference? You can't let a little bird crowd you off your land.*

> *We've been spraying herbicides for years with no complaints. It is deadly*

to marijuana crops and that's a big business in those places that are complaining now.

People used to stay in their own backyards to relax. Now that we're all affluent, everyone wants a piece of the woods.

When does a special interest like wilderness or deer protection become the public interest?

Company publications which mention "corporate citizenship" essentially are limited to social philanthropy.

Some of these comments reflect a reactive, crisis-battling mentality. This suggested weaknesses in the structure that was designed to act as an advance net for developing issues as well as in integration. A vice president for general management summed the problem of company attitudes by saying, "There's been too much focus on the trees and not enough on the forest." But even beyond this poor structural sensitivity was evidence of low cultural sensitivity. The interviews summed a limited social role of the corporation and a hostility to stakeholder interests. Characterizations of corporate citizenship included mention of the donations to local art organizations as well as the social benefit of forest products. There appeared to be a predilection for combat as opposed to exchange with the public.

American Forests

Reputation

Born out of a merger of forest products companies a quarter of a century ago, American Forests is easily the youngest company studied. While some of its acquired paper and timber operations represented older enterprises, this company's corporate identity is a full century younger than many of the other big companies in the industry. It has a moderate forest land base but relies strongly on federal timber purchases for raw materials.

Despite its lack of a long heritage, the company does not lack a distinctive history. Through the 1960s, the company's high growth through acquisition in forest products and also in presumably countercyclical businesses caused the company to be prominent for its earnings per share and return on equity. Finally, at the end of the decade, the chief executive was forced to resign. A large percentage of the company assets were sold off and many top-level executives left the company. In the wake of these events, the company has a young senior management corps with not too many years of company experience.

A second legacy of the poor performance during that decade was the accurately perceived need to establish an exchange with outside stakeholders. The investment community was especially targeted as a critical external audience. The company's new chief executive effectively introduced a communicating policy strictly of the style of Benjamin Franklin—"honesty is the best policy"—under the assumption that "folks suspect the worst when they sense secrecy." The chief executive and other top staffers began to meet regularly with investment analysts and brokers in large regional meetings. Several detailed but attractive and clearly written financial fact books are circulated, including quarterly shareholder reports and company newsletters. The company has since received much praise in investment journals such as *Institutional Investor* and *Value-Line* for both its constructive approach in communication and its markedly improved financial performance (for example, a 50 percent reduction in the debt ratio and impressive increases in earnings per share and return on investment). The year of this research was billed as the year of the company's best financial performance to date, despite a crippling 7-month paper-union strike, severe antitrust penalties, and other such industrywide events.

American Forests had tried to carry its philosophy of open discussion to other outside interests (for example, labor relations and environmental concerns). Company documents, instead of presenting a broad, sweeping hyperbole of corporate citizenship and codes of ethics, explain the company's social role as one of providing high-quality products and services that meet basic needs and offer fair value. One of the six strategic objectives laid out in company publications that specifically cater to the business society states that the company strives to "be capable of anticipating, constructively influencing, and adapting to the changing needs of society." This is a good illustration of how the culture has not tried to infuse a rich set of values, but rather has tried to effect a style of operation. The company has been a keystone of recent tough positions toward labor across the industry and has been deeply involved in an effort to increase the harvest on federal timberlands. Some industry executives acknowledge that American Forests has been particularly aware of certain obvious threats to the company but has lacked a wider view of how issues affect one another. Several trade association executives commented that the company's interest in candor has at times produced naive intransigence when compromise would have been desirable. While environmentalists and labor officials echoed these points, all parties agreed that American Forests was an honest and fair dealer.

Establishing Contact

American Forests promptly responded to the phone call follow-up to the solicitation letter and eagerly accepted the opportunity to participate in this study. The vice president of corporate communications (public relations and advertising) was a very gracious host, and he constructed an interview schedule to produce a thorough cross section of executive opinion, circulated the researcher's solicitation letter, and arranged a plane ride with the chief executive to a divisional headquarters. The company response rate to the questionnaire survey (77 percent) was somewhat below the responses of the three highest-responding companies (90 percent). Similarly, the response time (three months) was longer for American Forests than for most of the other companies. A representative of the company's communications department accompanied the researcher through the interviews and acted as a guide through the company. Public affairs executives appeared to have offices that were as close, if not closer, to the chief executive than non–public affairs executives. The government affairs and legal departments report through one vice president to the chief executive and the public relations and investor relations departments report jointly through another vice president to the chief executive. Each of these departments is comparable in size to the parallel departments of competitor companies.

Executive Themes

One of the most distinguishing qualities of the interviews with the executives in American Forests was a tendency to espouse a very determined stand on whatever was most salient to a particular executive. While American Forests' executives did not dispute the rights of outside critics, they did not seem willing to find common ground between the company and stakeholders. One senior executive said, for example, "There are a few issues we have an adamant posture on. For example, it'll be a cold day in hell before we participate in a cost-of-living labor agreement." Another senior general manager complained,

> *The federal government is operating at one-half efficient capacity. The United States should be exporting forest products. We will not yield to government encroachment on the industry's need for a timber supply.*

A financial executive complained about excessive disclosure requirements and also evaluated the environmentalist threat:

> *We face a constant confrontation with preservationists who want a total prohibition against the harvesting of trees. We will continue to fight for controlled multiple use.*

A vice president of one of the company's business divisions explained the company's open, confronting style:

> *A lot of companies in this industry are hiding in their own trees. These companies have been the battleships, damn hard to sink but easy to hit.*

*We, along with a few other companies, are trying for more maneu-
verability and striking back like aircraft carriers.*

A labor relations official elaborated how this approach works in his area:

*The union locals here are a strong part of the small-town environment.
Many of our mills have a third generation of family members. We go
directly to the employees who will pressure their unions. While our competitors freeze up in silence during a strike, we bring the press into our
mills. We maintain an around-the-clock hotline and distribute lengthy
fact sheets.*

A public relations executive concurred, stating:

*Most of our plants are in towns of 25,000 or less. If your employees are
bad-mouthing you, you have no chance to be understood by others.
When we clear-cut, we explain where, why, and how.*

This tough, but direct stance was echoed in statements about other
types of interactions with stakeholders. Executives frequently spoke in
harsh words about those companies who were less open in their
dealings either through deception and silence, "parasitic reliance on
the industry associations alone," or "weak-stomached conciliation."
The general prognosis inside American Forests about these companies,
who do not do their homework and who take a strong stand where
important, was: "They'll get theirs in the long run." In every department, executives were armed with examples where one company's
unfocused animosity or another company's outright laziness or a third
company's dishonesty caught up with the company.

   This value of candid expression was further evidenced in the surprisingly ready admission that even within American Forests the prevailing tendency had been to react to public events rather than anticipate them. One senior management executive confessed:

*We've gotten to where we are kicking and screaming. We had to concede
that there had to be a better way than running from presumed enemies.
With some foresight, we see that we can get involved in the process but
we're still frustrated as hell about our lack of influence in many subjects.*

A public relations executive complained:

*Too many issues such as environmental concern with toxic substances and
energy issues just fall through the cracks here. We have to assume that
someone is watching and will tell us if there is a problem in different
areas. That blind assumption is a problem.*

A company lawyer agreed, stating,

*We're far too decentralized in certain areas such as environmental prob-
lems. There is a definite need for the coordination of activities. Several
departments may hit a regional EPA office or a state department of*

environmental quality with no prior coordination. We work closely with government people but we use a regular briefing on, and they could use one on, legal issues.

A senior public affairs vice president further supported this perceived lack of coordination and foresight:

We've missed opportunities in issues such as recycling. We didn't spend enough time worrying about public expectations 10 to 15 years ago and could have anticipated a lot of our traumatic experiences. We still have to find some way to get involved earlier in issues.

The chief executive acknowledged such complaints as a valid representation of the past and expressed the belief that things were changing:

We've learned to address issues and consequences directly. We tended to be a company which said, "Let the other guy do it." The other guy has a different agenda. We'd only take on one issue at a time and focus on efficiency.

He further commented that overlap across staff departments is not a problem, stating:

Frankly, I don't lose sleep over such things; we're pretty informed, informal, and close. As far as organization goes, if something's not broken, why fix it? We don't have a lot of task forces. It's not our style.

Several senior executives pointed proudly to the integration across departments that followed from the scenario on public affairs required in a department's annual plan. Progress reports were used to update these projections of departmental activity. Some of these executives felt that top-level strategy committees waste time because people with no background or interest in one another's functional concerns must sit through discussions that have no implication for their own activities.

On the other hand, it was acknowledged that inconsistencies in plans have to be resolved too often at the chief executive's level. An executive for public affairs illustrated how the innocuous piloting of a survey on human resources in a small mill town caused a public relations nightmare because it accidentally hit a local nerve about job security. The issue got resolved through the CEO's involvement following the damage, whereas there should have been advance contact by public relations people. Furthermore, several people in government affairs complained that the annual time frame was inappropriate for business planning and performance appraisals in their area. They argued that legislative issues can erupt and even be resolved before it is possible to update the annual plan. These executives complained of company inflexibility in the absence of a system for clearing company policy and primary interests. They resolve competing demands for time and resources from other company departments by "following a reactive, squeaky-wheel pattern." A general manager of a business division said that the lack of internal coordination leads the company's skilled labor negotiators to become too fearful of being second-guessed by general management.

> *These labor guys can often take too hard a line to appear loyal, only to find the company would pull the rug out from under them and take different teams. These guys have as hard a time reacting on the inside as the outside. That sure hurts morale as well as credibility.*

Finally, one financial executive commented that the company's informal coordination would be even less satisfactory when the key jobs were filled by new people who have different personalities and are less familiar with each other.

These comments do not indicate peculiar weaknesses of American Forests, but rather reflect some definite strengths. The company clearly shares a willingness to openly confront internal and also external difficulties. There is a deeply felt belief that cover-ups are ineffective and only tempt observers to suspect the worst. The company respects the legitimacy and intelligence of its critics and also has the confidence to respond to these elements. It seems equally true, however, that owing to this company's comparatively brief but stormy history, it has not developed a rich sensitivity to the needs of its stakeholders. While various executives displayed an understanding of various community segments, there are few uniformly expressed values about the corporate role towards its stakeholders outside of forthright confrontation. Some other companies have espoused more concern for locating common ground with the stakeholders. The average executive tended to speak of efforts to convince rather than compromise.

U.S. Paper

Reputation

Despite a corporate history that dates back to the turn of the century, U.S. Paper has not cultivated the same tradition of social consciousness that is so prominent in the culture of the other century-old forest products firms (Pacific Timber, Central Paper, New York Paper). This company, created through the merger of twenty paper mills in New England and New York, came under the domination of family management for much of this century. A business journal commented that for much of this period, the company "was run as a feudal empire, the sole purpose being to cut trees to keep the mills running." Consequently, the company became an extremely large timberland owner to fuel its operations. According to the many public statements of a recent U.S. Paper chief executive, this mill-level perspective inhibited a companywide overview. Deprived of a corporate-level awareness, the firm became numb to its environment. Publications have characterized the company as a "sleeping giant" and a "plodding giant." Recent efforts to transform their stodgy, insensitive culture to a more alert atmosphere have produced a remarkable internal upheaval.

The company response to a stagnant atmosphere has been to pump in a steady stream of top executives from other industries. Unlike the home-grown flavor of other forest products companies, U.S. Paper history over the past decade has been marked by tumultuous senior management turnover. This uneasiness is exemplified by the four changes of chief executive officer in that decade. At a recent meeting of the top 200 company officials, those who had been with the company for over five years were asked to stand. Only about twelve executives then stood. None of these executives nor their many transplanted lieutenants had been from the industry. One journal termed the company "notoriously inept at developing its own management." Another journal labeled the effort "one of the more ambitious reorganizations in corporate history." The changes that followed included fundamental changes in information systems, financial control systems, formal strategic planning, production scheduling, plant siting, and management development plans.

These procedural changes have been brought about by massive structural reorganization as well as what one journal terms an attempt to transform "the very 'culture' of a venerable company that had always been painfully slow to change its ways." Much of this transformation was masterminded by the executive who at the time of the study was chairman of the board, only six years into the job; however there are limits to the degree of success achievable in this period. The organizational upheaval has followed on poor financial performance but has only partly corrected problems. Despite the looming obsolescence of its aging paper mills, the company embarked on an expensive acquisition program in the 1960s. Such an effort was designed to protect this relatively debt-free company from takeover threats. While other companies began to substitute scrap wood chips for logs in the production of paper, U.S. Paper continued to use the old technology. Through the 1960s, market share deteriorated; and profitability in 1970 declined to a 2 percent return on sales. The response to this crisis was to begin the external talent recruitment. Nevertheless, performance had continued to trail the other leading firms in the industry.

Investment analysts predicted that the company would continue to lose its market share through the 1980s. Analysts further stressed the importance of carefully scrutinizing company financial reports for possible distorting of actual performance, such as the sale of big assets. Through the period of this study, sales averaged at almost 15 percent above the previous year's performance and profits were virtually unchanged. By comparison, profits increased 15 to 25 percent at the other five companies studied. The company's ratio of debt to total capitalization still far exceeds this measure of outside obligations for each of the other five companies. The company still did not even supply half of its own wood requirement. It is fairly certain that soon-to-mature forests, however, will greatly increase self-sufficiency and lead to cost reduction. Even product price changes frequently have had no bearing on their rival's behavior. Thus, the company's financial and market performance had remained laggard despite the upheaval in management.

Some members of the industry trade associations suggest that part of the company's continued difficulty is because the company is run by individuals greatly inexperienced in the industry. Some other industry executives suggest that transfusion of outside executives introduced many senior executives who came from very different company cultures and spoke different languages of management. Consequently, it was not surprising to find an extremely wide variation of stakeholder attitudes toward U.S. Paper. Several labor officials characterized their view of the company's interactions with outsiders as "clumsy" and "awkward." Environmentalists frequently claimed to have established a constructive rapport in recent years. State regulators joined with environmentalists to praise the company's stepped-up commitment to community relations. Trade association executives and congressional staffers also praised the company's contribution to industrial governmental relations. Both this more casual sampling of industry stakeholders, and also formal independent surveys commissioned by the company, however, uncovered a poor rapport with the investment community.

The intensified commitment to public affairs was manifested in many formal and informal ways. First, the new currents of top-level management had brought in executives with previous experience in government and public affairs. The president and chairman were both extremely active in industry associations and business interest groups. A second, merger method, promoting corporate sensitivity to public affairs, brought about a relatively large public affairs staff (corporate communications with 30 staff members, government affairs with 20 staff members, and environmental compliance with 6 staff members, legal with 20 staff members). Through their large public affairs mechanism, the company was better able to extend corporate sensors out into the field and to improve communication internally. For example, the government affairs office annually brought several hundred company managers to Washington, D.C. for an orientation program. Many of these managers would return to see the government affairs officers as well as legislative and agency officials once this rapport had been established.

The corporate communications department published much material for internal as well as external consumption. One particularly sophisticated internal periodical stated its purpose was to best inform U.S. Paper officials, "so that they may more effectively represent the company to the people they contact daily and to further the purpose of the company." Through such efforts, the company indicated an awareness of the importance of developing and projecting a common perspective for the company on public affairs.

One of the most impressive of these public efforts was the company's widely admired "grassroots" program. Although this program could be traced back almost 20 years in this company's history, it was a small effort until five years ago, when it was expanded from 30 company operations to every operation of the company. At the time of this research, the company had appointed at least part-time public affairs representatives at 160 company locations across the country. This represented 127 congressional districts in 35 states. All 160 local representatives were brought together at least twice a year. They were required to establish a personal rapport with key stakeholders in their territory, with particular emphasis on state and federal legislators. Clear knowledge of the company's position on a wide array of issues was required.

The corporate government affairs department further attempted to establish a continuing two-way exchange directly with this network of local representatives. In addition, the government affairs department has 12 regional and state government affairs officials in places in which the company has important interests. These full-time public affairs professionals work at all three government levels (local, state, and federal) and help in coordinating the larger, part-time network.

Added muscle has been given to this program through the time and attention of the chief executive officer and the public affairs committee of the board of directors. Often after the introduction of the grassroots program, enthusiasm began to dissipate because it became a burden to the other, more traditional company duties of these representatives for public affairs. The chief executive quickly responded to this situation by citing that these responsibilities were not optional but a part of the official job descriptions. Furthermore, he stated in a company document, "Anyone who does not respond to a request for action from our Washington office should not be on the payroll the next morning."

Finally, the chief executive had helped bring weight to this commitment to public affairs by making the program's goals a part of the corporate incentive compensation plan. At times the company has specified particular company interests in a program called "Budgeted Non-Financial Objectives." A task force of top corporate officers set these goals in human resources, communication, government affairs, and strategic planning. Sixty organizational units (two-thirds were line units and one-third were staff units) were evaluated twice a year by the senior staff officers responsible for these areas. Units are evaluated by how well they formulate their objectives as well as by their results. These ratings equal ratings of financial performance in management incentive bonuses. This special plan represented the recent efforts to change the company culture by formal mechanisms.

Establishing Contact

U.S. Paper took longer than any of the other companies to agree to participate in this study, but four months after receiving the researcher's request letter, the company responded on its own initiative. This time lapse may be partly explained by the company's difficult and widely publicized negotiations for a large tract of timber acreage. The interviews took place at the company's modest executive headquarters, which had senior executives divided between two multi-occupant center-city office buildings. A new executive building was under construction in the same city.

The public relations department acted as the researcher's tool by arranging interviews, providing lunch, and distributing the follow-up questionnaires. A public relations executive acted as a guide through the interviews to introduce the researcher. The executive response rate to the questionnaire was low (70 percent) relative to the other companies, as was the three-month return time.

Executive Themes

One of the most prominent themes that emerged from the interviews with U.S. Paper executives was the consciousness of the massive amount of internal cultural readjustment in which the company was engaged. One public relations executive stated:

> *The job of corporate communications is to help give some consistency to company statements, but this is far harder here at [U.S. Paper] than at a company like [Pacific Timber]. The perspective of the world here has been a lot more limited. You have to realize things like the fact that we as a multi-billion-dollar company didn't even have a corporate personnel department as recently as 1971. There was no management development. It just took 25 years to become a mill manager. We've had a lot of cultural problems.*

Another public affairs executive explained that all the company's efforts haven't been as successful as desired because, "Most of our efforts didn't begin until 1974 and 1975. You can't change 75 to 100 years of culture overnight." A third public affairs executive added,

> *We've had some of the departments in place in the past but no managers were held to planning and communication. It's only recently that our people are seriously being held accountable for managing.*

The chief executive explained that this effort to change the culture was really brought about to merge operations issues with public affairs. He stated:

> *When I got here, most people seemed to feel that public affairs was something separate from business operations. I want everyone to feel responsible for public affairs. A mill manager is not just hired to run the mill. He is also responsible for the public-mill interactions in his community.*

A senior vice president of one of the business divisions suggested an area that demonstrates a change in U.S. Paper's behavior. He claimed that the new chief executive:

> *. . . has introduced a more responsible culture and a new public awareness. For example, we no longer treat our assets as readily disposable. We now want to recognize an obligation to the workers of community affected by a mill.*

A human resources executive explained:

> *. . . just five years earlier a nasty mishandled mill closing showed how primitive our community relations were. A prominent mill which provided primary employment and tax support for local services was closed with no advance warning. Employees heard about it on the radio.*

He added that there were "tremendous ripples all through the system." He described the stark contrast in the new style. Teams from various staff and line divisions have since been deployed to investigate worker resettlement and alternative uses of doomed facilities.

Despite the consensus around the difficult but successful move to turn around company culture, there was far less agreement about the quality of the company's management of public affairs. The chief executive stressed the role of the board's policy committee on public affairs in reviewing policies and programs. Furthermore, he insisted that the final integration should be done by the chairman. He explained,

> *It doesn't matter if the chairman is CEO or not. I can't think of any way to coordinate public affairs policy except by way of the chairman. The chairman is Mr. Outside. No one should try to be a public affairs synthesis as Mr. Inside. That's the mold at GE and Dupont and they do extremely well.*

A senior officer for public affairs indicated that hardly any more structure is needed beyond the creation of specialized departments. He felt
that there is already close daily contact between departments such as
government affairs and public relations. He said that no weekly or
monthly or other such regular steering committee meetings were
needed, since the chairman, president, and four or five executive vice
presidents set corporate policy through informal meetings. Other vice
presidents, both line and staff, however, claimed to take their position
on public affairs independently in their area of responsibility. A
member of the company's legal department stated:

> *If the sensitivity is already there and there is good common sense, you
> don't need that much structure. . . . Any one of the executive vice presi-
> dents can make something a critical corporate issue even if others dis-
> agree. No formal coordinating mechanisms are needed here. You can
> mess up goodwill inside by constantly pestering people for support. There
> is no one way to organize a company. Any professor who says so is an
> idiot. You have to deal with different cultures.*

Several other executives, however, provided rich illustrations of important issues that fell through the cracks under the poor coordination.
One staff vice president explained that cross department efforts in
environmental compliance and in planning mill closing ran into
difficulty getting corporate approval when needed because of prior
top-level agreement. He explained,

> *We always end up changing the structure after it's too late. We have
> tended to find easy fixes in the past. . . . We've been living with a
> structure that got slipped into place in the 1950s. Most staff units still do
> the planning and the times when we get together are when we're driven
> together out of fear.*

Another executive supplied examples of a failure to spot critical environmental issues that cut across departments (such as inadvertently
criminal construction without proper licensing, continued pumping of
pollutants through a broken pipe in a misguided effort to locate a leak,
or opportunities to persuade regulators to recognize company technological inventions not specified in the guiding regulation). He concluded, "A lot of people have been trying to do a good job, but in a
fragmented way."

There was no internal disagreement, however, that the company had
come a long way towards comprehending and responding to society's
expectations of the company. Not a single executive challenged either
this effort or the acknowledgement of its historical stodginess.

Thus, in this discussion of the history of U.S. Paper, we have
suggested that this company has been struggling to release itself from
the shackles of its cultural norms. Formal structural tools, such as

expert staffing, performance appraisals, reward plans, and communication vehicles have been the primary instruments for bringing about this cultural retreading. As the company has begun to assume a longer-run strategic perspective of both the market and the environment of public affairs, it has become a more alert actor. The sudden transformation of new executive talent, however, seemed to have introduced almost as much cultural collision as cultural cohesion. The mostly strongly shared company value was the need for the company to become active in its environment. Beyond this agreement, however, executives tended to value individual prerogative. Most executives spoke with the tenacity and independence of original soloists rather than cooperative orchestra members.

Conclusions

Specific data we have gathered suggest some relevant considerations of the informal culture of the sample companies. Certain enduring behavior patterns, corporate images, and traditional executive values seem to have implications for interpreting current company performance. The cultural qualities were necessarily detected by methods beyond the quantitative questionnaire survey. However, just as any tourist's impressions of a foreign culture are susceptible to viewer bias and overly hasty stereotyping, so too are our company impressions subject to distortion. Nevertheless, it is unmistakable that three of these companies had older, more stable cultures that enhanced the likelihood of the successful infusion of executive social values throughout the corporation. Hence, these companies appeared to be more culturally sensitive both to this researcher and to a panel of prominent outside stakeholders of the industry.

Faint clues from the questionnaires—response rate and executive tenure—turned out to be accurate predictors of a company's cultural sensitivity. Each of Pacific Timber, New York Paper, and Central Paper date back to the turn of the century. They have enjoyed longer executive tenure, smoother earnings, and smoother executive successions through this period than the other three companies have had over their briefer lifetimes. Pacific Timber, through its large timber base, loyal shareowners, stable management, and carefully articulated social values, has developed and maintained a traditional, empathetic respect for stakeholder claims. At New York Paper, the attentiveness to its dominant shareowner blocks, a humble management style, and long executive terms have similarly helped the company accept outside criticism. Finally, a tradition of socially conscious chief executives and community leadership along with executive stability has fostered a strong expression of corporate social responsibility. Company newsletters, codes of ethical business conduct, executive training, and expressed attitudes showed far more acceptance of a role in public affairs for each of these three companies. These companies were also more open in interviews and more responsive to the questionnaire stage of this research.

The other three companies displayed either reticence or defensiveness in the interviews and less responsiveness to the follow-up questionnaires. These companies, Northwest Forests, American Forests, and U.S. Paper, had shorter company histories but far more tumultuous sagas of external experience in their market and community interactions, as well as far more turbulent executive successions. Northwest Forests, not yet sixty years old, has already catapulted from a small regional operation to one of the very largest companies in the industry. In this period, this company has managed to offend nearly every important stakeholder group and faced a serious imposed divestiture. Each chief executive seemed reluctant to pass on the baton and his successor promptly introduced a big change in the location, operations, or market of the company. In thirty years of life, American Forests has faced near financial disaster, the forced exit of a chief executive, the sale of a large chunk of the business, and a disruptive executive turnover. Their image among stakeholders has been more ambiguous than antagonistic. Finally, U.S. Paper, although virtually as old as the culturally more sensitive companies, and a large landowner, failed to raise its eyes beyond the mill-level perspective to see itself as an important social actor. It has faced uncertain supply problems, weak clout in the market, antiquated equipment, an outdated bureaucratic structure, and five chief executives in just over ten years. Each new chief executive brought in a cadre of loyalists from his old company in an effort to realign this stodgy company. The company has used structural tools to bring about a more sensitive company culture. Mere recognition of outside stakeholder forces took preeminence over comprehension of their complex demands.

Thus, in essence, we see that the heritage of these companies has contributed to differences in their perceived social role. The first three companies recognized an obligation to understand and even compromise with outside stakeholders. The second three companies tended to express more resentment of outsiders as intruders. These less culturally sensitive companies tended to view their main goal as improved clarity in the articulation of company interests. They valued efforts to convince over efforts to understand. It was common for the researcher to find seemingly calm executives become enraged, red-faced and even fist-pounding at the innocent mention of certain topics. This situation never occurred at the more culturally sensitive com-

CULTURAL SENSITIVITY

		High	Low
	High	Pacific Timber	American Forests U.S. Paper
STRUCTURAL SENSITIVITY	*Low*	New York Paper Central Paper	Northwest Forests

Figure 10-1.

panies, where executives responded without displaying a sense of being threatened.

There are obvious discrepancies in structural and cultural sensitivity. Figure 10-1 diagrams the general findings of our research on company culture and on company structure. We suggested that Pacific Timber was both structurally and culturally sensitive, and that Northwest Forests was relatively insensitive in both characteristics. Furthermore, New York Paper and Central Paper were perhaps more ideologically committed but did not have the equipment to act on their cultural values. American Forests and U.S. Paper may have had the equipment in place to receive information from the outside but lacked the internal capacity to understand that material properly.

A logical next step is to consider the likelihood of how the combined culture and structure affects the management of corporate public affairs. After examining the differences in the current perceptions of public affairs, we shall then examine the current performance in public affairs of these companies. An important caveat to the reader is to avoid concluding that these descriptions of structure, culture, perceptions of performance in any way represent the actual current situation of these companies. Even in the midst of this research, none of the management teams was complacent about how a company managed its public affairs. Consequently, the companies may now be very different entities than as described above.

Chapter 11

EXECUTIVE PERCEPTIONS OF PUBLIC AFFAIRS

We have developed a model for managing public affairs in a corporation that stresses (1) the need for recognizing the challenging conditions of public issues, (2) the susceptibility of executives to inherent bias, and (3) the need for companies to use and coordinate diverse perspectives. These fundamental propositions of the model of corporate sensitivity to public affairs have been elaborated in connection with presenting the data. In Chapter 7 we noted the turbulence and complexity of public issues in the forest products industry. Virtually every aspect of business activity appeared constrained by stakeholder considerations. In many ways, departmental responsibilities bias executive receptivity to outside information. In particular, public affairs executives and non–public affairs executives have sharply different sources and types of information-gathering behavior, as we saw in Chapter 8. A study of six companies has revealed that they differ markedly in their sensitivity to public affairs. An environment that is difficult to read may be perceived differently depending on company structures for channeling information. With a highly uncertain environment and the chance for departments and hence companies to misread it, we can expect perceptual variation across companies. Group-level perceptions are harder to measure and identify than individual ones. We now report on executive perceptions of the importance of issues, of appropriate positions on issues, and of the internal company consensus on some issues the industry faces.*

---

* Factor analysis of these issues proved to be less helpful than a more straightforward issue-by-issue comparison. Each of the issues was so different that it was practically impossible to correlate them, and thus reduce the 40 items to significant dimensions. The items presented then are those that displayed significant difference across either companies or receptor units.

An important task for management is coordinating the diverse perceptions that company units have. Without such coordination, the different vantage of each receptor will lead to sharply conflicting perceptions within the parent companies. Despite varied integrating efforts by the companies, several interesting departmentally biased perceptions appeared in the data. We shall examine evidence of such receptor biases before turning to the differences in company bias.

Receptor Bias

Receptor bias was investigated by comparing executives, matched by receptor unit (that is, department), across the entire sample. The features studied were (1) weight given to the various issues and (2) tolerance for outside stakeholder claims. Figure 11-1 demonstrates, for example, that departments differ markedly in how they rate the importance of challenges to their practice of clear-cutting forest land ($x^2 = 35.04$, $df = 18$, $p < .01$). Environmentalist forces concerned about damage to wildlife refuges, even-age growth, watershed harm, and scenic beauty have long fought against the presumed over-reliance on clear-cutting. The industry has countered by discussing the economic necessity of such practices in certain regions and the development of more environmentally sound compromises. Federal and state legislatures have been the primary forum for such debate. It is not surprising, then, that the executives who rate this issue of high importance (those in government relations, public affairs, and general management) are those who spend more time with state and federal legislative bodies than any other stakeholder. Stakeholder profiles (Chapter 8) show that these three departments not only spend more time with legislatures than with other departments in this category (public affairs) but that legislative involvement represents one of the top two or three uses of their time devoted to public affairs.

Turning to the second aspect of receptor bias, expressed tolerance of stakeholders, we see a similar grouping of receptor units. Executives oriented to public affairs showed the least tolerance toward environmentalists. This attitude is evident in Figure 11-2, which presents executive ratings as to the accuracy of the following statement: "Environmentalists are Easterners longing for Bambi's woods." The significant pattern showed executives in government relations, public affairs, public relations, and general management very ready to agree ($F = 3.14$, $df = 9,121$, $p < .003$). Compared with executives in other departments, these executives had exceptionally prominent interaction with environmentalists. Time devoted to environmentalists represented far lower proportions of the total stakeholders interaction time

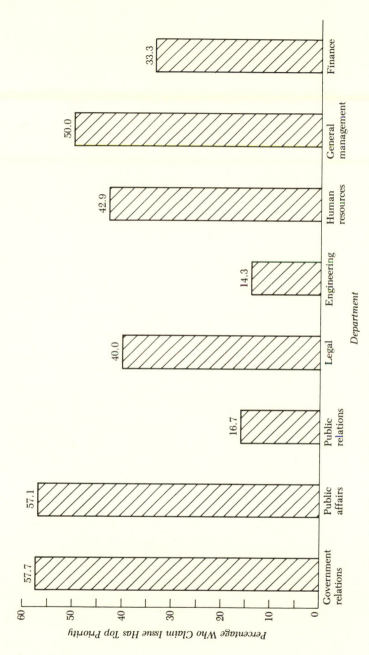

Figure 11-1 Department Perceptions of Clear-Cutting as a Company Priority. ($X^2 = 35.04$; ($df = 7$); $p < .01$.)

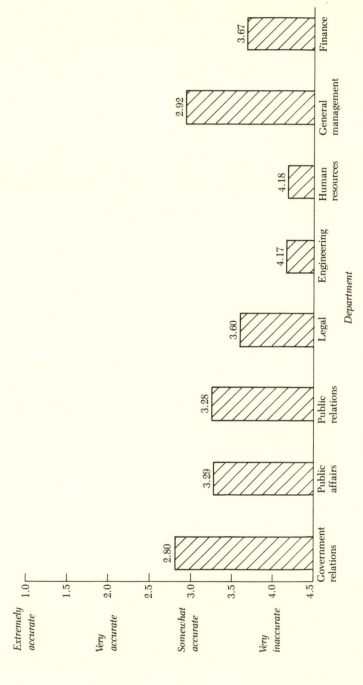

Figure 11-2 Department Ratings of Accuracy of Statement Against Environmentalists as Reflection of Company Position. ($F = 3.14$; $df = (9,121)$; $p < .005$.)

of other executives (for example, engineering, human resources, and financial executives). The particularly strong tolerance of environmentalists by engineering and human resource executives might be explained by additional data (see Chapter 8). It seems that these executives were more receptive; these two departments stood out in their much stronger appreciation of the information value of outside contacts.

A similar pattern of tolerance of environmentalist concerns was evident in another item. Figure 11-3 shows the accuracy ratios given to the statement, "Reasonable doubt exists as to the safety of using some herbicides" ($F = 1.97$, $df = 9$, 122, $p < .031$). As before, government relations, public affairs, and general management executives were less tolerant than engineering, human resources, and financial executives ($F = 2.10$, $df = 9$, 125, $p < .05$). Here once again less frequent interaction with environmentalists and greater appreciation of outsiders as information sources may help explain this pattern of perception across departments.

When this interaction time with a particular stakeholder group was increased for the "more tolerant" departments, the tolerance quickly disappeared. For example, Figure 11-4 shifted the spotlight to the investment community. This diagram shows that financial executives agreed strongly with the complaint "The investment community tends to overemphasize the short-term perspective." Meanwhile, engineering and human resource executives remained less critical of this stakeholder group also.

The tolerance of these last two departments, engineering and human relations, also diminish, as shown in Figure 11-5. Here we see a reversal of the tolerance pattern we originally saw in Figure 11-2. Engineering executives who have the greatest interaction with state and federal regulation appeared to be the most critical. Now they joined government relations executives, finance executives, and general managers in attributing high accuracy to the statement, "Regulators reflect more bureaucratic self-interest than public interest." Although the legal and general public affairs departments tend to spend a good deal of time with regulators, this interaction may seem to be more a part of regular duties than it is for engineers. This is suggested by the far higher scores these departments (public affairs and legal) had in attention to public affairs. Then, if engineers see themselves less as boundary spanners, they may feel that their time spent with regulators is more of an intrusion than a normal part of an engineer's job.

We then have evidence to support the existence of a perceptual bias associated with different departments. Our research looked at how outside stakeholders were perceived and suggested possible reasons why some departments regard stakeholder groups as annoying intruders.

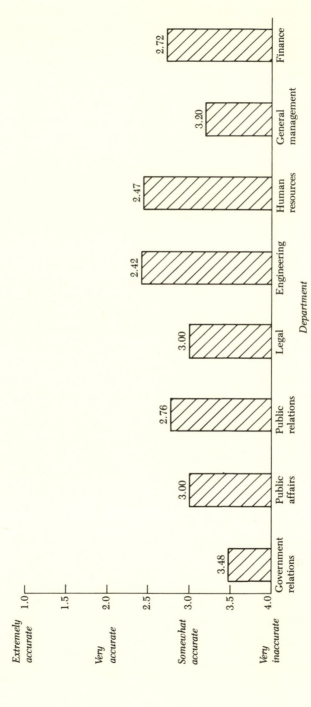

Figure 11-3   Department Ratings of Accuracy of Statement Acknowledging Reasonable Doubt About Herbicide Safety as Reflection of Company Position. $(F = 2.10; df = (9,125); p < .05.)$

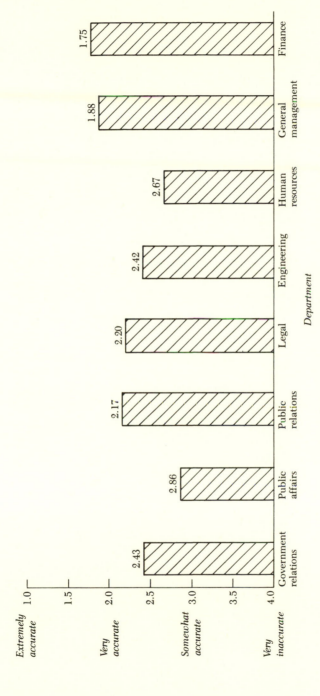

Figure 11-4   Department Ratings of Accuracy of Complaint Against Investment Community as Reflection of Company Position. ($F = 1.97$; $df = (9,122)$; $p < .05$.)

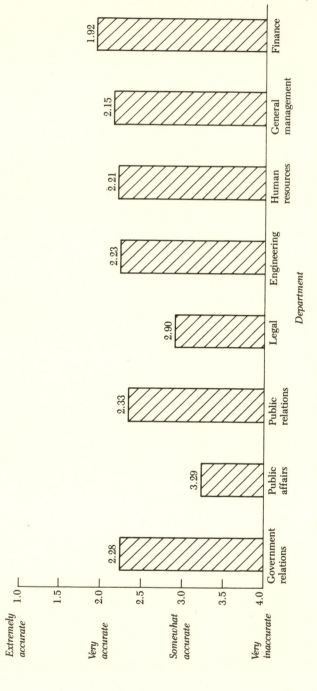

Figure 11-5 Department Ratings of Accuracy of Complaint That Regulators Reflect More Bureaucratic Self-Interest Than Public Interest as Reflection of Company Position. ($F = 2.66$; ($df = 9,127$); $p < .01$.)

Differences in Company Perceptions: Priorities

We again look at differences in (1) issue priorities and (2) issue posture (tolerance, or "accumulation") in the analysis of perceptual variations among the companies. In addition we examine a third measure, the degree of internal consensus on public issues.

The differences in rating priorities support the notion that companies simply cannot rely on trade associations to manage their public affairs while each company looks after its own market issues. The special market slot and the social role of each enterprise guarantee conflicting management interests and explanations to stakeholders across companies, even in the same industry. This premise was supported by this investigation of the forest products industry by comparing how each company ordered priority of industry issues relating to public affairs. There were 14 critical issues on which the differences in perception among companies were far more powerful than the different perception within a company (among departments). These issues appear below ranked in order of the chi square values:

1. Log exports ($X^2 = 91.68$, $df = 10$, $p < .001$)
2. Transportation issues ($X^2 = 83.55$, $df = 10$, $p < .001$)
3. Aerial spraying bans ($X^2 = 37.72$, $df = 10$, $p < .001$)
4. Formaldehyde dangers ($X^2 = 34.35$, $df = 10$, $p < .001$)
5. Herbicide restrictions ($X^2 = 34.34$, $df = 10$, $p < .001$)
6. Disposable bottle bans ($X^2 = 31.07$, $df = 10$, $p < .001$)
7. Solid waste control ($X^2 = 30.64$, $df = 10$, $p < .001$)
8. Slash burning ($X^2 = 28.51$, $df = 10$, $p < .001$)
9. Shareholder communication ($X^2 = 27.72$, $df = 10$, $p < .005$)
10. Timber taxation ($X^2 = 26.35$, $df = 10$, $p < .005$)
11. Clear-cutting restrictions ($X^2 = 23.80$, $df = 10$, $p < .01$)
12. Imports problems ($X^2 = 23.37$, $df = 10$, $p < .01$)
13. Financial disclosure ($X^2 = 20.65$, $df = 10$, $p < .05$)
14. Product standardization ($X^2 = 20.32$, $df = 10$, $p < .05$)

Five of these 14 issues are presented in Figure 11-6 as examples of the differences in preferential ratings across companies. Geographic location and product mix may explain the importance of exports at Pacific Timber and Northwest Forests. The companies more dependent on outside sources of supply were less enthusiastic about protecting the ability of suppliers to ship logs away. Companies with extensive forest land (Pacific Timber, U.S. Paper) seem to be more interested in valuation. Companies with primary emphasis on timber as opposed to paper (Pacific Timber, Northwest Forests, American Forests) were far more concerned about restrictions on aerial spraying and on clear-cutting. The other companies with a focus on paper prod-

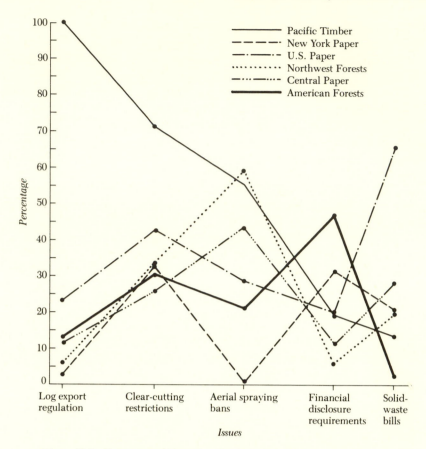

Figure 11-6 **Percentage of Executives Rating Issue as High Priority.** (Based on the rating of "high priority" from three-point range—(high, medium, low).)

ucts (Central Paper, U.S. Paper, New York Paper) were more concerned about solid-waste regulations, as were companies with weak market performance. Companies with weak market performance were more concerned about financial disclosure than strong performers (Northwest Timber) and more closely held companies (Pacific Timber). While a trade association can mediate rival demands for industry resources (lobbying, public posture, research), it is nonetheless necessary for companies to define their individual interests first and be prepared to act independently if necessary. These overlapping interests suggest that lasting clear-cutting alliances are also unlikely. Each firm is grouped with different firms, depending on the issue. Thus, beneath the surface of apparent homogeneity of interests may lurk sufficient heterogeneity to warrant homework on issues down to the level of the firm itself.

Differences in Company Perceptions: Company Posture

Not only is the relative importance of each of the public issues held differently by company, but the opinions on these issues vary substantially by company. In particular, there were 17 items on which differences by company showed high statistical significance. These items listed by topic were:

Energy
1. Nuclear reactor delays ($F = 4.29$, $df = 5,129$, $p < .001$).
2. Coal conversion pressures ($F = 5.11$, $df = 5,128$, $p < .001$).

Marketing
3. Log exports and timber prices ($F = 5.68$, $df = 5,126$, $p < .001$).
4. Canadian products ($F = 6.18$, $df = 5,126$, $p < .001$).
5. Log shipping ($F = 13.60$, $df = 5,112$, $p < .001$).

Finance
6. Investment tax credits ($F = 5.31$, $df = 5,122$, $p < .001$).
7. Tax assessment on growing timber ($F = 2.4$, $df = 5,129$, $p < .05$).
8. Financial disclosure ($F = 2.54$, $df = 5,129$, $p < .05$).

Conservation
9. Aerial spraying bans ($F = 4.78$, $df = 5,119$, $p < .001$).
10. Obligation to preserve scenic areas ($F = 8.30$, $df = 5,133$, $p < .001$).
11. Herbicide use ($F = 5.64$, $df = 5,109$, $p < .001$).
12. Reasonable fear of herbicide safety ($F = 5.40$, $df = 5,129$, $p < .001$).
13. Pesticide use ($F = 4.23$, $df = 5,123$, $p < .001$).

Labor
14. Swift and silent mill closings ($F = 5.70$, $df = 5,124$, $p < .001$).
15. Log exports and job losses ($F = 6.17$, $df = 5,130$, $p < .001$).

Regulators
16. Regulators reflect more self-interest than public interest ($F = 2.42$, $df = 5,131$, $p < .05$).
17. Regulators are really environmentalists ($F = 2.74$, $df = 5,131$, $p < .05$).

Thus, these companies significantly disagree with each other in virtually every one of the public affairs areas probed by the survey. These topics also represented many of the critical issues the industry faces (Chapter 7). Reflection on the findings leads one to question the wisdom of relying on industrywide postures. Even the most important issues for this industry allow only highly specific alliances.

Several examples of items that represent company differences on main issues appear in Figures 11-7 through 11-9. A company's position is very much affected by the particular constellation of operating, marketing, financial, and other such constraints. Figure 11-7 shows, for example, the varied positions on energy issues. Perhaps owing to different values about the environment and to community activism, the western companies felt far more constrained by delays in nuclear reactor construction. These western companies seemed to share the complaint, "Nuclear reactor delays are hurting the health of our industry" (Appendix B, question 17). Companies interested in alternative energy projects such as biomass fuel and cogeneration (Northwest Forests and U.S. Paper) felt particularly strongly about what were seen as inappropriate pressures to convert to coal fuel (Appendix B, question 17-s).

The financial and market situations of each company also affect a company's position on public affairs. Figure 11-8 indicates how Pacific Timber strongly disagreed with the criticism implied in the statement about log exports ("Log exports are raising the cost of timber throughout the country"). This company was unique in its reliance on foreign customers for logs. The other companies had far less export business in logs and consequently felt that the statement was "somewhat accurate."

Finances and marketing situation may also help explain a company's position on environmental issues. Figure 11-9 suggests that the timber-based companies (Pacific Timber, Northwest Forests, and American Forests) were stronger defenders of aerial spraying than the more paper-based companies (New York Paper, Central Paper, and U.S. Paper). This may be because herbicides and pesticides are important for the wood used in timber products. Or else this pattern may reflect a reaction to the greater community activity against aerial spraying in the West.

Even more interesting is the other environmental information in Figure 11-9. It seems that all the companies except Northwest Forests felt that the companies have some obligation to preserve scenic areas on private land (Appendix B, question 17-bb). Northwest Forest's position was a dramatic departure from the feeling of the rest of the sample. This possible lack of tolerance for external constituents may also explain their exceptionally strong agreement with the preceding item on aerial spraying ("We have used herbicides and pesticides without causing personal or property damage for decades. It's only now that we are

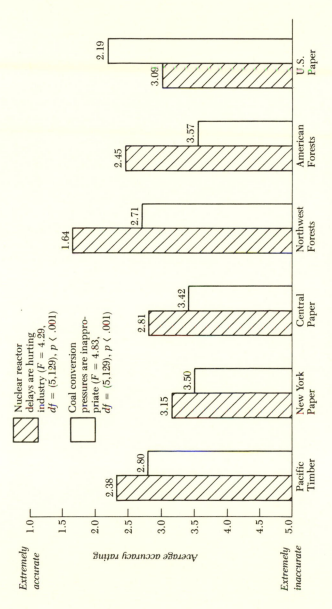

Figure 11-7   Company Ratings of Accuracy of Energy Issue Statements.

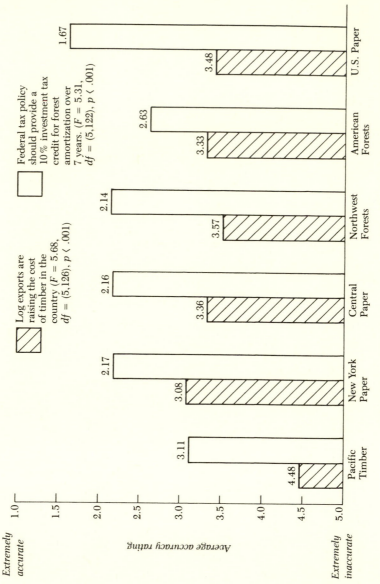

Figure 11-8 Company Rating of Accuracy of Statements on Exports and Taxes.

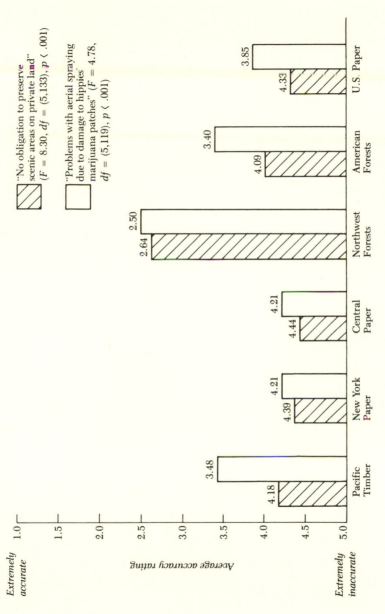

Figure 11-9   Company Ratings of Accuracy of Environmental Issue Statements.

spraying in woods where hippies have planted marijuana that we are having trouble"). There are no apparent explanations for such implied intolerance, except that the culture and structure of Northwest Forests seemed particularly insensitive to the public environment (Chapters 9 and 10).

This company's hostility towards outside stakeholder groups is also manifest in the questions that treated regulators and successful mill closings. Figure 11-10 shows that Northwest Forests, American Forests, and U.S. Paper have been more hostile towards regulators than the other three companies. These companies were significantly more in agreement with the following two statements:

1. Environmental regulators now tend to be environmentalists and, thus, suffer from a conflict of interests.
2. Regulators reflect more bureaucratic self-interest than the public interest.

A high score on these questions would indicate tolerance and also openness to new information. This tolerance of regulators suggests a basic recognition of their legitimacy. This tolerance was labeled "accommodation" in Chapter 4.

Characteristics such as product line, land ownership, finances, and operating practices are not helpful in explaining the different stands these companies have taken toward regulation. Consideration of structural and cultural sensitivity, however, may contribute to our understanding of these differences across companies. In violation of the predictions, two companies high in structural sensitivity did not appear accommodating (tolerant), and two companies that were structurally less sensitive appeared more accommodating. The sharply contrasting ratings of structural sensitivity between Pacific Timber and Northwest Forests were consistent with the dramatic differences in the degree of tolerance for outsiders. An even more striking pattern is the distinction in cultural sensitivity between the tolerant and less tolerant companies. Each of the three tolerant companies (Pacific Timber, New York Paper, and Central Paper) differed from the three less tolerant companies in the following characteristics:

1. A longer history of commitment to public affairs.
2. A tradition of long-tenured executives.
3. A higher response rate to this research.

(These corporate qualities were discussed in more detail in Chapter 10.)

Such sensitivity to public affairs seemed again the best explanation for differences in company perceptions when we look at a statement on community relations. Those companies expressed more agreement with the statement, "Mill closings should be done swiftly and silently to avoid internal community skirmishes." The distribution of company

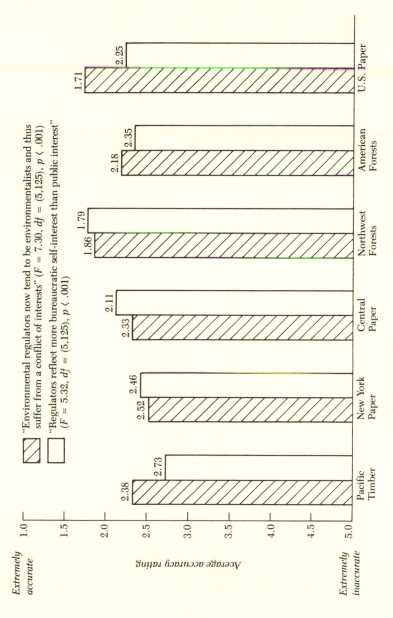

Figure 11-10 Company Ratings of Accuracy of Hostile Statements About Regulators.

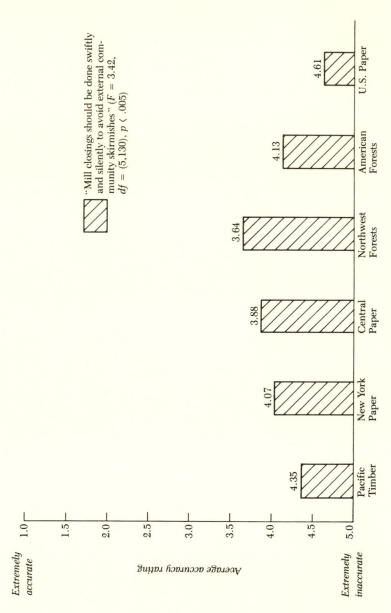

Figure 11-11   **Company Ratings of Accuracy of Statement Encouraging Swift, Silent Mill Closings.**

scores in Figure 11-11 suggests, instead of cultural sensitivity, a possible association between structural sensitivity and perception. As before, Northwest Forests displayed the least tolerance for outside stakeholder interests. On the other hand, companies that appeared better equipped to receive such local community influences, such as U.S. Paper, Pacific Timber, and, to a lesser degree, American Forests, were exceptionally willing to accommodate such stakeholders.

Differences in Company Perceptions: Internal Consensus

Lastly, we can learn something about how executives within each company agree about public affairs by examining the standard deviation values around each position taken by company executives. A high standard deviation means high internal variation, or a lack of consensus. Thus, Figure 11-12 displays the ranking within companies on each of the issues, with significant differences between companies. The obvious extreme differences are again between Pacific Timber and Northwest Forests. Comparing the actual averages for standard deviation, we find that Pacific Timber's consensus score (.19) is significantly different from the score of Northwest Forests (.27; $t = 5.28$, $df = 42$, $p < .001$). Northwest Forests is also significantly lower than each of the other companies. Northwest Forests differed from New York Paper (.20) and Central Paper (.20), ($t = 4.07$ and $t = 5.34$; respectively, $df = 46$, $p < .001$) as significantly as it did from Pacific Timber. However, American Forests (.22) and U.S. Paper (.22) also had significantly more internal perceptual consensus than Northwest Forests, but the differences were not so extreme ($t = 2.38$ and $t = 3.24$, respectively, $df = 16$, $p < .01$). Finally, there were no significant differences among the three high-consensus companies (Pacific Timber, New York Paper, and Central Paper) and between two of the three lower-consensus companies (American Forests and U.S. Paper). Thus, it may be best to think of Figure 11-12 in terms of three consensus levels.

1. High consensus: Pacific Timber, Central Paper, and New York Paper.
2. Moderate consensus: American Forests and U.S. Paper.
3. Low consensus: Northwest Forests.

Summary

Forest products executives do not interpret the public environment uniformly. How executives perceive the relative importance of issues

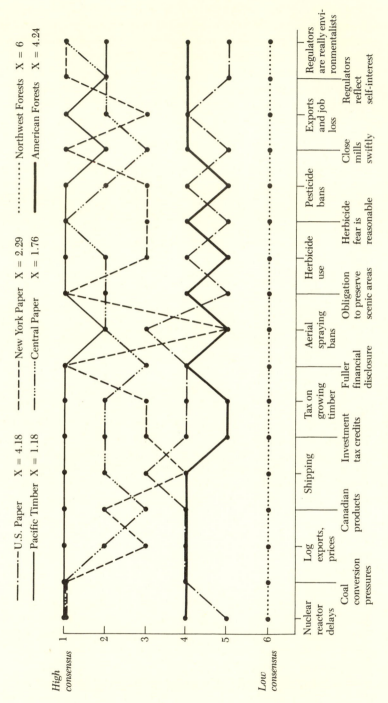

Figure 11-12   Ranking of Issues: Company Consensus. (X = average internal consensus scores.)

and the appropriate company stand on these issues is often associated with their departmental affiliation. In particular the tolerance towards outside stakeholders (financial community, regulators, environmentalists, and the like) seems to correspond with (1) the amount of time spent in contact, (2) the appreciation of the outsiders as information sources, and (3) the responsibility for paying attention to public issues. The apparent increase in hostility with increased contact may have a common cause, such as a need to spend more time to rectify problematic relations; alternatively, it may indicate a resentment that follows from increased interaction.

The differing priorities across the companies are more pronounced than the differences among companies. The relative importance of each of 14 main industry issues varies significantly. The nature of company land ownership, the emphasis on wood versus paper products, the company's financial performance, and other such characteristics are important considerations in explaining the differences in how issues are rated. Similarly, a company's stand on various public issues is affected by its special financial, market, and operating outlook.

Not all positions taken on public affairs can be explained by the particular self-interest of the company. A willingness to confer legitimacy on the expectations of environmentalists, regulators, and community members who depend on company operations may be a factor. Company sensitivity to public issues though either cultural value or company structure contributes to the differing degrees of company responses. When established responsibilities for public affairs such as interacting with regulators are viewed, the differences in companies may be accounted for by the cultural values of a company, as in Pacific Timber, Central Paper, and New York Paper. On other, more transient public issues, the sensitivity of the company's structure may be the critical factor, as in U.S. Paper, Pacific Timber, and American Forests.

Finally, both cultural and structural sensitivity may be associated with the observed company differences in the level of internal consensus on public affairs postures. Pacific Timber, Central Paper, and New York Paper, all culturally more sensitive to public affairs, had significantly more consistent perceptions about the outside. American Forests and U.S. Paper had less stable cultural sensitivity and hence less agreement in their views about the public affairs environment. These two companies, however, were at least far more structurally sensitive than most of the other companies. Perhaps this may explain why they have a significantly greater internal consensus than Northwest Forests does.

Thus, it is just as misleading to consider a single action or perception as it is merely to consider an objective environment. A corporation's position toward public affairs is affected by:

1. An executive's departmental outlook.
2. Interpreters of the company's peculiar business opportunities and posture in other business areas (marketing, finance, operations).
3. Its cultural value for involvement in public affairs.
4. The structural sensitivity of the corporate public affairs perceptual system.

The impressions from the environment to which a company responds can be understood only after assessing the above features.

These data pointedly challenge an often-echoed statement by executives who have not been active in managing public affairs. This assertion was, "We approach public affairs as an industry, not through fragmented company claims. The issues are not really company-specific." This belief in a shared fate is naive for several reasons. Stakeholder claims may affect competitors differentially (Chapter 7). It is extremely improbable that any two companies have even the same concept of the realities of the public affairs environment. The clarity and openness of company beliefs varied widely across the sample.

Chapter 12

COMPANY SOCIAL RESPONSIVENESS

Corporate social performance is frequently discussed but rarely clarified. Substantial company efforts have been dedicated to managing the corporate social performance of each of the six forest products companies in this study. Executives in these companies, however, were far less confident in discussing this sort of performance than they were when discussing market performance. Through literature reviews (Chapter 2), we have suggested that corporate social performance should be separated into social responsibility (ethical evaluations of company *outcomes* of corporate acts) and social responsiveness (a company's *process* for understanding its setting in public affairs). A model of public affairs management was developed (Chapter 4) in which responsiveness was construed as a function of the company's structure for gathering information. Social responsiveness is not easily measured. Seven possible subcomponents of this dimension are suggested. The underlying premise of these components is that corporate awareness is dictated by the firm's ability to be (1) trusted (credibility), (2) open to outsiders (accessibility), (3) knowledgeable (preparedness), (4) consistent (reliability), (5) alert (attentiveness), (6) respectful (legitimacy), (7) conscious of its role (clarity of interests). We shall pinpoint the distinction between social responsiveness and social responsibility. We shall also look at social responsiveness in the forest products industry relative to other industries and across the companies under study. Furthermore, we shall compare this general rating in responsiveness to the suggested specific subcomponents.

We have found that company efforts and perceptions vary relative to public affairs. The importance of both the cultural and structural qualities of sensitivity to public affairs, which seem important in understanding differences in company perceptions, may also yield some insight into why companies perform differently. Evaluating performance in public affairs is almost as challenging as identifying perception of public affairs. A company's placement may be inconsistent across issues as it is in perception. In connection with measurement (Chapter 5), it was pointed out that objective qualitative data are certainly available (for example, prosecutions, lawsuits, license granting time). There are three problems, however, with such data: (1) There is no basis for assessing the importance of one type of data relative to another. (2) Data are unavailable for most types of activities in public affairs. (3) This sort of data reflects situations where some companies face more difficulties than others (for example, operating in environmentally conscious geographic regions) but are still more effective.

It is not surprising, then, that the academic researchers reviewed (Chapter 2) and each of the companies in the present study have not developed appraisals of company social performance. The assessments to be presented are drawn from a survey of ten foremost outside stakeholder groups. These groups reflect the main public issues that were identified as industry concerns (Chapter 7). Furthermore, these stakeholders are the principal targets of company efforts in public affairs (Chapters 8, 9, and 10). Finally, because of the enduring nature of these issues, their exploration captures more of a continuing state of behavior than past isolated action. Companies may enjoy varied success with different segments of the public. This panel of 75 outside judges thus is designed to capture a very high within-group variance. Therefore, it will at times be appropriate to consider these judges in their stakeholder groups rather than as a single panel.*

Industry Responsiveness

The stakeholder panel rated the forest products industry just slightly better than average in its management of public affairs. Figure 12-1 shows that these judges rated five companies as substantially less responsive than the forest products industry (petroleum, steel, chemicals, tobacco, and mining) and six industries as comparable to or better than forest products (insurance, consumer products, banking, airlines, and broadcasting). In fact, the broadcasting and airlines industries were considered more socially responsive. This ordering of the industries is strengthened by the significant difference between the average of the

---

* Because (1) it is desired to show the variation among the 75 judges and (2) the cell size is low when broken down into stakeholder groups, inferential statistics will not be referred to heavily here. This procedure is safe, since the inter-rater reliability within each group was very high ($r = .98$) for each item. Labor union officials and public affairs officials were not included in such comparisons because of their low responses.

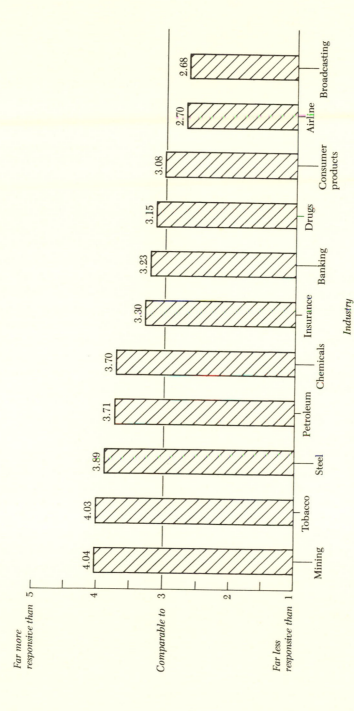

Figure 12-1 Social Responsiveness of the Forest Products Industry Compared with Other Large Industries (ratings by stakeholder). (Overall average = 3.43 (sd = .15); f = 4.69, df = 10, p < .001 (two-tailed).)

more responsive industries and the average of the less responsive industries ($t = 4.69$, $df = 11$, $p < .001$). Furthermore, these findings exactly parallel findings of a survey of the general public.[1] Finally, the mean of the ratings of the twenty largest forest products companies in social responsibility (ethics) and social responsiveness (alertness) placed the industry as "average" (3.10 and 3.17, respectively; $r = .81$, $p < .001$ for responsibility and responsiveness.

Stakeholder Bias

Having scored this industry relative to other important industries, we can look inward at our panel of judges. The judges seemed to vary markedly along stakeholder lines ($F = 3.62$, $df = 71$, $p > .001$). Figure 12-2 presents these differences in order of decreasing favorability. Industry executives, trade association members, and executives clearly rated the industry companies most favorably; these were followed in order by ratings of the investment community (representing local regulators), academicians, journalists, federal regulators, and environmentalists. The more favorable stakeholder groups tended to have a broader multi-issue interaction with forest products companies, while the less favorable groups have more interaction with the companies on specific issues. This pattern also resembles the company preferences for information sources (Chapter 8). That is, the more issue-focused the interactions with stakeholders, the less valued this group as an information source.

Not only do the judges of social performance vary by category, but there is also variance across the different dimensions of social performance itself. Since the industry scores on the two performance dimensions were so close, the proposed distinction between social "responsibility" and social "responsiveness" can be best demonstrated in the company comparisons that follow. It is possible, however, to observe industrywide differences in the proposed components of responsiveness. Figure 12-3 suggests that the industry demonstrated better "accessibility" to outsiders, more "preparedness" for public issues, and more "reliability," or consistency, than it does "credibility" for company statements relative to "perceived legitimacy of outsiders," displaying "attentiveness" (or leadership) towards outsiders, and distinguishing company interests from the public interest. In particular, accessibility, preparedness, and reliability were significantly higher than the average across the seven dimensions ($t = 2.64$, 3.34, and 2.64, respectively; $df = 74$, $p < .01$ for each), and the perceived legitimacy of outsiders was rated significantly below the average of these seven dimensions ($t = 4.24$, $df = 72$, $p < .001$).

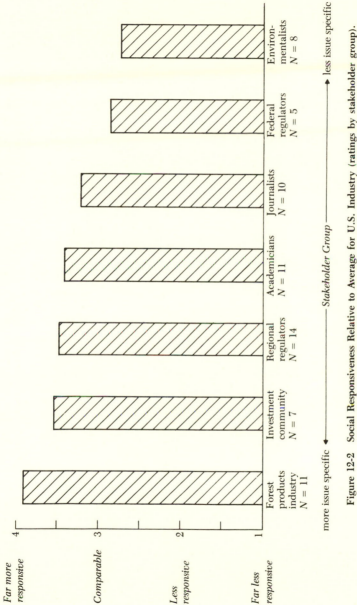

Figure 12-2 **Social Responsiveness Relative to Average for U.S. Industry (ratings by stakeholder group).** (Overall average = 3.42 (*sd* = 0.57); *F* = 3.62; *df* = 71; *p* < .001.) Groups with less than 5: labor, *N* = 3; congress staffers, *N* = 4; public affairs professionals, *N* = 2.

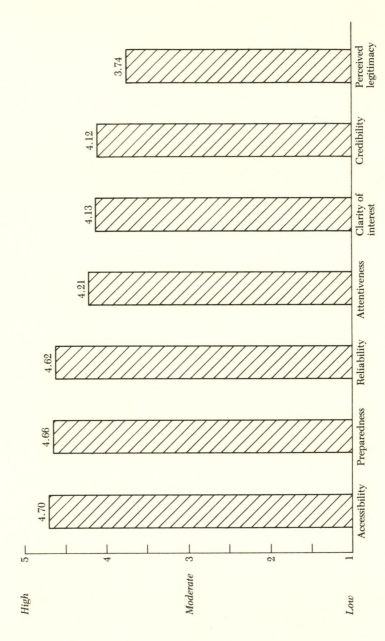

Figure 12-3 Stakeholder Ratings of Forest Products Industry's Responsiveness Along Seven Dimensions. (Based on industry sample studied more intensively in preceding chapters.) Overall average = 4.31; *sd* = .35.

These responsiveness components were compared with the initial general measure of responsiveness in several ways. First, the aggregate sum of the seven dimensions was positively related to responsiveness. The highest relations with total responsiveness were by preparedness of company officials (having done their homework), and clarity of company interests (as distinguished from the public interest) ($r = .88$, $p <$ .001 for each). Ratings of the reliability, or consistency, of company statements, the credibility, or believability, of company statements, and the perceived legitimacy of outsiders for the dimension that had the next-highest correlation with general responsiveness ($r = .69$, .63, and .61, respectively; $p < .01$). Thus it seems that the industry varies in its success across the different dimensions, but its success has no correspondence to the relative weighting given these characteristics in stakeholders' notions of responsiveness. The companies appeared to show their responsiveness more through their deliberate *actions* (reliability, preparedness, accessibility) and less through *attitudes* that show an understanding of outsiders (clarity of interest, perceived legitimacy, credibility, attentiveness).

Company Differences

It is important, in discussing the social performance of each of the six companies examined intensively, to view each in relation to the top twenty companies in the industry. Figure 12-4 diagrams the ratings of each of these companies on social responsibility and on social responsiveness. It appears, for social responsibility, that three companies were somewhat above the industry average, two companies were about average, and one company was far worse than the industry average. Specifically, Pacific Timber and Central Paper exceeded the industry average of 3.1 ($t = 6.36$, $df = 140$, $p < .001$ and $t = 4.33$, $df = 142$, $p <$ .001, respectively). New York Paper did not significantly exceed the industry average ($T = 1.66$, N.S.). American Forests and U.S. Paper were roughly at the industry average, while Northwest Forests was significantly below the industry average ($t = 4.33$, $df = 142$, $p < .001$).

Similarly, this sample hovered around the industry average in ratings of social responsiveness. Once again, Pacific Timber well exceeded the industry average ($t = 9.26$, $df = 132$, $p < .001$); however, this time Pacific Timber was immediately followed by American Forests and U.S. Paper. Again, Northwest Forests was closest to the industry average, with Central Paper and New York Paper fairly close to the industry average. Pacific Timber and Northwest Forests maintained their respective positions at the top and bottom of each of these dimensions of social performance. The pattern of the middle four companies is

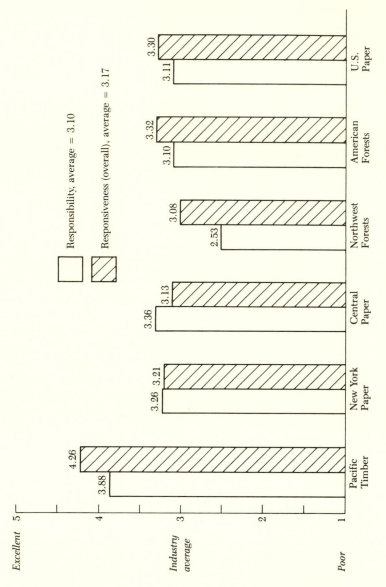

Figure 12-4   Comparisons of Company Social Performance (ratings by stakeholders).

ambiguous, since it appears as though New York Paper, while perceived as more ethical (responsible), is seen as less alert (responsive) than American Forests and U.S. Paper.

This performance appraisal of the extreme companies, Pacific Timber and Northwest Forests, is supported in pairwise t statistical comparisons in social responsibility and social responsiveness. When Pacific Timber and Northwest Forests were compared with each other, the differences in social responsibility and social responsiveness were extremely significant ($t = 7.05$, $df = 132$, $p < .001$, and $t = 5.88$, $df = 121$, $p < .001$, respectively). They also differed significantly in both dimensions when compared with the other four companies. Pairwise statistical comparisons among the other four companies on both performance dimensions still eluded statistical significance. The difficulty here stems from the great diversity among the judges. As we have cautioned, the goal of collecting the data was to maximize rather than minimize within-group variance across the complete panel of stakeholder judges. The response bias of each stakeholder group was unmistakably displayed in the range of judgments on the relative responsiveness position of our forest products companies among large U.S. industries (see Figure 12-2). It seemed as if the stakeholders with the least issue-specific interaction with the industry (like industry trade associations or the investment community) had far more favorable views than stakeholder groups with more issue-specific interaction with the industry (say federal regulators or environmentalists). Furthermore, it is probable that each stakeholder group has a somewhat different perspective and history of dealings with a particular company.

So that we should avoid the dulling effect of a mass of disparate data from the individual sources in the total stakeholder panel, scores relative to the companies were classified by stakeholder group for both categories—responsiveness and responsibility. Figure 12-5 shows the six companies as rated by several stakeholder groups (those with over five respondents), for social responsibility. Stakeholders are presented in order of favored view toward the industry, as shown in Figure 12-2. First, the general downward trend further illustrates the harsher ratings by certain stakeholder groups. The most striking feature is the consistently high assessment of Pacific Timber and the consistently low assessment of Northwest Forests. The slight deviations in this pattern are the relatively mild ratings given to Northwest Forests by the investment community and journalists, and the relatively harsh ratings given to Pacific Timber by the environmentalists. Also Central Paper and to a lesser extent New York Paper once again received fairly high ratings. U.S. Paper's ratings were a bit lower than New York Paper and certainly lower than Central Paper and Pacific Timber. American Forests' ratings by journalists and the investment community were

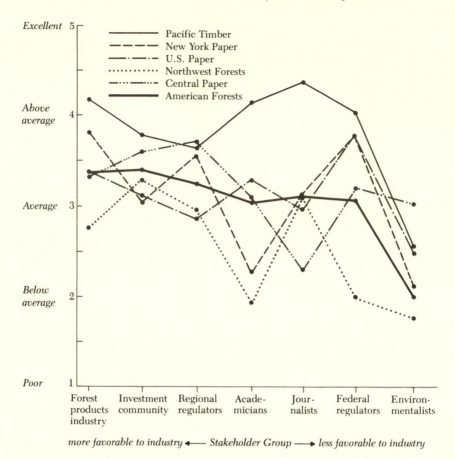

more favorable to industry ◄——— *Stakeholder Group* ———► less favorable to industry

Figure 12-5   **Company Social Responsibility (ratings by stakeholder group).**

exceptions to what was generally seen as the second least socially responsible company in the sample. These findings support the previous
results from the aggregate stakeholder panel.

Similarly, Figure 12-6 displayed ratings of company social responsiveness extended by the seven stakeholder groups. Once again Pacific
Timber received consistently very high ratings from each of the
stakeholder groups—except from environmentalists; the rating from
them well exceeded the group's downward bias towards the industry.
Northwest Forests was ranked at or near the bottom by each group
with the exception of the markedly kinder rating from the trade association judges (forest products industry) and the investment community.
The reversal in position among the middle four companies is also demonstrated more clearly in comparing this diagram with Figure 12-5. It
can now be seen that American Forests and U.S. Paper were ranked

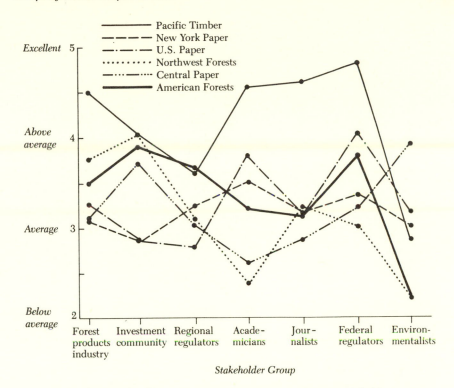

Figure 12-6   Company Social Responsiveness (ratings by stakeholder group).

near the top by every group, while New York Paper and Central Paper were ranked at the bottom by almost every stakeholder group. Thus, this comparison of company ratings by stakeholder groups has added to the confidence in our observations that (1) Pacific Timber and Northwest Forests represent the extremes in social performance, (2) the ratings of the middle-performing four companies indicated a poor correspondence between the more socially responsible (Central Paper and New York Paper) and the more socially responsive (U.S. Paper and American Forests).

Executives' ratings of their own company's social performance did not correspond to the outside ratings from stakeholders in even a general way. Executives were asked to rate the company's performance in public affairs relative to other companies in several areas. Four areas for which differences among company self-assessments were significant are presented in Figure 12-7.* No company rated itself relative to the other companies in the same order as the ratings by stakeholders. Even

---

* The following three self-assessments were not significantly different areas for the companies: labor relations, legal compliance, and community relations.

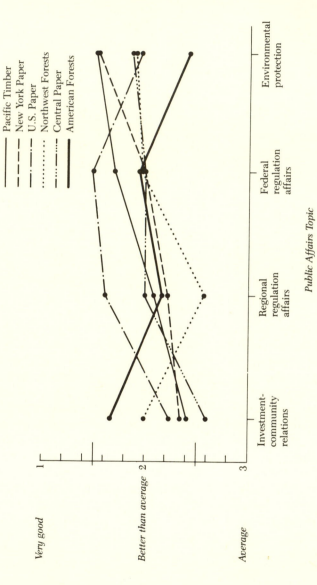

Figure 12-7 Self-Assessment of Social Performance by Company by Topic.
(Executives rated their own company performance.)

rough high-versus-low categories do not correspond for a company in more than two areas. Thus, there is reason to suspect a significant gap in how the companies in an industry are perceived from the inside and from the outside.

Summary

A large panel of outside stakeholders was used to evaluate the performance in public affairs of the forest products companies under analysis. This panel, in agreement with a sizable survey of the general public, placed the industry toward the center of American industry in social performance. These judges, however, varied significantly across stakeholder groups. In reflection on some earlier findings, we can note a striking resemblance between (1) the industry ratings of the value of particular stakeholder group as an information source (Chapter 8), and (2) the responsiveness ratings those stakeholder groups assigned to the industry. This suggests some common feelings between outsiders and insiders that probably make themselves known in both directions. Essentially the stakeholder groups who focus on specific issues, do not hold the industry in high favor.

The companies sampled within this industry were rated as roughly average in social performance. One company, Pacific Timber, was substantially higher in both the social responsibility and social responsiveness. This same company scored far higher in structural sensitivity, in cultural sensitivity, in tolerance (accommodation) and internal consensus. Another company, Northwest Forests, was rated as substantially less socially responsible and socially responsive. This company was also found to be lower in both structural and cultural sensitivity, as well as in the perceptual dimensions. Two other companies, Central Paper and New York Paper, were rated high only in social responsibility. These two companies were found to be strong in cultural sensitivity but weaker in structural sensitivity. They also seemed more tolerant of

		RESPONSIBILITY	
		High	*Low*
RESPONSIVENESS	*High*	Pacific Timber	American Forest U.S. Paper
	Low	New York Paper Central Paper	Northwest Forests

Figure 12-8   Summary of Company Performance.

the better-recognized concerns in public affairs. The last two companies, American Forests and U.S. Paper, were considered by
stakeholders to be higher in social responsiveness than in social responsibility. These companies were also found more structurally sensitive,
although less culturally sensitive, and to have less perceptual consensus. Therefore these findings generate further hypotheses about a possible link between structural receptivity and social responsiveness as
well as between cultural receptivity and social responsibility.

We have made four general observations about social performance.
First the ethical component, responsibility, may not be the same as the
state of alertness, or responsiveness. Second, general responsiveness
may be classified by specific performance dimensions, which vary in
contribution. This study did not try to similarly analyze social responsibility. Third, outside stakeholder groups may view an industry differently from how they view companies within that industry, depending
on each group's relation to the industry; the more issue-specific
stakeholders appeared to be more critical judges. Fourth, company
executives seem to have very different estimates of relative company
social performance from those of outside stakeholders.

Endnote

1. Yankelovich, Skelly, and White Inc., *Public Policy Pressures on the Forest Products
   Industry*, prepared for the American Forest Products Institute (1979).

Chapter 13

CONCLUSIONS

We have long known that a company acts toward the outside world in a way it deems appropriate with the particular market environment it encounters. We have tried to extend the notion of appropriate and inappropriate external relations from the marketplace to the company's environment provided by public affairs. By holding industry as a constant, we have found that six comparably sized competing firms all face a public affairs environment that is at least as challenging as their marketplace. Furthermore, we have found strong differences in the efforts these companies have directed towards managing public affairs. These efforts seemed to be associated with difference in company effectiveness. Certain company efforts were manifested by the current *structure* of executive responsibilities within the company. Other company efforts were manifested by the *cultural* traditions that have emerged over the company's history. Companies whose corporate structure displayed greater sensitivity to public affairs were rated by external constituencies as having acted with greater alertness or more *responsively*. Companies whose corporate culture displayed greater sensitivity to public affairs were rated as having acted more ethically or *responsibly*. We shall relate these findings to the original hypothetical model and reflect on the implications beyond this study.

The Business Constituency beyond the Market

The increased public encroachment on the historical prerogatives of management in the private sector have caused an extensive realignment in the attention of business people. In the last two decades the most important institutions in U.S. society have been forced to explain how they are meeting changing public expectations. Organized religion, government, labor, and business have been forced to become conscious of a volatile public constituency beyond the market. Business, in particular, has historically had an easily identified constituency of suppliers, competitors, and employees.

Continuous attention to customers, suppliers and employees, along with periodic consideration of governmental activity was once enough to guarantee sensitivity to the business environment. Accordingly, academic literature on organizational behavior has advanced an anachronistically narrow definition of the business environment that rarely looks beyond market and technology issues to adaptation to a perceived environment. Such literature has frequently spoken with incomplete notions of the environment and inadequate explanations of who in the organization reads the environment.

Today's management, however, must be sensitive to a much larger audience than what has been previously recognized. The surging influence of interest groups beyond the marketplace represents the dynamic force in what Parsons called the "institutional" environment.[1] By this theory, the firm's goal is not the mere procurement of the resources needed for operating nor the securing of consumers of output:[2]

> *The problem concerns rather the compatibility of the institutional patterns with which the organization operates with those of other organizations and social units as related to the integrative agencies of the society as a whole.*

Thus the critical task is to maintain society's legitimizing of corporate activities. The legitimate status was symbolically conferred with the granting of the corporate charter and figuratively comes up for frequent renewal.

This renewal requires a broad responsiveness to competing social claims. Companies designed strictly for sensitivity to the market environment will be less capable of interacting with the environment for purposes other than procuring input or disposing of output. Businesses have not had the luxury of ignoring these claims by outside stakeholders. Every aspect of company activity can, in some way, be fundamentally altered by the environment of public affairs. Therefore, executives in various locations in a corporation may feel a pressing obligation to respond to events in this institutional environment, regardless of their level of awareness. Accordingly, there is a high likelihood of overlapping, conflicting, and ill-informed actions by executives in the same company.

Such muddled management of the business-society interface is plainly implied through recent business and academic publications on managing public affairs. This flurry of literature has contributed to a chaotic map of assigning responsibility for public affairs. Depending on the article, the board of directors, chief executives, government affairs officers, public relations officials, legal officers, divisional general management, corporate planners, futurists, and technical compliance officers have each been identified as the primary agent to deal with public issues. These different company officials have been variously labeled "the panel of outside reviewers," "the chief architect of the organizational purpose," "the company's representative to the political process," "the company voice," "the corporate conscience," "the person in the center of the action," and "the visionary with the long-range perspectives." This literature has failed to offer a comprehensive consistent view of the entire set of company executives who should be aware of the public; furthermore, this literature has used unsystematic, anecdotal data on isolated issues to represent overall social responsiveness.

A Sensory-System Model

This study of the management of public affairs has offered a framework for analyzing a company's preparedness through a comparison with the human sensory system. The basic components consist of three fundamental concepts: (1) the *structural sensitivity* of the company (2) the quality of the company's *public affairs perceptions,* and (3) the consequent state of *social responsiveness* to stakeholder expectations. This model is based on the proposition that the public affairs environment of large U.S. corporations is a complex mosaic of specialized stakeholder interest groups. Furthermore, the claims of these stakeholders are dynamic, both in intensity and location. As specific stakeholder issues travel through their independent life stages, the locus of debate may be anywhere—community discussions, public campaigns, legislative battles, regulatory rulings, or courtroom debates.

The shifting locus of issue debate, along with the technical specifics of these issues, requires the coordinated functional expertise of many departments within a company. The primary component of structural sensitivity is the *receptivity* of company departments to public affairs signals. This departmental receptivity is analogous to the diverse sensory receptors with which the human detects external stimuli (receptors for light, sound, taste, touch, and smell). Units may be in place to receive information but not designed to receive the signals. Next, the information from these receptors must be *transmitted* back into the organization for further processing. Company units may acquire important information but not be able to share it. This transmitting strength can be conceived of as the influence of public affairs information on corporate activity. The final aspect of structural sensitivity is the assimilation of diverse bits of information through *integrating* devices. A consistent picture of the outside world must be drawn to ensure proper allocation of internal company resources and a consistent image among stakeholders. Therefore, internal coordination is necessary to reconcile conflicting views of the public from the different windows of each department.

This information net is held to affect the quality of two dimensions of public affairs perceptions. These dimensions are (1) the *tolerance* toward the specific claims of stakeholders rather than stereotyped reaction, and (2) the internal agreement, or *consensus*, on company position on important public issues. Finally these perceptions are translated into corporate actions, which can be measured by corporate *responsibility* (ethics) or corporate *responsiveness* (alertness). Responsiveness embraces dimensions of performance such as the advance preparedness on issues, the credibility of company communication, and the reliability of company actions.

Public Affairs and Corporate Structure

This model was applied to the forest products industry, and the profiles of six of the ten largest firms in this industry were compared. This test of the model supported several fundamental propositions of the model. First, we found that public issues were sufficiently important and uncertain to warrant a sophisticated apparatus to react to the signals from this environment. Second, we saw that departments varied in their receptivity to public affairs. Third, we found that the companies could be meaningfully distinguished from each other by their structural sensitivity to public affairs. Finally, these differences in structural sensitivity seemed to correspond with the performance of these companies toward public affairs. This meant that those companies with a sophisticated structure for gathering and interpreting outside information showed greater responsiveness to outside stakeholders of this industry.

On the first proposition, relative to the significance of public affairs, we have seen that special public interests powerfully influence each main business function. The supply of *raw materials* is very much affected by public forest land, tax and zoning legislation, and the regulation of forest management practices (size of clear-cutting lots, soil conservation, fire control, herbicide and pesticide restrictions). Company *production* is affected by limits on air and stream pollution and by labor relations. *Financial* issues are affected by taxation of land and equipment and by reporting requirements. Finally, *market* activities are restrained by limits on log exports, strict price penalties for fixing prices, and proposed product standardizations. These issues exist at the national and local level and affect each company differently. This review of the environment of industry indicated that the public affairs part of the business environment easily rivals the importance of the market and technological sectors. More important, however, this environmental analysis of the forest products industry has illustrated the need for individual company mechanisms to manage public affairs. Because of the company-specific local pressures, the different effects of regulation across competitors, and the different strategic priorities of companies within the same industry, simple reliance on industrywide approaches through trade associations is far from sufficient to represent a company's interests. Finally, the unstable and diverse nature of the public claims has demonstrated the need for individual companies to draw from a wide array of internal executive talents.

When we looked at how these individual companies, in fact, used varied internal executive expertise, we found that interactions with stakeholders accounted for at least 25 percent of the working time of executives in every department, whether line or staff. Executives across all departments were alike in their preference for impersonal sources of information about public affairs (literature) over personal contact with stakeholders. Executives differed across departments in that public affairs executives (government affairs, public affairs, legal, and public relations) tended to (1) spend more time with outside stakeholders, (2) maintain contact with a broader array of outside stakeholders, and (3) recognize a greater formal obligation to watch over public affairs. Non–public affairs executives (general management, human resources, engineering, and finance) tended to be more issue-specific in their interaction with stakeholders, more respectful of outsiders as information sources, and more interested in listening to outsiders than expounding. Given such differences, then, we further see that a realistically broad view of corporate exposure to public issues regulates the coordination and balance of executive perspectives across departments to expose a broad view of public affairs. A failure to consider departmental bias would allow certain distorting factors to triumph.

At last, looking at such measures of departmental receptivity across the companies, we found that characteristics such as the breadth of outside contact, the ability to appreciate the information value of interaction with stakeholders, the amount of attention directed towards public affairs, the readiness to listen to outsiders, and the depth of involvement in issues differed significantly across the companies. These dimensions of company receptivity are essentially company attributes that allow for empathy with stakeholder claims or an understanding of them. Similar to the differences in receptivity across companies were significant differences in the influence of the information about public affairs (transmission strength) as well as differences in internal coordination (integration) of this information. It was suggested that these company traits—receptivity, transmission, and integration—could be considered distinct dimensions of how structurally sensitive a company is in perceiving public affairs. Companies with superior structural sensitivity were hypothesized to be more socially responsive.

Responsiveness and Corporate Structure

The relation between structure and performance is central to this study, and it was supported by the data. The most structurally sensitive companies—Pacific Timber, American Paper, and U.S. Paper—were rated by stakeholders as the most responsive to public affairs. Accordingly, the least structurally sensitive companies were rated by stakeholders as the least responsive to public affairs. While the stakeholder groups differed from each other in their appraisal of the industry, the rough listing by rank of company responsiveness was remarkably consistent across the groups. Companies that were seen as alert to more than one set of outside constituents were seen as alert by essentially all their constituencies. While a company's responsiveness relative to other companies could be generalized across stakeholder groups, it was not uniformly rated by each stakeholder group. For example, some companies received their strongest ratings from federal regulators. Such a difference may be explained by how companies differ in their internal emphasis on external matters. For example, a stronger internal focus on financial matters at Northwest Forests, American Forests, and Central Paper can be recognized from their histories. Thus, the favorable rating given by the investment community, relative to other stakeholder groups, to these companies may have indicated this difference in focus within companies.

Public Affairs and Corporate Culture

Reference to company history was critical in explaining an even more significant set of results. Although we found a link between company structure and performance as measured by responsiveness, structural sensitivity did not seem to correspond with either a company's perception of public affairs or its social responsibility. The consideration of each company's cultural context, however, was helpful in shedding some light on differences in both company perception and company social responsibility.

While this concept of cultural sensitivity was not originally designated in the proposed model, it became unavoidably important to the research. The appreciation of company culture was initially suggested through the differing levels of graciousness that the companies extended towards this research. Some companies seemed to respond to the researcher's initial overture faster and took greater pains to accommodate him than other companies did. Such differences were also manifest in the response rate and the speed of return of questionnaires distributed to each company. Further investigation into the history of these companies uncovered likely explanatory conditions for these company differences. Three companies—Pacific Timber, New York Paper, and Central Paper—were old, established companies with stable market and financial histories. These companies had long-standing well-articulated codes of business conduct, long traditions of community awareness, and smooth executive succession. These companies were enthusiastic about this research despite their inherent feeling that their performance was uneven. Finally, the distinct internal quality that distinguished these three culturally sensitive companies from the other three was their curiosity about stakeholder interests.

The three other, less culturally sensitive companies—Northwest Forests, American Forests, and U.S. Paper—were somewhat younger and far more unstable in their market and financial histories. This suggests some spillover in performance towards the different external sectors. Further, the last-mentioned companies lacked strong traditions of public concern. Finally, each had suffered volatile executive transitions. The atmosphere that was apparent from this cultural setting suggested suspicion rather than curiosity. While many executives in these culturally less sensitive companies were socially conscious individuals, the overall goal of their corporate approach to public affairs seemed to be directed towards *persuasion* rather than *understanding*.

The differences in these cultural patterns were parallel to how the companies beheld public issues. We saw first that company backgrounds helped explain company priorities and stands on various issues. For example, log-exporting companies were naturally the most concerned about proposed restriction on exporting logs; large land-owning companies were the most concerned about land taxation and timber harvesting issues; and companies oriented to paper products were the most concerned about pollution control. Beyond such background differences in operations, company differences in cultural sensitivity seemed to correspond with current perceptual openness (tolerance) towards outside stakeholders. Those companies who seemed least culturally sensitive were also more likely to agree with statements that expressed hostility or resentment towards stakeholders. Furthermore, the culturally sensitive companies had a greater degree of internal agreement about the company position on issues and about the primary interests of the company. This internal sharing of values would probably mean less dysfunctional internal squabbling over limited resources as well as a more consistent set of actions toward the outside.

Finally, when we apply this notion of cultural sensitivity to company public affairs performance, we see that outside stakeholders also detected parallel differences in those companies. While social responsiveness and social responsibility is often blurred in the academic literature, the constituents of the business environment were able to make these distinctions in judging company social performance. Cultural sensitivity did not correspond with responsiveness; it did with responsibility. Thus, those companies that were the most culturally sensitive in their traditions were also viewed by their actions as demonstrating the most ethical commitment. Thus, cultural sensitivity and structural sensitivity may contribute to different dimensions of company performance.

A Revised Model

Given this last statement then, we should revise the original model to the model diagrammed in Figure 13-1. The importance of this model is that the company needs to have both the equipment in place to receive information from the outside and the internal capacity to understand what has been gathered. The original model was inadequate because it proposed a mechanical sensory system without allowing for the nonrational context of this system. This resembled the mistake of studying human perceptions and behavior strictly on the basis of physiological structures. To understand the human character, we must supplement our knowledge of sensory organs with insight into individual personality and setting. Perceptual blockages occur as readily through personality extensions like expectations and fears as through faulty receptors. Certainly we should expect at least as much complexity when we consider the social character of a large corporation.

Selznick described this notion of organizational character as the infusion of value, which he called the "institutional embodiment of purpose." Using a comparison like that developed above, Selznick elaborated:[3]

> *The study of institutions is in some ways comparable to the clinical study of personality. It requires a genetic and developmental approach, an emphasis on historical origin and growth stages.*

Only one company in the study, Pacific Timber, had institutionalized the structural and cultural aspects of its character. Only one company, Northwest Forests, was relatively poorly developed in both of these dimensions. The character of the other four companies were at differ-

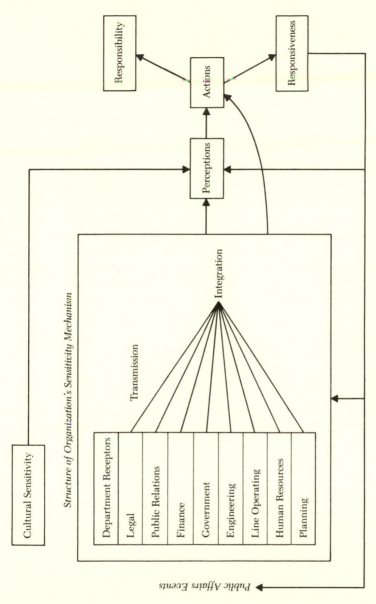

Figure 13-1   Corporate Sensitivity to Public Affairs (revised model).

ent stages of development in these two sensitivity characteristics. It is not surprising, then, that Pacific Timber and Northwest Forests were polar opposites in perception and performance in all the measured items, while the other companies alternated in assessments of strengths.

Managerial Implications

The message to management in its simplest form in that planning for effective communication with influential forces in the public affairs environment is now required of the big corporation. Society's demands on the high-profile firms studied (and categorized as important social institutions) have become too forceful to ignore and too complex to understand without prior and intensive sophisticated efforts. The effect does not require a big army of corporate guardians or loud shouting and fist-pounding histrionics. Instead it requires intelligent listening. Efforts to communicate without listening represent a monologue, not a dialogue.

An exchange is needed to achieve the ends desired by the business, the conferral of social legitimacy. But what does this amorphous term *social legitimacy* mean? Parsons defined the legitimizing of an institution as:[4]

> *the appraisal of action in terms of shared or common values in the context of the involvement of the action in the social system.*

The integration of company actions into the social system, then, requires the discovery of common values with other social actors. Common values cannot be discovered if the company does not understand what motivates stakeholders and does not accept their legitimacy as critics.

Management must remain sensitive to a wide range of stakeholder groups because of the influence that diverse community segments wields and because the company reputation is at stake. Stakeholders regularly described the ease they have in gaining allies to fight companies who have already tarnished their image. Even Pacific Timber has lost its effectiveness with environmentalists around the nation because of isolated examples of insensitivity.

This sensitivity is not secured by dragging overburdened chief executives through the halls of legislature corridors or by the reliance on functional technocrats. Varied functional expertise is needed to understand properly the appropriate language and to tap the relevant personal and professional networks behind public affairs. The chief executive alone cannot possibly be skilled enough for this task. On the other hand, merely staffing new offices and assigning novel job titles does not guarantee that departments will be alert receptors. Nor does the accumulation of diverse bits of information from the outside sources guarantee that companies will be able to understand what they have seen and then translate this into action.

The *role* of *senior management* is not to be chief lobbyist but to focus attention on *managing* the *environmental sensitivity of the corporate structure and culture*. This infusion of broad purpose is "institutional leadership" rather than defensive management. Such institutionalization of purpose is reflected in the company's management system for public affairs through three structural components of a company's character: (1) externally attentive experts, (2) internally coordinated experts, and (3) internal public affairs influence.

To help develop attentive experts, senior management must do more than pencil in added boxes on organization charts. The various professional skills, languages, and personal networks will demonstrate why various company officials such as the lawyers, the lobbyists, the human resource experts, the public relations executives, the engineers, and the financial executives all have distinct information sources, and hence relevant contributions to overlapping issues. Staffing departments with such experts is not enough, however, if they are not effectively receiving information from the outside.

Each of these functional experts has so many competing tasks that listening to stakeholders may be too often forgotten. For example, the Education Committee of the Public Relations Society of America outlined the following eight job classifications of work in public affairs:[5]

1. *Writing*—reports, news releases, films, booklets, broadcast copy, technical information.
2. *Editing*—internal newsletters, employee publications, shareowner reports.
3. *Placement*—contact with the general and trade press.
4. *Promotion*—exhibits, conferences, celebrations, awards.
5. *Speaking*—speechwriting and public appearances.
6. *Production*—technical skills for producing printed material, photographs, and films.
7. *Programming*—designing the stages needed for completing public relations projects.
8. *Institutional Advertising*—making the company's name and image prominent.

Noticeably missing from this list is any mention of listening and interacting with various company audiences. A survey of 96 public relations consulting firms asked the officials in these firms to compare the importance of the various services they provide to client companies for 1970 and for 1977. The two largest increases in importance are "legislative intelligence" and "opinion research."[6] Perhaps, then, companies have had to turn to outside experts for the sort of listening tasks that inside company officials should have undertaken. Senior managers must evaluate company departments on the breadth and number of sources they use, on the ways they use their time, and finally, on their ability to detect significant unusual occurrences.

Turning now to the other two structural components of sensitivity to public affairs, we see further opportunity for contributions from senior management. The second structural component, the internal coordination of experts, is essential for enlightened piecing together of the information that was fragmented in its gathering. Executives frequently confused their frightened, defensive handling in response to perceived external threats with a more ready and cooperative review of issues. Many issues only surface as corporate interests when their implications across functions and business divisions surface through internal cross-function discussions. Senior management can help promote this cooperation through formal procedures such as annual planning and cross-department rotation in management training.

While these efforts can stimulate greater recognition of the overlapping nature of issues across departments, however, the nature of these issues also thwarts the effectiveness of long-range efforts. The volatility of the issues and the difficulty of securing useful quantitative data indicate that more frequent joint reassessment is needed. This approach, recently labeled "logical incrementalism," suggests a more constant process when formal strategic planning alone is inadequate. Internal newsletters and bulletins are common ways of sharing information. Temporary task forces can be created for cooperatively meeting specific issues. Top-level steering committees can be created to provide a continuing review of serious issues.

The last component of a company's structural sensitivity, the internal influence of public affairs, requires similar attention from top management. The information about public affairs that has been gathered and disseminated must also be taken seriously in the company's decisions. Valuable information is often obtained but ignored. Company lawyers were frequently ignored in the rampant fixing of prices until severe prosecution and punishment resulted. Labor relations officials suddenly rose in importance when a strike broke out. Crisis response is seldom an effective inspiration for management action. However, public affairs executives must rely on crisis-generated clout.

When no immediate external threat exists, executives in public affairs do not control what are generally recognized as critical resources for production. Therefore, it should not be a surprise to find public affairs officials who magnify or perpetuate external difficulties so that they can acquire internal status. The public affairs mechanism is too important to be thus fueled by power-seeking insiders or explosive outside events. The public affairs significance attached to previously mentioned procedures such as annual planning, management training programs, and interdepartmental collaboration are naturally good opportunities for increasing the internal status of public affairs. Other formal tools, such as public affairs specifications in job descriptions in various departments and public affairs department involvement in performance appraisals may be helpful for raising a consciousness to these issues. Finally, senior management can increase the perceived importance of public affairs through some less formal actions. The time and attention of senior management that is dedicated to these issues, the direct access to top-level public affairs executives, and including some public affairs executives in key decisions, are important symbols of company commitment.

Besides these three main *structural* features of public affairs sensitivity are three main cultural *features:* (1) leadership continuity, (2) social values, and (3) company reputation. Here too exists opportunity for top-level guidance. First, we saw that relative to leadership, unstable internal conditions seem to inhibit the infusion of corporate purpose into the organization. Executive succession is inevitable as executives age or perform unsatisfactorily. The board of directors and senior management should recognize the need to pass along the baton of leadership without upset. Disruptive top-level executive housecleaning seems as endemic to certain firms as the dismissal of coaching staffs of professional sports teams. In such companies, the changes in priorities and structure are too rapid for insiders ever to trust proclaimed company commitments. In other firms, strategies may shift and individuals may change jobs with no loss in the valuable momentum in all company efforts.

The second cultural feature, the corporate values, are also very much guided by senior management. Ethical stands are importantly established, according to the model, by the behavior of top officials. Lawbreaking and ideological hostility to outside constituencies are readily detected by organization members. Senior management has the responsibility for openly articulating the company's social purpose. Poorly articulated values or antagonistic reflexes damage the company's ability for understanding its external stakeholders and its interest in them.

The third cultural feature of sensitivity to public affairs, corporate reputation, calls for managers to recognize the handicap or advantage presented by their company's heritage. Every company has a history of interaction with its stakeholders that colors the public's perception of its actions. The likely success of company efforts in legislatures, in courts, and in communities is very much affected by the social goodwill that has been established. Past management mistakes may have preceded the tenure of current executives, but a company's public image does not change quickly. Some companies with poor reputations have been mystified that their gestures to environmentalists, labor unions, and investors have been rebuffed while similar efforts succeeded for other companies. On the other hand, some companies have so confidently relied on their good reputations that they have carelessly confused their own interest with the public interest. Management attention is required to guide the development of this corporate asset.

A final set of implications to managers concerns the measures of whether the above kinds of public affairs sensitivity have been effective. Certainly objective outcomes such as successful legislature lobbying, limited regulatory challenge, courtroom victories, permit clearances, and infrequent labor difficulty represent critical performance feedback. A company's objective social performance by such criteria may be due to its specific situation (its industry, its geographic location, and the like) rather than to any insensitivity. Well-informed efforts may still initially fail because of complex problems.

In addition, then, to actual events, two worthwhile dimensions of performance are social responsibility and social responsiveness—more subjective considerations. An assessment of social responsibility can tell company management if a company is seen as a valuable and ethical contributor to society beyond its focal products and services. Social responsiveness assessments are distinct, however, and convey to management whether a company is perceived as successful in its process for understanding the public environment. Thus, responsibility may indicate how effectively management has institutionalized corporate culture and convictions. Responsiveness, on the other hand, may indicate how effectively management has organized itself to listen and gather information. Various dimensions of responsiveness such as the company's credibility and preparedness can identify special strengths and weaknesses.

Unlike other sorts of performance appraisals, these performance assessments are best made by outsiders rather than insiders. Audience ratings are a valuable measure of the effectiveness of communication. Therefore, a survey of key stakeholders is an essential ingredient for determining a company's success in developing intentions into actions.

Academic Implications

The chief academic implication of this study has been the call for more internal study of organizations to understand their external behavior.

The recent trends in organizational behavior that highlight evolutionary explanations of company existence as well as trends that stress analyzing company actions as a series of strategies chosen to control external resource dependence remind us to consider the immediate and long-term potency of environmental threats.

Certainly the inability of some organizations to adapt to environmental change has led to their demise. Similarly, it cannot be denied that there is great value of studying organization efforts to (1) accept challenges, (2) form alliances with outside enterprises, and (3) diversify operations, thus minimizing external forces. However, an overemphasis on such perspectives can put the analyst strictly on the outside of the organization. Prior research has considered "proactive" and "reactive" behavior without effectively explaining how this comes about.

Organizational analysis must therefore not lose its insight into the internal workings of companies. The dynamics of the institutional battleground is important but not novel. Political science has properly studied company activities from the outside. Analysis of organizational behavior can contribute not by similarly accepting the corporation as a black box but by understanding the internal dynamics that lead to external actions. Given identical external circumstances, different companies will perceive and act differently. This study has suggested that company structure and culture may help explain some of that variation.

In addition, this research has called for an extension of our definition of the organizational environment from the marketplace to the public affairs arena. Organization theory has treated this environmental sector far too lightly. Some leading theorists reviewed here even suggest that organizational attention to this sector through scanning and monitoring is possibly harmful. Through the present study of a leading U.S. industry, we have found that large corporations do, in fact, encounter another sector of their environment that may threaten their survival as powerfully as the marketplace does. All the functional areas of this industry were influenced by public affairs.

We have also found that the companies studied differed in their success in managing relations with this environment. This success seemed to relate to the sensitivity the company already had toward its environment. It was clearly demonstrated that companies and departments vary in their susceptibility to distorted communication with the environment. depending on the vulnerability of an existing information-processing structure to departmental bias. In this sense, contrary to arguments of strictly "process"-oriented schools of thought, structure may precede strategy.

This debate has limited value since it must be conceded that both structure and strategy can be anticipatory or reactive. The attempt to explore the sources of company perceptions best illustrates the simplicity of "process" versus "structure" debates. The cultural values, historical process, and varied structures over the life of the firm may contribute as much to company perceptions as any current structures or processes. This effort to move beyond phases such as an "enacted environment" and probe the determinants and dimensions of organization-level *perceptions* deserve further attention. Gricar's work on the relevance of management ideology to regulatory compliance is a valuable step in this direction.[7] Consideration of a structure-culture model is not novel but nevertheless is underdeveloped.

Additionally, far more work in measuring social performance is needed. This work has shown that company performance in social responsibility is different from social responsiveness. Evidence in support of this distinction is helpful but the specific components of each of these dimensions must be better developed. The strength of various aspects of social responsiveness were studied here. These need to be refined and parallel definitions and systematic evaluation of responsibility is warranted.

Beyond the substance of this research, its methodology has implications for future research in this area. Important attempts to further our understanding of business-society relations have all too often led to large-scale surveys of many firms on isolated issues. Such endeavors ignore what has been learned about the inner complexity of organization life. Typically such studies rely on a single questionnaire from a single company official to represent that organization's perspective. As we have seen, however, it is probable that such data tell us more about the perspective of that individual company official than about the company itself. To study a company, it is essential to take multiple readings. Many different executives in different departments and at different hierarchical levels must be studied to approximate the collective stance within that company.

Similarly, companies are not well understood by tracing individual actions or isolated issues. To understand how organizations adapt to their environment, researchers must forgo the convenience of creating an artificial and simplistic view of the environment, realizing instead the overlapping complex conditions companies actually face. A company's quality of environmental response can be appreciated only by recognizing its total set of priorities.

Furthermore, multi-data types are essential. For example, corporate environmental behavior should be studied by methods that use both external and internal assessments. Organization self-concepts vary greatly from objective external views. Outsiders, because of their different locations, are not fully aware of what was intended, and insiders are not fully aware of what was achieved. In fact, mixed data sources are valuable even within companies. Analysis of corporate publications and on-site interviews led to the discovery of possible "cultural" variables not indicated in the company questionnaire survey. For these reasons it may be advisable to encourage small-sample studies, from which we can learn a lot about a few organizations, as opposed to large-sample studies that reveal very little about many organizations.

Finally, the business-society interaction must be studied at the level of interpersonal as well as institutional relations. This area should not become the domain of macro-level organizational research any more than leadership or motivation should be studied strictly through macro-level, systemwide analysis. The quality of personal communication and empathy between individuals on either side of a company's walls are not completely determined by macro structures and processes. The readiness for opposing sides to build resolvable deliberations into larger, symbolic statements introduces unnecessary hostility and rigidity. The work here on labor relations can be usefully broadened to other management-stakeholder interactions.[8]

A previously stated caveat is important enough for repetition in these closing comments. The six companies that cooperated in this study must be congratulated for their generous donation of time and their candid comments. Company names were not disclosed, to help protect individual identities. However, the findings in this book only approximately represent the current state of management in these companies. First, only selected portions of the company's character were studied. Second, the instruments used for analysis were largely new and untested. Finally, each of these companies has changed considerably along intended directions in cultural and structural dimensions. Several chief executives and senior officers studied are in fact no longer in office.

Due to its history of and breadth of exposure to public affairs, the forest products industry has learned a good deal about the management of public affairs. In the past, alert management and business scholars have studied employees and customers as management constituencies. An important next step is to borrow from that knowledge base where possible and learn more about other types of management-constituent relations.

One regulator commented in this study,

Environmental problems occur in the best-managed companies. The key is the way they each respond. Some of these forest products companies have fought regulations on environmental protection or employee safety before they understood them. If we'd worked together they could have had both better rulings and equipment purchased at a lower price. Further, when a company develops a nasty reputation with us and with the community, politicians are less likely to come to their defense. In that situation, where regulatory agencies have a chip on their shoulder, that company is in real trouble.

Each company exerts individual actions and particular frames of reference to develop its own social character. The extent to which a company shapes its character to seek understanding of its principal stakeholders will determine its success in developing a partnership with the public to secure its survival.

Endnotes

1. T. Parsons, *Structure and Process in Modern Societies* (New York: Free Press, 1960).
2. *Ibid.*, p. 36.
3. P. Selznick, *Leadership in Administration* (New York: Harper & Row, 1957), p. 141.
4. Parsons, *op. cit.*, p. 175.
5. "Education Committee of the Public Relations Society of America Report," as cited in S. M. Cutlip and H. H. Center, *Effective Public Relations*, 5th ed. (Englewood Cliffs, N.J.: Prentice-Hall, 1978), p. 22.
6. Cutlip and Center, *op. cit.*, pp. 24–26.
7. B. G. Gricar, "Responses to Regulation," presented at the Eastern Academy of Management meeting in Buffalo, N.Y. in May 1980.
8. E. Walton and R. McKersie, *A Behavioral Theory of Labor Negotiations* (New York: McGraw-Hill, 1967).

Appendixes

THE INTERVIEW INSTRUMENTS

Appendix A

HARVARD UNIVERSITY

GRADUATE SCHOOL OF BUSINESS ADMINISTRATION

GEORGE F. BAKER FOUNDATION

SOLDIERS FIELD
BOSTON, MASSACHUSETTS 02163

1/31/80

RESEARCH ON PUBLIC AFFAIRS MANAGEMENT - STATEMENT OF PURPOSE

As many of you already know, I am in the midst of some research on the management of public affairs by major U.S. corporations. I have been working intensively with seven of the top forest products companies in an effort to understand how one industry confronts multiple pressures from the outside. The forest products industry has a long history of facing a wide range of public affairs issues (labor union problems, environmentalist challenges, anti-trust prosecution, community pressures, and taxation issues, etc.) In many ways, forest products companies serve as lightning rods for the types of public affairs exposure awaiting much of the rest of American industry.

The attached questionnaire is being mailed to thirty executives in each participating company. I have asked for people's names to be sure that all questionnaires are received and returned, but individual identities WILL NOT BE DISCLOSED. I intend to maintain the Harvard Business School's reputation for and my personal policy of respecting anonymity.

The questionnaire covers the ways your company allocates responsibility for public affairs management and its posture on several public affairs issues. Many of these issues are likely to be quite remote from your daily concerns, but please respond to each of these questions using your best estimate of the appropriate response. Please do not skip any questions or delegate this request to any other company officials.

This questionnaire is based on information gathered from interviews with over two hundred executives in the industry, including many of the senior executives of your company. The style of this questionnaire and several of the topics raised resemble the questionnaires of similar recent studies of large corporations in other industries.

Answer the questions with respect to YOUR COMPANY OVER THE PAST 12 MONTHS and not just the immediate situation you face. Please mail your questionnaire to me as soon as is convenient. Allow 20 minutes to complete this questionnaire.

Thank you very much for your time and assistance.

Sincerely,

Jeff Sonnenfeld
Baker 109
(617) 495-6485

259

Appendix B

1. Which of the following titles best identifies your department?
   Please place a mark (X) beside the title.

Legal ____	General Management ____	Public Relations ____
Finance ____	Government Affairs ____	Human Resources ____
Planning ____	Line Operations ____	Engineering/
Other (specify) _____		Environmental ____

2. In the course of an average week, how much time are you likely to spend in
   direct contact (e.g., telephone, letters, visits, etc.) with the following
   groups?

					HOURS PER WEEK						
Investment Bankers	0	1	2	3	4	5	6	7	8	9	10
Shareholder groups (individual/institutional)	0	1	2	3	4	5	6	7	8	9	10
Stock Analysts	0	1	2	3	4	5	6	7	8	9	10
Financial Consultants	0	1	2	3	4	5	6	7	8	9	10
Securities and Exchange Commission	0	1	2	3	4	5	6	7	8	9	10
American Institute of CPAs	0	1	2	3	4	5	6	7	8	9	10
Financial Accounting Standards Board	0	1	2	3	4	5	6	7	8	9	10
American Bar Association	0	1	2	3	4	5	6	7	8	9	10
American Institute of Tax Executives	0	1	2	3	4	5	6	7	8	9	10
American Management Association	0	1	2	3	4	5	6	7	8	9	10
American Society of Personnel Directors . . .	0	1	2	3	4	5	6	7	8	9	10
Public Affairs Research Council	0	1	2	3	4	5	6	7	8	9	10
Public Relations Society of America	0	1	2	3	4	5	6	7	8	9	10
Business Roundtable	0	1	2	3	4	5	6	7	8	9	10
Conference Board	0	1	2	3	4	5	6	7	8	9	10
U.S. Chamber of Commerce	0	1	2	3	4	5	6	7	8	9	10
National Association of Manufacturers	0	1	2	3	4	5	6	7	8	9	10
American Paper Institute	0	1	2	3	4	5	6	7	8	9	10
National Forest Products Association	0	1	2	3	4	5	6	7	8	9	10
American Forest Institute	0	1	2	3	4	5	6	7	8	9	10
Western Timber Association	0	1	2	3	4	5	6	7	8	9	10
Southern Forest Products Association	0	1	2	3	4	5	6	7	8	9	10
Forest Farmers Association	0	1	2	3	4	5	6	7	8	9	10
American Plywood Association	0	1	2	3	4	5	6	7	8	9	10
Packaging Council of America	0	1	2	3	4	5	6	7	8	9	10
Folding Box Association	0	1	2	3	4	5	6	7	8	9	10
Western Forest Association	0	1	2	3	4	5	6	7	8	9	10
U.S. Senators	0	1	2	3	4	5	6	7	8	9	10
U.S. Congressmen	0	1	2	3	4	5	6	7	8	9	10
State Senators	0	1	2	3	4	5	6	7	8	9	10
State Congressmen	0	1	2	3	4	5	6	7	8	9	10
State Governors	0	1	2	3	4	5	6	7	8	9	10
Congressional Staffs (Federal)	0	1	2	3	4	5	6	7	8	9	10
Municipal and County Officials	0	1	2	3	4	5	6	7	8	9	10

(continued)

	0	1	2	3	4	5	6	7	8	9	10
Environmental Protection Agency (Federal) . .	0	1	2	3	4	5	6	7	8	9	10
Regional Environmental Protection Agency . .	0	1	2	3	4	5	6	7	8	9	10
Occupational Health and Safety Admin.	0	1	2	3	4	5	6	7	8	9	10
U.S. Federal Trade Commission	0	1	2	3	4	5	6	7	8	9	10
U.S. Food and Drug Administration	0	1	2	3	4	5	6	7	8	9	10
U.S. Forest Service	0	1	2	3	4	5	6	7	8	9	10
U.S. Dept. of Agriculture (not Forest Service)	0	1	2	3	4	5	6	7	8	9	10
U.S. Fish and Wildlife Commission	0	1	2	3	4	5	6	7	8	9	10
U.S. Department of the Interior	0	1	2	3	4	5	6	7	8	9	10
U.S. Department of Commerce	0	1	2	3	4	5	6	7	8	9	10
State Environmental Regulators	0	1	2	3	4	5	6	7	8	9	10
State Health and Safety Regulators	0	1	2	3	4	5	6	7	8	9	10
Local Zoning Officials	0	1	2	3	4	5	6	7	8	9	10
Conservation Foundation	0	1	2	3	4	5	6	7	8	9	10
Sierra Club	0	1	2	3	4	5	6	7	8	9	10
National Resources Defense Council	0	1	2	3	4	5	6	7	8	9	10
Nature Conservancy	0	1	2	3	4	5	6	7	8	9	10
Audubon Society	0	1	2	3	4	5	6	7	8	9	10
Common Cause	0	1	2	3	4	5	6	7	8	9	10
Congress Watch	0	1	2	3	4	5	6	7	8	9	10
Academic Institutions	0	1	2	3	4	5	6	7	8	9	10
Management Consultants	0	1	2	3	4	5	6	7	8	9	10
National Wildlife Foundation	0	1	2	3	4	5	6	7	8	9	10
Local Environmentalist Groups	0	1	2	3	4	5	6	7	8	9	10
Other Public Interest Groups	0	1	2	3	4	5	6	7	8	9	10
Local Civic Associations	0	1	2	3	4	5	6	7	8	9	10
Trade Press	0	1	2	3	4	5	6	7	8	9	10
Local Journalists	0	1	2	3	4	5	6	7	8	9	10
National Media	0	1	2	3	4	5	6	7	8	9	10
Labor Unions	0	1	2	3	4	5	6	7	8	9	10
UPPW	0	1	2	3	4	5	6	7	8	9	10
IWA	0	1	2	3	4	5	6	7	8	9	10
LPIU	0	1	2	3	4	5	6	7	8	9	10
AWPPW	0	1	2	3	4	5	6	7	8	9	10
Teamsters	0	1	2	3	4	5	6	7	8	9	10

Other Outside Groups (name)

	0	1	2	3	4	5	6	7	8	9	10
_____	0	1	2	3	4	5	6	7	8	9	10
_____	0	1	2	3	4	5	6	7	8	9	10
_____	0	1	2	3	4	5	6	7	8	9	10

3. How much do you *rely* on the following *information sources* for your opinions on *public affairs issues* facing your company?

	Not at all	A small amount	Somewhat	Quite a bit	A good deal
Trade Press	1	2	3	4	5
Trade Associations	1	2	3	4	5
Trade Contacts	1	2	3	4	5
Internal Company Sources......	1	2	3	4	5
Environmentalist Publications.	1	2	3	4	5
Environmentalist Contacts.....	1	2	3	4	5
Other Public Interest Groups..	1	2	3	4	5
Labor Union Publications	1	2	3	4	5
Labor Union Contacts	1	2	3	4	5
Consultants	1	2	3	4	5
Investment Community Contacts.	1	2	3	4	5
Wall Street Journal	1	2	3	4	5
New York Times................	1	2	3	4	5
Business Week.................	1	2	3	4	5
Fortune	1	2	3	4	5
Forbes	1	2	3	4	5
Duns and other Business Press.	1	2	3	4	5
Harvard Business Review.......	1	2	3	4	5
Radio and Television	1	2	3	4	5
Other Popular Press...........	1	2	3	4	5
Professional Press	1	2	3	4	5
Government Publications.......	1	2	3	4	5
Government Contacts...........	1	2	3	4	5
Business Research Firms (eg. Conference Board, AMA, etc.)	1	2	3	4	5
Books or classes	1	2	3	4	5

4. Size of your Department (# of professional people) _____

5. Your experience (# of years):   this company _____ present dept. _____
                                     other companies _____
                                     government _____
                                     journalism _____
                                     other _____

6. Do you anticipate working in public affairs (government relations, public relations, legal, environmental) in the foreseeable future?   yes ____
                                                                                 no ____

7. To what extent is your unit actually performing the following activities? (circle one numerical alternative for each activity)

	Not at all	A small amount	A moderate amount	Quite a bit	A great deal
Representing – Providing information about your company to outside organizations, groups, or individuals.	1	2	3	4	5
Scanning – Searching for and identifying emerging events and trends that might provide threats or opportunities for your company.	1	2	3	4	5
Monitoring – Tracking already identified public affairs issues affecting your company.	1	2	3	4	5
Protecting – Warding off outside pressures which might disrupt the ongoing operations of your company.	1	2	3	4	5
Transmitting – Analyzing, translating, and communicating information about public affairs issues to key decision makers in corporate and divisional levels in your company.	1	2	3	4	5
Transacting – Acquiring the resources needed by your company or marketing company products.	1	2	3	4	5

8. On the average, over how long a period of time do you generally stay involved with any particular public affairs issue?

___ 1 day or less ___ 2-5 days ___ 1 week-1 month ___ 2-6 months ___ a year +

9. How many of the ten most influential executives in your company have their primary responsibilities in public affairs management? (circle one)

0   1   2   3   4   5   6   7   8   9   10

10. Relative to other management topics, how important are public affairs issues to your company's operations in each of the following areas? (circle one)

	Much less Important	Less Important	As Important	More Important	Much more Important
General Management	1	2	3	4	5
Operations	1	2	3	4	5
Marketing	1	2	3	4	5
Finance	1	2	3	4	5
Human Resources	1	2	3	4	5
Planning	1	2	3	4	5
Control	1	2	3	4	5

11. Relative to other management topics, how important are public affairs
     issues to the following features of your company?   (circle one)

	Very Unimportant		Moderately Important		Extremely Important
The time and attention of the Chief Executive Officer	1	2	3	4	5
The time and attention of the Board of Directors	1	2	3	4	5
The company's annual planning process	1	2	3	4	5
Your career progress	1	2	3	4	5
Performance appraisals of line units	1	2	3	4	5
Management career paths, in general	1	2	3	4	5
Management training programs	1	2	3	4	5

12. How often are temporary task forces established to respond to public
     affairs events? (circle one)

Never	Rarely	Occasionally	Regularly	Quite Often
1	2	3	4	5

13. How well established are any permanent top management steering
     committees for strictly public affairs issues? (circle one)

Not at all	Being Considered	Just Beginning	Settling In	Well Established
1	2	3	4	5

14. Do such task forces and committees have more line operations executives
     or more public affairs executives?   (circle one)

More Line Operations		Even Balance		More Public Affairs
1	2	3	4	5

15. Which company departments have a policy-making role in the following list of
     issues? Mark (X) beside each public affairs issue for which the designated
     management group has a policy-making influence.

	Chief Exec.	Business Divisions	Finance	Engineering/ Environment	Planning	Legal	Human Resources	Gov't Affairs	Public Relations
Energy	( )	( )	( )	( )	( )	( )	( )	( )	( )
Pollution Air/Water	( )	( )	( )	( )	( )	( )	( )	( )	( )
Solid Waste	( )	( )	( )	( )	( )	( )	( )	( )	( )
Herbicides	( )	( )	( )	( )	(·)	( )	( )	( )	( )
Timber Supply	( )	( )	( )	( )	( )	( )	( )	( )	( )
Log Exports	( )	( )	( )	( )	( )	( )	( )	( )	( )
Union Relations	( )	( )	( )	( )	( )	( )	( )	( )	( )
Mill Closing	( )	( )	( )	( )	( )	( )	( )	( )	( )
Land Management	( )	( )	(.)	( )	( )	( )	( )	( )	( )

Shareholder Relations	( )	( )	( )	( )	( )	( )	( )	( )	( )
Local Press Interaction	( )	( )	( )	( )	( )	( )	( )	( )	( )
National Press Interaction	( )	( )	( )	( )	( )	( )	( )	( )	( )
Pesticides	( )	( )	( )	( )	( )	( )	( )	( )	( )

16. How well is your company performing in managing the following types of public affairs concerns compared to other companies in this industry?

	Very Well	Better Than Average	Average	Worse Than Average	Very Badly
Environmental Protection	1	2	3	4	5
Community Relations and Communication	1	2	3	4	5
Federal Government Affairs	1	2	3	4	5
Local Government Affairs	1	2	3	4	5
Legal Compliance	1	2	3	4	5
Labor Relations	1	2	3	4	5
Investor Relations	1	2	3	4	5

17. a) How *accurately* do the statements on the following pages reflect the position of your company?

b) How high a *priority* are the italicized issues?

(a)	ACCURACY OF STATEMENT				(b)	PRIORITY	
Extremely Accurately	Very Accurately	Somewhat Accurately	Very Inaccurately	Extremely Inaccurately	High	Medium	Low
1	2	3	4	5	A	B	C

(circle a number and a letter for each statement)

a. *Log exports* are raising the cost of timber throughout this country.

    accuracy 1 2 3 4 5   priority A B C

b. Fuller *financial disclosure* is in the interest of informed shareholders.

    accuracy 1 2 3 4 5   priority A B C

c. The *Eastern U.S. market* has been overtaken by Southern and Canadian lumber supply and the Pacific Northwest can't compete in that market.

    accuracy 1 2 3 4 5   priority A B C

d. It is cheaper to *ship logs* from the Northwest to Tokyo than to Long Beach, CA.

    accuracy 1 2 3 4 5   priority A B C

e. *Antitrust* issues are no longer as important in this industry as we have all learned the lessons from the past prosecution.

    accuracy   1   2   3   4   5   priority   A   B   C

f. *Log exports* are leading to substantial job loss in wood products manufacturing.

    accuracy   1   2   3   4   5   priority   A   B   C

g. *Shareholder suits* can be limited through strong shareholder communication.

    accuracy   1   2   3   4   5   priority   A   B   C

h. *Solid waste* restrictions are silly because we can't run a business waiting for Boy Scout paper drives every other month.

    accuracy   1   2   3   4   5   priority   A   B   C

i. Producers of virgin pulp should be taxed or recycled usage should be given a tax credit to assist *solid waste* control.

    accuracy   1   2   3   4   5   priority   A   B   C

j. *Litter* is almost as important to the public as inflation.

    accuracy   1   2   3   4   5   priority   A   B   C

k. We are in favor of *bans* on non-returnable *bottles*.

    accuracy   1   2   3   4   5   priority   A   B   C

l. The *capital gains tax* on timber should be improved to stimulate supply.

    accuracy   1   2   3   4   5   priority   A   B   C

m. Federal tax policy should be revised to provide a 10% *investment tax credit* for Forestry and amortization over seven years.

    accuracy   1   2   3   4   5   priority   A   B   C

n. The *value of growing timber* should be eliminated from inheritance taxes.

    accuracy   1   2   3   4   5   priority   A   B   C

o. The *investment community* tends to overemphasize the short term perspective.

    accuracy   1   2   3   4   5   priority   A   B   C

p. *Nuclear reactor delays* are hurting the health of our industry.

    accuracy   1   2   3   4   5   priority   A   B   C

q. Congress should offer incentives for *wood combustion* as an energy source.

    accuracy   1   2   3   4   5   priority   A   B   C

r. We avoid suspicion of *water pollution* by informing regulators as soon as we see we are in violation instead of waiting for inspections.

    accuracy   1   2   3   4   5   priority   A   B   C

s. *Coal conversion* pressures are often inappropriate in our industry.

    accuracy   1   2   3   4   5   priority   A   B   C

t. *Slash burning* is a major contributor to air pollution in the Northwest.

    accuracy   1   2   3   4   5   priority   A   B   C

u. *Air pollution* of pulp plants is often overstated as a problem.

    accuracy   1   2   3   4   5   priority   A   B   C

v. Changes in *standards* and lumber grading by the government would be too disruptive.

    accuracy 1   2   3   4   5   priority A   B   C

w. Environmental *regulators* now tend to be environmentalists and thus suffer from
    a conflict of interests.

    accuracy 1   2   3   4   5   priority A   B   C

x. Biological and natural predator control is preferred over *pesticides*.

    accuracy 1   2   3   4   5   priority A   B   C

y. Ambient *noise* control is becoming a worrisome concern.

    accuracy 1   2   3   4   5   priority A   B   C

z. We have used herbicides and pesticides without causing personal or property damage
    for decades. It's only now that we are *spraying* in woods where hippies have planted
    marijuana that we are having trouble.

    accuracy 1   2   3   4   5   priority A   B   C

aa. *Formaldehyde* may pose a significant danger to our workers and our customers.

    accuracy 1   2   3   4   5   priority A   B   C

bb. Forest products companies have no obligation to preserve *scenic areas* because they
    can do what they want on their own land.

    accuracy 1   2   3   4   5   priority A   B   C

cc. Reasonable doubt exists as to the *safety* of using some herbicides.

    accuracy 1   2   3   4   5   priority A   B   C

dd. The *lead time* required for planning and construction of a new plant has been
    generally reduced through less EPA regulation.

    accuracy 1   2   3   4   5   priority A   B   C

ee. *Clear cutting* is by necessity unsightly.

    accuracy 1   2   3   4   5   priority A   B   C

ff. The Sierra Club says that you should never *cut* in a *forest*.

    accuracy 1   2   3   4   5   priority A   B   C

gg. *Clear cutting* leads to even aged forests.

    accuracy 1   2   3   4   5   priority A   B   C

hh. *Environmentalists* are often Easterners longing for Bambi's woods.

    accuracy 1   2   3   4   5   priority A   B   C

ii. *Chloroform* in our bleaching operations may be hazardous.

    accuracy 1   2   3   4   5   priority A   B   C

jj. Rather than preserving *wilderness* land, public forest land
    should be managed for more multiple use.

    accuracy 1   2   3   4   5   priority A   B   C

kk. We do not support the Dow chemical suit to allow the use of *herbicide*
    2, 4, 5-T.

    accuracy 1   2   3   4   5   priority A   B   C

ll. *Regulators* reflect more bureaucratic self-interest than the public interest.

    accuracy 1   2   3   4   5   priority A   B   C

mm. Unions have been *whipsawing* us for years and it's about time that the companies fought back.

    accuracy   1   2   3   4   5   priority   A   B   C

nn. *Union leaders* generally have lost touch with the interests of their constituents.

    accuracy   1   2   3   4   5   priority   A   B   C

oo. *Mill closings* should be done swiftly and silently to avoid external community skirmishes.

    accuracy   1   2   3   4   5   priority   A   B   C

pp. Labor union rigidity seriously curtails our efforts at improved *productivity*.

    accuracy   1   2   3   4   5   priority   A   B   C

qq. The dangerous nature of work in this industry makes it extremely unlikely that there is much room for *handicapped workers*.

    accuracy   1   2   3   4   5   priority   A   B   C

rr. With the increasing *wage compression* between ranks, we are finding it difficult to fairly compensate our managers.

    accuracy   1   2   3   4   5   priority   A   B   C

ss. *Employee privacy* is not much of a concern of our workers.

    accuracy   1   2   3   4   5   priority   A   B   C

tt. We need to improve the career opportunities of *mid-career* and *older workers*.

    accuracy   1   2   3   4   5   priority   A   B   C

18. For administrative purposes and data analysis please supply the following two piece of information. No individual <u>identities</u> will be disclosed or will be presented in a recognizable format.

        a. Your Name _____ _____

        b. Your Title_____

THANK YOU VERY MUCH FOR YOUR TIME AND INTEREST.
TO GUARANTEE YOUR PERSONAL ANONYMITY PLEASE
MAIL YOUR COMPLETED QUESTIONAIRE DIRECTLY TO
ME IN THE ENCLOSED ADDRESSED, STAMPED ENVELOPE.

PLEASE MAKE SURE YOU ANSWERED EACH QUESTION.

Jeff Sonnenfeld
Baker 109
Harvard Business School
Boston, MA 02163
Phone: (617) 495-6485

Appendix C

HARVARD UNIVERSITY

GRADUATE SCHOOL OF BUSINESS ADMINISTRATION

GEORGE F. BAKER FOUNDATION

Baker 109
SOLDIERS FIELD
BOSTON, MASSACHUSETTS 02163

July 15, 1980

Dear

    The attached questionnaire is being mailed to a carefully selected
sample of individuals who are familiar either directly or indirectly with
the public affairs practices of several of these companies. I am conducting
a study of the management of public affairs by major U.S. corporations.
As many of you are already aware, I have been working intensively with
seven of the top forest products companies in an effort to understand how
one industry confronts multiple pressures from the outside. The forest
products industry has a long history of facing a wide range of public
affairs issues (labor union problems, environmentalist challenges, antitrust prosecution, community pressures and taxation issues, etc.). In
many ways, forest products companies serve as lightning rods for the
types of public affairs exposure awaiting much of the rest of American
industry.

    The way I have defined public affairs refers to all the NON-PRODUCT-
MARKET interactions which businesses have with outside constituent groups.
The questionnaire asks you to glance down the list of the top ten forest
products companies and evaluate them in terms of both their (1) Social
Responsibility - Corporate Citizenship and (2) Social Responsiveness -
Corporate Adaptiveness. The distinction will be made more clearly in the
questionnaire.

    Please answer each question to the best of your ability even if
your opinion is based on very limited or second-hand knowledge, indicating
where you have absolutely no basis for even a rough estimate. These
questionnaires will be treated with utmost respect for the anonymity of
the respondents, as is the tradition of this institution. The questionnaire is structured so that it should be completed in under 10 minutes.

    Thank you very much for your time and assistance. Feel free to call
me if you have any questions or suggestions.

                                Sincerely,

                                Jeffrey A. Sonnenfeld
                                Assistant Professor

269

Appendix D

1. Based on either your direct or indirect knowledge, please rate the reputation of each of these companies for <u>social responsibility</u> (ethical behavior) in their external performance.

	Poor	Below Average	Average	Above Average	Excellent	Don't Know
Georgia Pacific	1	2	3	4	5	X
International Paper	1	2	3	4	5	X
Weyerhaeuser	1	2	3	4	5	X
Champion International	1	2	3	4	5	X
Boise Cascade	1	2	3	4	5	X
Crown Zellerbach	1	2	3	4	5	X
Mead	1	2	3	4	5	X
St. Regis	1	2	3	4	5	X
Kimberly Clark	1	2	3	4	5	X
Scott	1	2	3	4	5	X
Great Northern Nekoosa	1	2	3	4	5	X
Union Camp	1	2	3	4	5	X
Hammermill	1	2	3	4	5	X
Louisiana Pacific	1	2	3	4	5	X
Westvaco	1	2	3	4	5	X
Diamond International	1	2	3	4	5	X
Potlach	1	2	3	4	5	X
Brown	1	2	3	4	5	X
Southwest Forest	1	2	3	4	5	X
Willamette	1	2	3	4	5	X

2. Based on your direct or indirect knowledge, please rate the reputation of each of these companies for <u>social responsiveness</u> (alertness) in managing their external behavior.

	Poor	Below Average	Average	Above Average	Excellent	Don't Know
Georgia Pacific	1	2	3	4	5	X
International Paper	1	2	3	4	5	X
Weyerhaeuser	1	2	3	4	5	X
Champion International	1	2	3	4	5	X
Boise Cascade	1	2	3	4	5	X
Crown Zellerbach	1	2	3	4	5	X
Mead	1	2	3	4	5	X
St. Regis	1	2	3	4	5	X
Kimberly Clark	1	2	3	4	5	X
Scott	1	2	3	4	5	X
Great Northern Nekoosa	1	2	3	4	5	X
Union Camp	1	2	3	4	5	X
Hammermill	1	2	3	4	5	X
Louisiana Pacific	1	2	3	4	5	X
Westvaco	1	2	3	4	5	X
Diamond International	1	2	3	4	5	X
Potlach	1	2	3	4	5	X
Brown	1	2	3	4	5	X
Southwest Forest	1	2	3	4	5	X
Willamette	1	2	3	4	5	X

3. Is the forest products industry <u>more</u> socially responsive or <u>less</u> socially responsive than the following industries?

	far less responsive	less responsive	comparable to	more responsive	far more responsive
Oil and petroleum	1	2	3	4	5
Insurance	1	2	3	4	5
Consumer Products	1	2	3	4	5
Banking	1	2	3	4	5
Steel	1	2	3	4	5
Chemicals	1	2	3	4	5
Airlines	1	2	3	4	5
Tobacco	1	2	3	4	5
Pharmaceuticals	1	2	3	4	5
Broadcasting	1	2	3	4	5
Mining	1	2	3	4	5

4. The following leading companies have been selected for in-depth analysis. Please rate these seven companies, rank listing as much as possible, on the following dimensions: (Try to rank each company even if you must rely on indirect or incomplete information.)

a) the <u>credibility</u> of company statements (Do they mean what they say?):

	Low			Moderate			High
Georgia Pacific	1	2	3	4	5	6	7
International Paper	1	2	3	4	5	6	7
Weyerhaeuser	1	2	3	4	5	6	7
Boise Cascade	1	2	3	4	5	6	7
Crown Zellerbach	1	2	3	4	5	6	7
Mead	1	2	3	4	5	6	7
St. Regis	1	2	3	4	5	6	7

b) the <u>accessibility</u> of company officials (Can you easily reach company officials for responses?):

	Low			Moderate			High
Georgia Pacific	1	2	3	4	5	6	7
International Paper	1	2	3	4	5	6	7
Weyerhaeuser	1	2	3	4	5	6	7
Boise Cascade	1	2	3	4	5	6	7
Crown Zellerbach	1	2	3	4	5	6	7
Mead	1	2	3	4	5	6	7
St. Regis	1	2	3	4	5	6	7

c) the <u>preparedness</u> of company officials (Have they done their homework in advance on the major public affairs issues?):

Georgia Pacific	1	2	3	4	5	6	7
International Paper	1	2	3	4	5	6	7
Weyerhaeuser	1	2	3	4	5	6	7
Boise Cascade	1	2	3	4	5	6	7
Crown Zellerbach	1	2	3	4	5	6	7
Mead	1	2	3	4	5	6	7
St. Regis	1	2	3	4	5	6	7

d) the <u>reliability</u> of company statements (Do they stand by their agreements?):

Georgia Pacific	1	2	3	4	5	6	7
International Paper	1	2	3	4	5	6	7
Weyerhaeuser	1	2	3	4	5	6	7
Boise Cascade	1	2	3	4	5	6	7
Crown Zellerbach	1	2	3	4	5	6	7
Mead	1	2	3	4	5	6	7
St. Regis	1	2	3	4	5	6	7

e) the <u>attentiveness</u> of company officials (Do they listen or does information
    tend to mostly flow one way -- from the inside?):

Georgia Pacific	1	2	3	4	5	6	7
International Paper	1	2	3	4	5	6	7
Weyerhaeuser	1	2	3	4	5	6	7
Boise Cascade	1	2	3	4	5	6	7
Crown Zellerbach	1	2	3	4	5	6	7
Mead	1	2	3	4	5	6	7
St. Regis	1	2	3	4	5	6	7

f) the <u>perceived legitimacy</u> of outsiders (Do company officials respect the
    purposes of outside critics?):

Georgia Pacific	1	2	3	4	5	6	7
International Paper	1	2	3	4	5	6	7
Weyerhaeuser	1	2	3	4	5	6	7
Boise Cascade	1	2	3	4	5	6	7
Crown Zellerbach	1	2	3	4	5	6	7
Mead	1	2	3	4	5	6	7
St. Regis	1	2	3	4	5	6	7

g) the <u>clarity of their interests</u> (How clearly does the company distinguish its
    interests from the public interests?):

	Low			Moderate			High
Georgia Pacific	1	2	3	4	5	6	7
International Paper	1	2	3	4	5	6	7
Weyerhaeuser	1	2	3	4	5	6	7
Boise Cascade	1	2	3	4	5	6	7
Crown Zellerbach	1	2	3	4	5	6	7
Mead	1	2	3	4	5	6	7
St. Regis	1	2	3	4	5	6	7

5. What would you list as the major public affairs issues likely to confront forest
    products companies in the next year?

    1. _____

    2. _____

    3. _____

6. How many years have you worked in a forest product company?

    _____ never   _____ 5-10 years

    _____ 1-5 years   _____ 10 or more years

7. For administrative purposes and data analysis, please supply the following two
    pieces of information. NO INDIVIDUAL IDENTITIES WILL BE DISCLOSED or will be
    be presented in a recognizable format.

          Name   _____

          Profession _____

Thank you very much for your time and interest.

Please mail your completed questionnaire to me in the enclosed addressed, stamped envelope.

PLEASE BE SURE YOU ANSWERED EACH QUESTION!!

Jeffrey Sonnenfeld
Baker 109
Harvard Business School
Boston, MA 02163
Phone: (617) 495-6485

INDEX

Acadia National Park, 102
Accommodation, 57, 218, 223, 237
Ackerman, R. W., 35–36
Adaptation theory, 4, 12–13, 27
  and external sources, 27, 28–34, 44
  and internal structure, 27, 34–44
  market issues in, 4, 12, 21
  public affairs in, 4
  technology in, 4, 12, 21
Administrative subsystem, 14
Aetna Life and Casualty, 37
AFL–CIO, 104
Aguilar, F. J., 37, 67
Aiken, M., 31
Air pollution, 6, 91, 107–114, 120–21,
  242
  regulations and, 16
Alabama, 98
Aldag, R., 11
Allowable emissions, definition of, 110
American Can and Container Corporation of America, 79
American Forest Institute, 76, 120–21
American Forestry Association, 81, 93
American Forests Company
  and company differences in percep-
    tions, 210–11
  and cultural sensitivity, 200–201, 245
  and departmental receptivity,
    144–56
  establishing contact, 188–89
  executive themes and, 189–92
  and internal integrations, 156–59
  and public affairs influence, 156
  reputation of, 187–88
  and social responsiveness, 231–38
  and structural sensitivity, 161, 165
American Paper Institute, 76–77, 116,
  120, 165
Andrews, K. R., 35
Angle, H. L., 41

Antitrust, in forest product study, 6,
  91, 117–19
Appreciation, 30, 135–39, 141, 152–55,
  159, 243
Argyris, C., 32, 37
Arkansas, 98
Assimilation (see Integration)
Association of Western Pulp and Paper
  Workers (AWPPW), 105
Attention, 1, 12, 20, 139, 155, 149, 243

Barnard, C. I., 35
Bauer, B., 36
Bendix Company, 3
Best available technology (BAT), 109–
  110
Best current technology (BCT), 109
Bias, perceptual, 7, 36–37, 42, 71, 132,
  142–43, 203–210
  company, 204–10
  department, 204–10
  receptor, 204–10
  stakeholder, 227–31, 233
Bledsoe, R., 98
Boise Cascade Company, 83, 101, 115
Boulware, L., 13
Boundary spanners, 68, 139
  in contingency theory, 40–43
  influence of, 55
  "institutional adaptive" functions of,
    41
  as sensory mechanisms, 53–54
Breadth of interactions, 135, 141,
  151–52, 159, 243
Brown, J. K., 39, 42
Bubble concept, 16
Buffering, 32–33
Burns, T., 10, 40
Burton, P., 95
Business-labor relationship, 17–18
Business policy approach, 35–39, 44

Business Round Table, 3
Business-society relations, 9, 13–14,
    239–41, 254–55
Business Week, 2–3, 165

California, 95–97
Capital investment, 82–83
Carroll, A. B., 20
Carter, J., 94–96, 100
Cartwright, D., 7
Center for Science in the Public Inter-
    est, 113
Central Paper Company
    and company differences in percep-
        tions, 210–21
    and cultural sensitivity, 199–201, 245
    and departmental receptivity,
        144–56
    establishing contact, 178–79
    executive themes, 179–81
    and internal integration, 156–59
    and public affairs influence, 156
    reputation of, 177–78
    and social responsiveness, 231–38
    structural sensitivity of, 161
Chamberlin, N. W., 10
Champion International Company, 78,
    83
Change, 10, 30, 32, 34
Chase, H., 20
Chatlas, W., 18
Chief executive officer (CEO)
    in business policy approach, 89
    in contingency theory, 42, 44
    in cultural sensitivity study, 166,
        168, 174, 176–77, 187–88, 191,
        195, 197–201
    interviews in forest products study,
        6–7, 61–62, 64–65, 71
    in perceptual process, 54–56
    and public affairs, 3–5, 121–22, 156
    questionnaire surveys and, 61–62,
        65–70, 71
Chrysler Corporation, 28
Civilian Conservation Corps, 75
Clean Air Act of 1967, 109, 113
Clean Air Act of 1970, 109, 110, 113
    1977 Amendments to, 110–11
Clean Streams Act (Pa.), 102
Clean Water Act of 1972, 109
Coalitions, 40–41
Community groups, 12–14, 16, 19,
    218–21

Competition, 83
Complexity, 11, 51, 53, 246
Conference Board study, 38–39
Conservation
    and company perception, 213–14,
        223
    and forest products industry, 108,
        121
    vs. timber supply, 91–99, 100–102,
        120–21
"Contingency school" theory, 9, 39–44,
    57
Cooperative Farms Forestry Acts of
    1937 and 1950, 102
Corporate culture (*see* Cultural sen-
    sitivity)
Corporate process, 20 (*see also* Social
    responsiveness)
Corporate purpose, 20 (*see also* Social
    responsibility)
Corporate response, stages of, 20
Corporate structure (*see* Forest prod-
    ucts study; Structural sensitivity)
Cost
    energy, 81
    labor, 80
    of noise-abatement equipment, 105
    of pollution abatement, 80, 91, 109,
        112–13
Council on Environmental Quality, 114
Council on Wages and Price Stability, 118
Crisis response (*see* Proactive behavior;
    Reactive behavior)
Crown Zellerbach Company, 78, 99,
    101, 118
Crude Oil Windfall Profits Tax Act of
    1979, 115
Cultural features, of public affairs sen-
    sitivity, 251–52
Cultural sensitivity, 163–66, 174,
    199–201
    and accommodation, 218
    and company perceptions, 218,
        223–25, 237–38
    and establishing contact, 165,
        170–79, 183–84, 188–89, 196
    and executive themes, 165–66,
        171–72, 184–87, 189–91
    in forest products study, 239,
        241–46, 253
    and reputation, 165–70, 173–74,
        177–78, 192–96, 251–52
Cyert, R. M., 29, 31, 37

Dearborn, D. C., 12, 29, 37
Decentralization, 32–33
Deep-Portage Conservation Reserva-
    tion, 87
Department(s)
    bias, 204–210
    in cultural sensitivity study, 170
    differentiation in, 40, 43–44, 142,
        148–51
    perception, 142–43, 159, 223–24
    receptivity, 127, 141–42, 204–207,
        242–43
Department perceptions vs. company
    perceptions
    and company posture, 203, 213–21
    and internal consensus, 203, 221, 223
    and issue priorities, 211–12
Depth of interaction, 155, 159, 243
Diamond International Company, 78,
    117
Differentiation, 40, 43–44, 142, 148–51
Dill, W. R., 40
Downey, K., 11
Downs, A., 13
Drucker, P., 3
Duncan, R. B., 11, 40
DuPont Company, 3

Economics, of forest products industry,
    73, 79–88, 120, 122
Education Committee of the Public
    Relations Society of America,
    249
Emery, F. E., 10
Emissions, 110–11
Employees, 13–14
Employment, in forest products indus-
    try, 106–107
Energy issues
    and company perceptions, 213–14,
        223
    and forest products industry, 81,
        114–15, 120–22
Engineering department, 127–41, 207
Environmental Defense Fund, 113
Environmental impact statement (EIS),
    95
Environmental issues, 253–56
    and company perceptions, 213–18,
        223
    and evolutionary approach, 28–30,
        44
    in perceptual process, 51, 53, 59

and strategic choice approach,
    30–34, 44
Environmental issues, in forest prod-
    ucts study, 6, 91, 92–99, 120–22,
    242–43
    industry's response to, 99–103
    and pollution control, 107–114, 121
Environmental Protection Association
    (EPA), 80, 95, 99, 108–14
Establishing contact, and cultural sen-
    sitivity, 165, 170–71, 174–75,
    178–79, 183–84, 188–89, 196
Evolutionary approach, 28–30, 43–44
Executive-initiative approach, 37
Executives (*see also* Executive themes)
    bias, 204–210
    in business policy approach, 35–38
    within company differences, 240, 243
    and cultural sensitivity study, 244–46
    in evolutionary approach, 29–30
    as labor negotiators, 17–18
    and perceptions, 203, 221–24
    rating of social performance, 235–37,
        238
    receptor bias of, 204–207
Executive themes, in cultural sensitiv-
    ity study, 165–66, 171–73,
    175–77, 179–81, 184–87, 189–92,
    196–99
Extension Service of Department of
    Agriculture, 102
External control theory, 10–12
External factors, 12, 239–40
    and appreciation, 135–39, 141,
        152–55, 159
    in business policy approach, 37, 44
    in contingency theory, 40–41, 44
    and departments, 135–39, 141–42,
        159
    in forest products industry, 242–44
    and research, 254–55
External factors, in adaptation theory,
    27, 28–34, 44
    and evolutionary approach, 28–30,
        43
    and strategic choice approach,
        30–34, 44, 57
Externally attentive experts, 249–50
    (*see also* Public affairs sensitivity)
Exxon Company, 28

Farmers Home Administration Service,
    102

Farmland and Forest Land Assessment
    Act (Pa.), 102
Federal economic regulatory agencies,
    1–2
Federal government, and forest prod-
    uct industry, 99–103, 104–105
Federal Land Bank, 102
Federal Land Policy and Management
    Act (FLPMA), 100
Federal social regulatory agencies, 2,
    15
Federal Trade Commission (FTC), 118,
    182
Federal Water Pollution Control Act of
    1972, 111
Feedback loops, 57–59
Finance department, 127–41, 166, 207
Finances
    and company perceptions, 213–14,
        223
    in cultural sensitivity study, 166,
        173, 177, 182, 188, 194, 199
    in forest products industry, 115–17,
        120, 122, 242
Financial Accounting Standards Board
    (FASB), 18, 116
Fleming, J. E., 39
Forbes, 79, 165
Forecasting, 37–38
Foreign Corrupt Practices Act, 115
Forest management, 74, 76, 83–88, 99,
    120
Forest Management Act of 1976, 99
Forest Pest Control Act of 1947, 102
Forest Products Association, 165
Forest products industry, 6–7, 61,
    242–44, 255–56
    archives in, 6–7, 61, 71
    and cultural sensitivity, 199–201,
        239, 241–46, 253
    economics of, 79–82, 88
    energy and transportation, 114–15,
        120
    and environmental issues, 99–103
    and financial issues, 115–17, 120,
        122, 242
    history of pulp and paper industry,
        76–79
    history of timber industry, 75–76
    industry setting, 73–74, 88
    and institutional sector, 119–21, 242
    interviews in, 61–62, 64–65, 70–71
    labor-related issues, 103–107, 121

    marketing perspective of, 117,
        119–22
    methodology of study, 6–7, 61, 71
    and pollution control, 107–114,
        120–22
    questionnaires for, 61–62, 65–71
    recession and, 82–83
    and social responsiveness, 226,
        231–38, 242, 244
    and stakeholders, 73–74, 91
    and structural sensitivity, 67–69,
        161, 165, 242–44
    and technology advances in forest
        management, 74, 83–87, 88
Fuel wood, 86–87

General Electric Company, 3
General management departments,
    127–41, 204
General managers, 1, 37–40 (*see also*
    CEO; Executives; Executive
    themes)
Georgia, 98
Georgia-Pacific Company, 78, 84, 86,
    101, 115
Glueck, W. F., 17
Gould, S., 28
Government, 1, 12–16, 99–105 (*see
    also* Federal government)
Government relations department,
    127–41, 204
Grant national park, 82
Great Northern Company, 78
Green, R., 38
Green Acre Bond Act (NJ), 102
Gross National Product (GNP), 81, 83
Grunig, J. E., 20
Guillion, G., 87

Hacker, A., 15
Hage, J., 31
Hagenstein, W. D., 95
Hall, R. H., 12
Hammermill Company, 78–79, 117–18
Hansen, K., 15
Harris poll, 2, 15
Harvard Business Review, 15, 62, 138
Harvard Business School, 3
Hatch, O., 100
Heavily regulated industries, and GNP,
    2, 15
Hellriegal, D., 11
Hirsch, P. M., 31

Holmes, S. L., 38
Humanistic-environmental values, 15
Human resources department, 127–41, 207
Hyton, L. F., 31

IBM, 28
Ichan, Carl, 117
Independent Association of Western Pulp and Paper, 104
Industrial Forestry Association, 95
Influence, 5, 41, 44, 143, 156, 241
    in forest products study, 68–69, 211, 243–44
    and structural sensitivity, 54–56, 67–68
Information acquisition, 5, 53–54, 61, 228, 237
    and cultural sensitivity, 169
    and departments, 135–39, 141–42, 143–56, 159, 203
    in forest products industry, 242–44
    and labor management, 17–18
    in sensory-system model, 241–42
    and structure, 54, 225
Innovation, 37
Institutional environments, 2–3, 12–13, 14, 119–21, 240, 249
Interactions
    breadth of, 135, 141, 151–52, 159
    corporations, and public affairs, 51, 58–59, 62
    departments with stakeholders, 127–35, 143–51, 159, 204–210, 223–24
    depth, 155, 159, 243
    in forest products industry, 243
    issue specific, 20, 228, 233, 237–38
    and public affairs sensitivity, 249
    time, 128–32, 141, 143–44, 159
Interaction time, 128–32, 141–44, 159, 204–10, 223–24
Interactive mode, 36
Integration, 5, 40, 43–44
    in forest products study, 69, 243–44
    and structural sensitivity, 55–56, 67, 143, 156–61, 241, 244
Interest groups, 12, 14, 19
Internal consensus, 57–58, 203, 221, 223, 237, 242, 245–46
Internal integration, 55–56, 58, 67, 143, 156–61, 244

and cultural sensitivity, 166–68, 179, 191, 196–97, 200–201
Internal structure, 27, 34–44, 57–58
International Paper Company, 76, 78, 96, 101
International Woodworkers of America (IWA), 104, 106
International Woodworking, 107
International Workers of the World (IWW), 104–105
Interviews
    and cultural sensitivity, 165–67, 200
    and forest products study, 61–62, 64–65, 70–71
Investors, 14, 17–19, 58–59, 91, 116–17, 122
Issues
    and company perceptions, 203, 213–14, 223
    executive perception of, 203
    internal consensus and, 203, 221, 223
    market, 4, 12, 21, 213–14, 223
    priorities, 203, 211–12, 223
    public affairs, 13–14, 14–19, 19–21, 33, 99, 120, 226
    and receptor bias, 204
    in sensory systems model, 241
ITT, 28, 116

Jackson, J. E., 16
Jemison, D. B., 41
Jones, B. W., 20

Kandwalla, P. N., 40
Kimberly-Clark Company, 78–79, 83
Koester, Terri, 96
Kotter, J. P., 31

Labor Reform Act of 1978, 17
Labor relations
    and company perceptions, 213–14, 223
    in forest products study, 6, 17–18, 19, 91, 103–107, 121
Land taxes, in forest products study, 6, 91, 103, 122, 242, 245
Lawrence, P. R., 2, 10–11, 29, 37, 40, 42
Legal department, 127–41
Legislation, 15–16, 19, 94–96, 100–103, 107, 120
LeMaster, D., 96
Leone, R. A., 15–16

Lewin, K., 7
Listenership, 139–41, 155, 159, 24,
    248–50
Literature
    academic, 4–6, 11–13, 165–66, 225,
        240–41
    in cultural sensitivity study, 165–66,
        188, 200
Litwak, E., 31
Lockheed Corporation, 28
Lorsch, J W., 11, 29, 37, 40, 42
Lumber Production and Industrial
    Workers Union (LPIW), 104

McGrath, P. J., 39
McGraw-Hill Econometrics, 82
McKersie, R., 17
Maine, 97, 99, 108
Management, and public affairs, 1–3,
    239–41
    in cultural sensitivity study, 169–74,
        176–79, 187–89, 199–201
    and revised model, 248–52
    in sensory-system model, 241–42
Managers, as negotiators, 17–18 (see
    also Executives; General man-
    agers)
March, J. G., 29–31, 37
Market issues, 1, 239–40
    in adaptation theory, 4, 12, 21
    and company perceptions, 213–14,
        223
    and forest products study, 119–22,
        242–43
    vs. public affairs, 61–62, 73, 88
Mazis, M., 38
Mead, 78–79, 116
Megacorporations, 6, 19, 27, 30, 51–53
Merrill Lynch Econometrics, 82
Methodology
    in forest products industry study,
        6–7, 61, 71
    in organization theory literature, 5–6
Miles, R. H., 2, 12, 27, 29–30, 41
Mills, D. Q., 17
Morse, J. J., 40
"Multiple-use Sustained Yield" Act of
    1960, 76, 93–94
Murray, E. A., 36

Nader, R., 97–98, 104
National Coal Association, 114

National Council of the Paper Industry
    for Air and Stream Improvement,
    109
National Energy Conservation Policy
    Act of 1978, 115
National Forest Management Act of
    1975, 94, 96
National Forest Products Association,
    75–76, 120
National Forest Timber Conservation
    and Management Act of 1969, 99
National Highway Beautification Act,
    102
National Labor Relations Board, 17
National Park Service, 182
National Pollutant Discharge Elimina-
    tion System (NPDES), 112
National Recovery Act, 75
National Wilderness Preservation Sys-
    tem, 94, 100
Naylor, M., 87
Negandhi, A. R., 40
Nekoosa Company, 78
Newgren, K., 38
New Jersey Natural Lands Trust, 102
New York Paper Company
    and company differences in percep-
        tions, 210–11
    and cultural sensitivity, 199–201, 245
    and department receptivity, 144–56
    establishing contact, 174–75
    executive themes, 175–77
    and influence, 156
    and internal integration, 155–59
    reputation, 173–74
    and social responsiveness, 231–38,
        244
    structural sensitivity of, 161, 244
North Carolina University Industry
    Cooperation Tree Improvement
    Program, 84
Northwest Forests Company
    and company differences in percep-
        tions, 210–21
    and cultural sensitivity, 200–201,
        245, 246–48
    departmental receptivity of, 144–56,
        159
    establishing contact in, 183–84
    executive themes in, 184–87
    and internal integration, 156–59
    and public affairs influence, 156

reputation of, 182–83
and social responsiveness, 231–38
structural sensitivity of, 161, 246–48

Objective reality, 10–13
Occidental Petroleum, 116
Oklahoma, 98
"One-issue thinking," 5
Open Space Acquisition Act (Pa.), 102
"Open systems" theory, 10
Organizational environment
and corporate preparedness for pub-
lic affairs issues, 19–21
dimensions of, 10–13
and public affairs boundary, 13–14
and similarities across public affairs
issues, 14–19
"Organizations as coalitions," 31
Organization theory, 51–53, 253–56
Osborn, W. C., 98, 104, 108
OSHA, 105, 108

Pacific Timber Company
and company differences in perception, 210–21
and cultural sensitivity, 199–201,
245, 246–48
and departmental receptivity,
144–56
establishing contact in, 170–71
executive themes in, 171–73
and internal integration, 156–59
and public affairs influence, 156
and reputation, 166–70
and social responsiveness, 231–38
and structural sensitivity, 159–61,
244, 246–48
Packaging industry, 78–79, 88
Parsons, T., 12, 14, 34, 240
Pennsylvania, 102
Perceived uncertainty, 11
Perception of public affairs, 4–5, 27, 29
and behavior of organizations, 11–13
bias in, 7, 36, 42, 71, 132,
142–43, 203–210
and department receptivity, 142,
143, 159, 223–24
and executives, 203
in forest products industry, 6–7, 61,
69–70, 121
in perceptual process, 51, 57, 59
in revised model, 241–48

in sensory-system model, 241–42
in strategic choice approach, 32
influence on structural sensitivity, 61
Perception, company
and cultural sensitivity, 244–46
vs. department perceptions, 203,
211–21, 223
differences, and company posture,
203, 213–21, 223
and internal consensus, 203, 221, 223
and issue priorities, 211–12, 223
Perry, J. L., 41
Pesticide Control Act (Pa.), 102
Pfeffer, J., 12–13, 31–33, 42
Pfizer Company, 3
Pinchot, G., 93
Pinelands Environmental Council Act
(NJ), 102
Polaroid Company, 37
Politics
of protection, 92–97
of regulatory policy, 16
Pollution, 6, 16, 91, 107–114, 120–21,
242, 245
control, 107–114, 120–22
Post, J. E., 2, 14, 19–20, 27, 36
Potential emissions, definition of, 110
Potlach Company, 78
Power, 1, 31–32, 41
Powerplant Industrial Fuel Use Act of
1978, 115
Pressure-response style, 36
Prestige, as objective, 1
Preston, L. E., 14, 20
Price fixing, 168, 173–74
Private sector, 100–103, 117–19, 239
Proactive approach, 27, 30, 32, 36,
42–43, 253
Profits, as objective, 1
Public affairs
and company's internal integration,
156–59, 244
and company perceptions, 203,
223–24, 225–26, 239
and corporate culture, 244–46
and corporate structure, 242–44
and cultural sensitivity, 163–66,
169–70, 173, 175, 177, 179,
182–83, 189–91, 194–95, 198–201
definition of, 65
and departmental receptivity,
143–56, 159–61

Public affairs (*continued*)
  and forest products industry response
    to, 91, 99–103, 242
  influence, 143, 156, 249–51
  issues, 13–21, 33
  management, 27, 225
  in revised model, 246–48
  in sensory-system model, 241–42
Public affairs environment, 19–21, 51,
  53, 59, 73, 119–22, 240–42 (*see
  also* Institutional environment)
  in perceptual process, 51, 53, 59
Public Affairs Leadership Manual,
  120
Public affairs, perceptions of, 51, 57,
  59, 225
  and company posture, 203, 213–21,
    223
  and internal consensus, 203, 221, 223
  and issue priorities, 203, 211–12, 223
Public affairs receptivity, 1, 6–7, 9,
  15–16, 19, 239
  and appreciation, 135–39, 141,
    152–55, 159, 243
  and attention, 1, 12, 20, 139, 149,
    155, 243
  departments as receptors, 127,
    141–42, 204–207, 242–43
  differences in perceptions, 203–23
Public affairs responsiveness (*see also*
  Social responsiveness)
  differences in social responsiveness,
    226, 231–38
  and interactions with stakeholders,
    127–35
  learning process in, 28–29
  and listenership, 139–41, 155, 159,
    243, 248–50
  perceptual process for, 51–59
Public affairs sensitivity, 248–52
  and cultural features, 251–52
  and structural features, 249–51
Public expectations, 19, 27, 33, 53
Public forest lands, 6, 91–96, 100, 120,
  242
"Public issues life cycle," 19
Public policy, 15–16, 19
Public relations departments, 57,
  129–41
  and appreciation, 135–39
  in cultural sensitivity study, 166,
    171, 176, 184–85, 203

  and interactions with stakeholders,
    127–35
  as receptor, 127–42, 143, 152–56
Pulp and paper industry, 76–79, 83, 88

Questionnaire surveys, for forest product industry, 61–62, 65–71
  and company structure, 67–69
  of perceptions, 69–70
  of responsiveness, 70–71

RARE II (*see* Roadless Area Review
  and Evaluation)
Reactive approach, 27, 30–33, 36–37,
  51, 253
Receptivity, 132, 135, 141–42, 241
  departmental, 143–56, 159, 203
  of executives, 203
  in forest products study, 67–68,
    243–44
  and structural sensitivity, 55–56, 67
Receptors, for corporations, 53–54,
  55–56, 132, 142
Receptors, departments as, 127,
  141–42
  and appreciation, 135–39, 141,
    152–55, 159
  and attention, 139, 155, 159
  and depth, 155–56, 159
  and interactions with stakeholders,
    127–35, 143–51, 159
  and listenership, 139–41, 155, 159
Regions, geographic, 64, 75, 77, 88,
  100–101
Regulations, 15–16
  and company perceptions, 213–14, 223
  and forest products industry, 101–
    103, 115, 120–22, 242–43
Regulatory agencies, 1–2, 12–13,
  15–16, 19
Reidel, C., 81
Reimann, B. C., 40
Reputation, and cultural sensitivity
  study, 165–70, 173–74, 177–78,
  182–83, 187–88, 192–96, 251–52
  (*see also* Public affairs sensitivity)
Research
  in forest management, 84–85
  on organizations, 4–5, 11–13, 252–56
  on structure and perception, 29–30
Resource Conservation and Recovery
  Act (1976), 112

Resources, 10, 31–33, 242
Responsibility (*see* Social responsibility)
Responsiveness (*see* Social responsive-
    ness)
Rittenhouse, W., 77
Roadless Area Review and Evaluation
    (RARE II), 94–96, 100
Robinson, Gordon, 97

"Sagebrush Rebellion," 100
St. Regis Company, 78
Salancik, G. R., 12–13, 31–33, 42
Scanning, 1, 4, 33–34, 41, 68
Schmenner, R. W., 16
Schon, D., 32
Scott, R. D., 106
Scott Paper Company, 78–79, 116, 118
Securities and Exchange Commission,
    18, 182
Seiberling, J., 95
Selznick, P., 31, 35, 246
Sensory-system model, 5, 53–56,
    241–42
Sequoia national park, 92
Sethi, S. P., 36
Shapiro, I ., 3, 5
Sierra Club, 95–97, 99, 113–14, 165
Simon, H. A., 12, 29, 35, 37
Simpson Timber Company, 85
Single loop learning, 37
Size of company, 62, 74, 88
Skelly, 121
Slocum, Y., 11
Snow, C. C., 12, 30
Social issues, 20, 38–39
Social performance theory, 12–14, 20,
    252, 254
Social responsibility, 1, 20, 200, 225,
    237–38, 242, 254
    company differences in, 231–33,
        237–38
    and cultural sensitivity, 244–46
    in forest products study, 71, 121
    and public affairs sensitivity, 252
Social responsiveness, 1, 12, 20, 59,
    225–26, 237–42, 244, 254 (*see also*
    Attention)
    company differences in, 231–38
    and cultural sensitivity, 246
    in forest products study, 70–71, 242,
        244
    industry responsiveness, 226–27

influence of perception on, 61
and public sensitivity, 252
in sensory-system model, 241–42
and stakeholder bias, 227–31
and structural sensitivity, 225, 244
and structure, 225
Soil Conservation Program, 102
Solid waste issues, 6, 91, 108–114, 121,
    212
Sonnenfeld, J., 2, 10, 12, 29, 37
Spaeth, G., 114
Stakeholders, 2, 13–14, 62, 224, 240
    bias, 227–31, 233
    company differences in responsive-
        ness, 231–38
    in cultural sensitivity study, 165–67,
        171–73, 175, 190, 199–200,
        244–46
    and forest products industry, 73–74,
        91, 121, 242–44
    and industry responsiveness, 226–27,
        237
    interaction with departments,
        127–35, 141–42, 143–51, 159
    interviews in forest products study,
        6–7, 61, 70–71, 165
    and management, 248–52
    and questionnaire surveys, 61, 70–71
    in sensory-system model, 241–42
    tolerance for, and receptor bias,
        204–210, 223–24
Stalker, G. M., 10, 40
Starbuck, W. H., 11, 29
State implementation plans (SIPs), 111
State Recreation and Conservation
    Land Acquisition Fund (NJ), 102
State Trails system (NJ), 102
Staw, B. M., 10, 31
Stigler, G., 10
Storey, 11
Strategic choice approach, 10, 30–34,
    44, 57
Structural features, of public affairs sen-
    sitivity, 249–51
Structural sensitivity, 34, 143, 149–51,
    239, 253
    and accommodation, 218
    and company perceptions, 218,
        223–24, 225, 237–38
    vs. cultural sensitivity, 163–66
    and departmental receptivity,
        143–56

Structural sensitivity *(continued)*
  in forest products questionnaire,
    67–69, 242–44
  and internal integration, 143, 156–61
  in perceptual process, 51, 53–56, 59
  and public affairs influence, 143, 156
  in sensory-system model, 241–42
Structure, of organizations
  and business policy approach, 35–39
  and contingency theory approach,
    39–44
  and environment, 28–30
  and evolutionary approach, 29
  and perceptions of public affairs envi-
    ronment, 27, 29
  and social responsiveness, 225
  and strategic-choice approach, 29,
    32–33
  in systems theory, 34–35
Subjective reality, 11–13
Subunits, in organizations, 14, 18,
  32–33, 44, 53–56, 132, 142 *(see
  also* Departments)
Suhl, M., 117
Swajakowski, E., 10, 31

Taxation *(see* Land taxes)
Technical phase, of regulatory policy,
  16
Technology, in adaptation theory, 4,
  12, 21
Technology issues, and forest products
  industry, 73–74, 83–87, 88, 119,
  122
Texas A&M, 85
"Thirteen Mile Woods," (NH), 102
Thompson, J. D., 11, 40, 43
Timber harvests, and public affairs,
  97–99
Timber industry, 75–77, 88
Timber supply, 91–99
Time, Inc., 116
Tolerance, 242, 245
Tosi, H., 11
Transactions, 68, 139
Transmission *(see* Influence)
Transportation system, and forest
  products industry, 75, 80, 114–15,
  120
Trist, E. L., 10

Udall, M., 95

Uncertainty, 1, 40
Union Camp, 78, 118
United Paper Workers International
  Union (UPIU), 104, 106
U.S. Army Corps of Engineers, 108
U.S. Bureau of Labor Statistics, 106
U.S. Bureau of Land Management
  (BLM), 100, 114
U.S. Congress, 93–94, 96, 107, 109,
  113–14
U.S. Department of Commerce, 82,
  109
U.S. Department of Energy (DOE),
  87, 115
U.S. Department of the Interior, 93,
  100
U.S. Department of Justice, 114, 118
U.S. Forest Service, 75–76, 93–95, 99,
  114
U.S. Paper Company
  and company differences in percep-
    tions, 210–21
  and cultural sensitivity, 200–201, 245
  departmental receptivity in, 144–56
  establishing contact in, 196
  executive theme in, 196–99
  and internal integration, 156–59
  and public affairs influence, 156
  reputation of, 192–96
  and social responsiveness, 231–38,
    244
  structural sensitivity of, 161
University of Minnesota Forest Wildlife
  Project, 87

Vickers, G., 30
Volatility, 10–11, 19, 53, 83, 250
Votaw, D., 36

Wall Street Journal, 2–3, 165
Walton, R. E., 17
Water pollution, 6, 91, 107–114,
  120–21, 242
Water Quality Act, 109, 111–12
Weeks Act of 1911, 93, 102
Weick, K. E., 29
Weir, Robert, 84
Western Lands Distribution and
  Equalization Act, 100
Westvaco Company, 78
Weyerhaeuser Company, 76, 78, 92,
  101

White, 121
Wilderness Act of 1964, 93–94, 101
Wilderness Society, 165
Williamson, D. E., 10
Wright, Keith, 98

Yankelovich, 121
Yellowstone National Park, 76, 92

Zobel, Bruce, 85